THE FIVE PILLARS OF ISLAM

THE FIVE PILLARS OF ISLAM

Laying the Foundations of Divine Love and Service to Humanity

A practical manual for learning essential Islamic beliefs and practices and understanding the true spirit of worship

MUSHARRAF HUSSAIN

KUBE
PUBLISHING

First published in England by Kube Publishing Ltd,
Markfield Conference Centre
Ratby Lane, Markfield,
Leicestershire LE67 9SY
United Kingdom
Tel: +44 (0) 1530 249230
Fax: +44 (0) 1530 249656
Email: info@kubepublishing.com
Website: www.kubepublishing.com

A Cataloguing-in-Publication data record is available from the British Library.

ISBN 978-1-84774-023-6 *paperback*

Typesetting by: N. A. Qaddoura
Cover Design by: Nasir Cadir

Printed by Imak Offset, Turkey

The Essence of the Five Pillars

THE FIRST PILLAR OF ISLAM:
SHAHĀDAH – THE DECLARATION OF FAITH
The Foundation of Divine Love

THE SECOND PILLAR OF ISLAM:
ṢALĀH – THE PRAYER
The Deepening of Divine Love through Devotion

THE THIRD PILLAR OF ISLAM:
ZAKĀH – THE ALMSGIVING
The Growth of Divine Love by giving Charity

THE FOURTH PILLAR OF ISLAM:
ṢAWM – FASTING IN RAMAḌĀN
The Expression of Divine Love through Self-Discipline

THE FIFTH PILLAR OF ISLAM:
ḤAJJ – THE PILGRIMAGE
In the Presence of Divine Love

Transliteration Table

Consonants. Arabic
initial: unexpressed; medial and final: ء ʼ

a	ا	d	د	ḍ	ض	k	ك
b	ب	dh	ذ	ṭ	ط	l	ل
t	ت	r	ر	ẓ	ظ	m	م
th	ث	z	ز	ʻ	ع	n	ن
j	ج	s	س	gh	غ	h	هـ
ḥ	ح	sh	ش	f	ف	w	و
kh	خ	ṣ	ص	q	ق	y	ي

Vowels, diphthongs, etc.

Short:	a ـَ	ـِ i	ـُ u
long:	ā ـَا	ـُو ī	ـِي ū
diphthongs:		ـَوْ aw	
		ـَيْ ay	

Contents

Acknowledgements xiii

Introduction xiv

THE FIRST PILLAR OF ISLAM

***SHAHĀDAH* – The Declaration of Faith**

1. The Meaning of Faith and Its Development 3
   The Significance of the *Shahādah* 3
   The Cultivation of Faith 5

2. *'Aqā'id al-Nasafī*: A Summary of Islamic Beliefs 9
   About *'Aqā'id al-Nasafī* 9
   Translation of *'Aqā'id al-Nasafī* 10
   Belief in Allah 11
   Belief in *al-Ākhirah* (the Hereafter), its Punishments and its Rewards 14
   The Nature of *Īmān* (Faith), Belief in the Messengers, Angels and Revealed Books 15
   The Beliefs and Practices of the Ahl al-Sunnah wa al-Jamā'ah 17

THE SECOND PILLAR OF ISLAM

Ṣalāh – The Prayer

3. Introduction to the *Sharī'ah* and the Science of *Fiqh* 27
The *Sharī'ah* 27
Fiqh 28
The Categories of Rulings in Islamic Jurisprudence 29
Islamic Rituals of Worship 31

4. The Meaning, Wisdom and Benefits of *Ṣalāh* 35
The Meaning of *Ṣalāh* 35
The Spiritual Benefits and Wisdom of *Ṣalāh* 36
Developing Concentration (*Khushū'*) in *Ṣalāh* 39
The Moral Benefits and Wisdom of *Ṣalāh* 41
The Social Benefits and Wisdom of *Ṣalāh* 42
The *Masjid* – The Most Blessed Place on Earth 43
Women in the *Masjid* 44

5. Preparation for *Ṣalāh*: *Ṭahārah, Adhān* and *Iqāmah* 51
The Importance of preparing for *Ṣalāh* 51
Introduction to *Ṭahārah* (Purity) 52
Purification with *Ghusl* (Bath) and *Tayammum* (Dry Ablution) 52
Ghusl 53
Tayammum 55
Purification with *Wuḍū'* (Ablution) 57
Making the *Adhān* (Call to Prayer) and *Iqāmah* (Call made immediately preceding prayer) 67

6. How to Pray *Ṣalāh* 71
The Obligation to pray *Ṣalāh* 71
The Six Conditions for Prayer 72
The Six Compulsory (*Farḍ*) Acts in Prayer 77
The Nine Necessary (*Wājib*) Acts in Prayer 78
The *Sunnah* Acts in Prayer 80

The Special *Sunnahs* for Congregation 82
The Desirable (*Mustaḥabb*) Acts in Prayer 82
The Undesirable (*Makrūh*) Acts in Prayer 83
The Invalidating (*Mufsid*) Acts in Prayer 85
How to perform the *Ṣalāh* 86
Summary of the Procedure for *Ṣalāh* 94
The Nafl Prayers (Voluntary *Ṣalāhs*) 96
Combining Two Prayers 99
Making Up for Missed *Ṣalāh* (*Qaḍā'*) 99

7. Special Congregational *Ṣalāh*: The Friday, ʿĪd and Funeral Prayers 103
The Friday Prayer 103
The Conditions for establishing the Friday Prayer 106
The ʿĪd Prayer 109
The Funeral Prayer 113
The Procedure for the Funeral Prayer 116
The Traveller's Prayer 117
How to pray whilst travelling on an Airplane, Train or Coach 118

THE THIRD PILLAR OF ISLAM

***Zakāh* – The Almsgiving**

8. The Meaning and Wisdom of *Zakāh* 123
The Spiritual Benefits and Wisdom of *Zakāh* 124
The Moral Benefits and Wisdom of *Zakāh* 126
The Social Benefits and Wisdom of *Zakāh* 128

9. The Payment of *Zakāh* 132
Who must pay *Zakāh*? 132
What Types of Wealth necessitate *Zakāh*? 133
Who deserves to receive *Zakāh*? 134
How is *Zakāh* paid? 135
The Manners of paying *Zakāh* 137

THE FOURTH PILLAR OF ISLAM

Ṣawm – The Fasting in Ramaḍān

10. The Blessings of Ramaḍān and Fasting 143
Ramaḍān is the Spring of Righteousness 143
A Month of Mercy, Forgiveness and Deliverance 147

11. Fasting: A Means of Moral and Spiritual Growth for the Individual and Community 151
Fasting was prescribed for Us to develop in *Taqwā* 151
Spiritual Growth 153
Using Ramaḍān as a Programme for Spiritual Growth 154
Using Fasting as a Means for Moral Development 158
The Social Benefits and Wisdom of the Obligatory Fast in Ramaḍān 160
The Health Benefits of Fasting 160

12. The *Fiqh* Rulings for Ramaḍān 164
Beginning and ending Ramaḍān 164
The Obligation to fast the Month of Ramaḍān 165
Who is exempt from Fasting? 166
What is the Fast and when does it begin and end? 169
What nullifies the Fast? 170
The Rulings of *Kaffārah* (Atonement) 171
What does not break the Fast? 172
What is Undesirable (*Makrūh*) whilst Fasting? 173
The Meaning and Practice of *Tarāwīḥ* Prayer 173
How did the Blessed Messenger fast? 174

13. *I'tikāf*: Spiritual Retreat 177
The Meaning and Virtues of *I'tikāf* 177
The Three Types of *I'tikāf* 179
What nullifies the *I'tikāf*? 180

The Permissable Reasons to temporarily Leave *I'tikāf* 180
The Undesirable Acts in *I'tikāf* 181

14. *Laylat al-Qadr*: The Night of Power 182
The Significance of the Night of Power 182
When is this Night? 184
What is the Wisdom in keeping the Exact Date secret? 186
What happens on this Night? 186
Is there any Special Devotion on this Night? 186

15. *'Īd al-Fiṭr*: A Time for Celebration and Charity 188
A Time to celebrate 188
Almsgiving at the End of *Ramaḍān*: *Ṣadaqah al-Fiṭr* 191

THE FIFTH PILLAR OF ISLAM

Ḥajj **– The Pilgrimage**

16. The Meaning and Significance of *Ḥajj* 197
Ḥajj – A Journey Back to Our Roots 197
The Spiritual Benefits and Importance of *Ḥajj* 200

17. An Overview of the *Ḥajj*: Rules and Conditions 203
The Types of *Ḥajj* 203
On Whom is *Ḥajj* Obligatory? 204
The Conditions for the Performance of *Ḥajj* 204
Performing *Ḥajj* on the Behalf of Somebody Else 205
The Five Days of *Ḥajj* in Brief 205
The Conditions for the Soundness of *Ḥajj* 207
The Obligatory (*Farḍ*) Rites of *Ḥajj* 207
The Necessary (*Wājib*) Rites of *Ḥajj* 207

18. The Rites of *Ḥajj*: Meaning and Practice 209
Iḥrām – The State of Sanctity 210
'Arafah – Preparation for the Day of Judgement 212

Ṭawāf – Turning around the Spiritual Pivot of the World 213
Sa'y – Running between *Ṣafā* and *Marwah* 215
Ramy – The Stoning of the *Shayṭāns* 219
Qurbānī – The Sacrifice 220
Ḥalq and *Qaṣr* – Shaving and Cutting the Hair 222
Jināyāt – *Ḥajj* Offences and their Penalties 223

19. Performing *Ḥajj* 227
The Five Days of *Ḥajj* 227
Before 8th Dhū al-Ḥijjah: The Months of *Ḥajj* 227
8th Dhū al-Ḥijjah: The First Day of *Ḥajj* 228
9th Dhū al-Ḥijjah: The Second Day of *Ḥajj* 230
10th Dhū al-Ḥijjah: The Third Day of *Ḥajj* 231
11th Dhū al-Ḥijjah: The Fourth Day of *Ḥajj* 234
12th Dhū al-Ḥijjah: The Fifth Day of *Ḥajj* 235
The Steps of *'Umrah* and *Ḥajj* 235

20. Performing *'Umrah* 237
The Rites of *'Umrah* 237
How to Perform *'Umrah* 237

Appendix: Moon Sighting 249

Selected Scholarly Biographies 261

Glossary 267

Bibliography 283
Islamic Source Texts 283
Classical and Modern Scholarly Texts 283
Reference Works and Internet Links 285

Acknowledgements

Allah is al-Shukūr, the One who gives us very great rewards for our efforts: He acknowledges our works no matter how small or big they are. This book is a product of many fertile minds: students, friends and teachers who have been working with me for nearly two decades. Its contents have evolved slowly over this period. I want to convey my deep sense of gratitude to my wife Shakila for her constant patience with me, to all my students who have typed and edited the drafts, particularly Ghufran Shah, Atif Hussain, Sajid and Majid, to Ibrahim Harvey for doing a brilliant edit of the initial draft of this book, to all my teachers for their selfless and pure souls that just wanted to give, and to Yahya Birt at Kube Publishing for his constant encouragement, insightful feedback, and in helping me to understand the difference between vanity and professional publishing.

Introduction

ISLAM – *The Path of Divine Love and Service to Humanity*

All praise is due to Allah, the Loving, Caring and Generous Lord and may countless blessings and salutations be conveyed to His beloved Messenger Muḥammad, 'the mercy sent for all'.

The Qur'ān describes Muslims as people who passionately love their Lord: *the believers have intense love for Allah* (Q2: 165) and the Qur'ān shows that this love goes both ways, for Allah also loves His faithful servants. The Messenger, may Allah bless him and grant him peace, gave us a simple yet practical action-based programme to develop this Divine Love when he said that *'Islam is founded on five pillars: to bear witness that there is no God but Allah and Muḥammad is His Messenger and servant, the five daily prayers, fasting in Ramaḍān, paying* zakāh *and performing the pilgrimage.'* (Bukhārī)

This book is a practical manual that will enable the reader to learn and understand the religious duties as prescribed by the Qur'ān and *Sunnah*, and it is based on classical sources. The first pillar, or the *shahādah*, is a translation of *'Aqā'id al-Nasafī* by Abu Hafs 'Umar al-Nasafi (d. 537 A.H.). This is a famous primer on Islamic beliefs, whilst the other four pillars of worship – prayer, fasting, *zakāh* and pilgrimage – are described in the minutest detail in another classical work of jurisprudence (*fiqh*): *Nūr al-Īḍāḥ wa Najāt al-Arwāḥ* by Ḥasan ibn ʿAmmār al-Shurunbulālī (d. 1069 A.H.). I have tried to follow faithfully these two most authentic books which are taught in seminaries all over the world. I have attempted to translate them into lucid and clear contemporary English and to present them in an appealing manner.

Whilst al-Shurunbulālī gives us accurate details of how to perform these wonderful acts of worship, that is, to scrupulously follow the Prophetic Way (*Sunnah*), I have attempted to explain their rationales in order to help Muslims to move from the outward performance of worship – in which there is the danger that it merely becomes a mindless mechanical exercise – to understanding how these acts of worship can influence our moral development, improve our social relationships with each another and, above all, bring us closer to the Almighty and develop the Divine love.

We live in an age of reason where science is constantly revealing the secrets of nature, yet whilst it gives an explanation of the outward world it remains deafeningly silent about spiritual ideals. I have tried to explain how the five pillars can influence our spiritual growth. This I hope has enriched the jurisprudence (*fiqh*) that is explained so beautifully by al-Shurunbulālī. My hope therefore is that this book will not only be used as a *fiqh* manual but also as a guide to the moral, social and spiritual values that inculcate perfect harmony between the outward and the inward realities of life.

There is an underlying logic to the order of the five pillars. The affirmation of the *shahādah* lays the foundations of Divine love, which is the yearning for one's Creator and Sustainer. However, this love needs a mode of expression which comes in the performance of the five daily prayers, the second pillar of Islam. The Divine love must be further cultivated by the paying of *zakāh* – the third pillar of Islam – which is an outward manifestation of growth in Divine love. The fourth pillar leads one to self-discipline through fasting and the final and fifth pillar sets one on the path of Divine love as one performs the pilgrimage (*ḥajj*).

I earnestly hope to achieve the Divine love and pleasure through this humble effort. Oh Lord, on You do we rely, to You we turn in prayer, and unto You is the final returning. Oh Lord, forgive me and my parents and all the believers. Amīn.

Nottingham, England
Rabīʿ al-Awwal 1433
January 2012

Musharraf Hussain

1st
Pillar

SHAHĀDAH

(The Declaration of Faith)

The Foundation of Divine Love

CHAPTER 1

The Meaning of Faith and its Development

The Significance of the *Shahādah*

أَشْهَدُ أَنْ لآ إِلَـهَ إِلاَّ اللهُ وَأَشْهَدُ أَنَّ مُـحَمَّدًا عَبْدُهُ وَرَسُوْلُهُ

Ashadu an lā ilāha illa Allāhu wa ashadu anna Muḥammadan ʿabduhu wa rasūluhu

I bear witness that there is no god except Allah and that Muhammad is his Servant and Messenger.

The *shahādah*, or declaration of faith, is the first pillar of Islam and the foundation of every act that follows it. This is because it is an affirmation of belief in *tawḥīd* (the Absolute Unity and Transcendence of God) and the messengership of the Prophet Muḥammad, which is the fundamental condition for felicity in the Hereafter and the acceptance of the acts of *ʿibādāt* (worship) that are performed in this life. It also signifies entrance into the Islamic *ummah* (community) and the obligation to observe the provisions of the *sharīʿah* (sacred law and ethics), which encompass an individual's entire life, including the prescribed acts of worship (*ʿibādāt*) that make up the four other pillars.

Allah (Most High) says in the Qur'ān:

> *Allah bears witness that there is none worthy of worship except He. So do the angels and those possessing knowledge, standing up for justice. There is none worthy of worship except He, the Mighty, the Wise.*[1]

Those '*possessing knowledge*' here includes, in a general sense, all who believe in Allah amongst humankind, as a person must know that to which he is bearing witness to if it is to be a meaningful act.[2] On a deeper level, the recognition of the presence of the One whose constant action underlies all of creation is certainly the most priceless knowledge.

He Most High also says:

> *Muḥammad is not the father of any one of your men, but he is the Messenger of Allah and the Seal of the Prophets.*[3]

These words allude to the fact that Muḥammad is the final Prophet sent by Allah to humankind, confirming the truthfulness of all those who preceded him. Every single one of the previous messengers followed Islam, although some of the practical laws in their *sharīʿah*s were different in accordance with the needs of their times. Since the coming of the Prophet Muḥammad it is necessary for all those who believe in God Most High to also accept His beloved messenger.

He, Most High, says:

> *The Messenger believes in that which has been revealed to him by his Lord and so do the believers. All of them believe in Allah, His angels, His books and His messengers.*

They say, 'We make no distinction between any one of His messengers, and we hear and obey. Grant us Your forgiveness our Lord, as to You is the final journey.'[4]

The Cultivation of Faith

As we shall see in the translation of *Aqā'id al-Nasafī* that follows, an individual either has faith (*Īmān*) or not and in that sense it can neither be said to increase or decrease.[5] However, this faith may be cultivated and made to shine forth in the heart dispelling darkness and whispering doubts, thus bringing a believer to higher levels of certainty and reliance on God Most High.

Allah Most High, says:

Do you see how Allah strikes a parable? – A goodly word is like a goodly tree, its root firm and its branches in the heavens, giving its fruit at every season by permission of its Lord. Allah strikes parables for humanity so perhaps they may reflect. The parable of an evil word is that of an evil tree, uprooted from the earth and possessing no stability. Allah will strengthen those who believe with a firm statement in this worldly life and in the Hereafter and will leave to stray those who do wrong. Allah does what He wills.[6]

Imām al-Samarqandī (d. 375 A.H.) comments on this as follows:

> '*A goodly word*' is the word of sincerity: there is none worthy of worship except Allah ... Allah strikes this parable for the believer, saying that the knowledge (of *tawḥīd*) in the heart of the '*ārif* (perceiving; gnostic) believer is firm like the tree that is rooted in the earth. In fact, it is firmer, because the tree can be cut, while it is not possible for anyone to remove the '*ārif*'s knowledge from his heart, except for the One

> who gave it to him. It is said that *'and its branches are in the heavens'* means that the deeds of the believer who affirms the truth are raised to the heavens, as actions are not accepted without faith. This is because faith is the root, while deeds are its ascending branches.[7]

Allah Most High also says:

> *The believers are only those whose hearts tremble when Allah is mentioned, and when His verses are recited to them they increase in faith and they trust in their Lord.*[8]

Al-Samarqandī refers faith here to affirmation (*taṣdīq*) of the truth and certainty (*yaqīn*), citing al-Zujāj who states that this is done by the believers when the Qur'ān is pronounced and in this manner they increase in affirmation verse by verse.[9] This also indicates two excellent methods to cultivate faith: *dhikr*, or remembering Allah Most High, with awe and reverence; and *tilāwah*, the recitation of the Qur'ān that should be accompanied with profound reflection.

Imām al-Bukhārī narrates on the authority of Anas that the Prophet, may Allah bless him and grant him peace, said, "There are three qualities that when present in an individual, he finds the sweetness of faith: that Allah and His Messenger are more beloved to him than anyone else; that he loves a person only for the sake of Allah; and that he hates to revert to disbelief like he hates to be thrown into fire."[10]

This *ḥadīth* vividly expresses the intensity with which faith should be felt by the believers, so that they come to experience a spiritual state that is sweeter than honey. It reminds us of how precious our *īmān* is, because by it we are saved from the punishment that Allah will deal out in the Hereafter to those who do not recognise, love and thank their Creator. 'Allāmah Badr al-Dīn al-'Aynī comments that love for Allah and His Messenger is the very foundation of faith and that these qualities are only truly present in someone whose *īmān* becomes strong in their soul, expanding their chest and mixing with their very flesh and blood.[11] A means by which we should try to acquire this state is to make an effort to internalise the noble character of the Prophet, which include such traits as his truthfulness, good manners, mercy and justice. These can be learnt through reading about his life and blessed sayings, but must be patiently applied in the chaotic environment of everyday life, if they are to have a lasting and transformative effect.

Notes

1 *Sūrah Āl ʿImrān* (Q3: 18).

2 Al-Shaʿrānī, ʿAbd al-Wahhāb, *Asrār Arkān al-Islām*. (Dār al-Turāth al-ʿArabī, 1980), p. 25.

3 *Sūrah al-Aḥzāb* (Q33: 40).

4 *Sūrah al-Baqarah* (Q2: 285): to *'make no distinction between any one of His messengers'* means that the believers fully accept the prophethood of every one of them. [Cf. Al-Rāzī, Fakhr al-Dīn, *Mafātīḥ al-Ghayb*, commentary on Q2: 285.]

5 This view, which is that of the Maturīdī School of Theology, is based upon the fact that the real essence of belief is assent by the heart in acknowledgment of the truth, which is not, in itself, susceptible to gradation; see al-Taftazānī, *Sharḥ ʿAqā'id al-Nasafī*, translated as *A Commentary on the Creed of Islam*, by E. E. Elder (Columbia University Press, 1950), p. 121. It can still be argued that the certainty with which this belief is established in the heart can become stronger, an example being the dialogue between the Prophet Ibrāhīm and Allah:

> *He said, 'My Lord, show me how You revive the dead.' He said, 'Do you not believe?' He said, 'I do, but I ask so that my heart becomes at ease.'* (Q2: 260).

The real motivation for the position that faith neither increases nor decreases, and the context within which this tenet must be understood, is that of a concern to make a definition of *īmān* that excluded deeds. This was important in the early centuries of Islam, because the Khawārij sect would consider a Muslim who neglected deeds to be an unbeliever. It was argued by some, including Imām Abū Ḥanīfah, that the logical step from considering faith itself to increase with the performance of acts of worship and decrease with sins, is to hold that it can disappear entirely through neglecting deeds thus leading to this extreme position. With these distinctions in mind and staying firm on the principle that deeds are not a component of faith, it has been held by some that the difference between increase and decrease of *īmān* (held by the 'Ash'arī s) and of its certainty (Maturīdīs) is more one of definition than substance. Cf. Nu'mānī, Shiblī, *Sirāt-i-Nu'mānī*, translated as *Imām Abū Ḥanīfah: Life and Works*, by M. H. Hussain, (Darul Ishaat, 2000), p. 91.

6 *Sūrah Ibrāhīm* (Q14: 24-7).

7 Al-Samarqandī, *Baḥr al-'Ulūm*, commentary on (Q14: 24).

8 *Sūrah al-Anfāl* (Q8: 2).

9 Al-Samarqandī, *Baḥr al-'Ulūm*, commentary on (Q8: 2).

10 Narrated in *Ṣaḥīḥ Al-Bukhārī.*

11 Al-'Aynī, *'Umdat al-Qārī*, (Dār al-Kutub al-'Ilmiyah, 2001), Vol. 1, p. 242.

Imam Abu Hassan Al-shari

CHAPTER 2

ʿAqā'id al-Nasafī: A Summary of Islamic Beliefs

Aqidah - 60 articles of our faith
Recognised by all the word esp hanafi's

About *ʿAqā'id al-Nasafī*

This chapter comprises a translation of *ʿAqā'id al-Nasafī*, a short, succinct and accurate summary of the authentic Muslim beliefs by Al-ʿAllāmah Imām Abū Hafs ʿUmar ibn Muḥammad al-Nasafī.[1] *ʿAqā'id* is the plural of *ʿaqīdah*, which means, 'to believe in something because of the certainty of its truth.'[2] This short treatise soon gained acceptance amongst the *ummah* because of its comprehensive summary of the beliefs of Islam. It has been highly praised by scholars for its brevity, accuracy and completeness and some 25 commentaries have been written on it. One of the most popular was the commentary written by Saʿd al-Dīn Taftazānī (d. 793 A.H.). Since then, it has been taught in Islamic schools and seminaries throughout the world, particularly in Central and South Asia.

In this work, the author compiled and enumerated some 60 points of belief, each one of them being established directly or indirectly by a Qur'ānic *āyah* or a *ṣaḥīḥ ḥadīth*. Although written from the perspective of the Maturīdī School of Theology, there is a consensus about all the fundamental beliefs mentioned in its pages amongst the Sunnī scholars and they have only differed on a few of the subsidiary issues dealt with in this work.

Our aim in translating this masterpiece is to enable every Muslim to read and learn about his beliefs in a short period of time. This may also be used as a textbook for studying the Muslim creed, in which students are encouraged to memorise the creed and the teacher explains the comments on the text.

Translation of *'Aqā'id al-Nasafī*

Knowledge and the Universe

Al-Nasafī begins his text with analysing the different means by which knowledge in general can be obtained. He does this in order to be able to affirm the articles of belief, so that it is established that they are known with certainty. In Islam there is no concept of 'blind faith', which means that Muslims are encouraged to reflect deeply on their fundamental beliefs and to become intellectually convinced of the truth of the message conveyed in the Qur'ānic revelation and the life of the Prophet Muḥammad, may Allah bless him and grant him peace.

The Sources of Knowledge

1. The people of truth declare that the reality of the existence of things is an established fact. Knowledge of it is certain, in disagreement with the Sophist philosophers.[3]

   There are three sources from which knowledge of creation can be acquired:

   i. The unimpaired senses
   ii. The truthful report
   iii. The intellect

   The senses are five: hearing, sight, smell, taste and touch. Each sense organ is endowed with a specific faculty (in order to perceive an aspect of reality).

The (certainly) truthful report is of two kinds:

a. The *mutawātir* (continuously narrated) report, which is affirmed by a number of people large enough for it to be inconceivable that they could have colluded upon a lie.[4] It entails necessary knowledge, such as that of kings in past times and of distant lands.
b. The report from a prophetic messenger assisted by miracles. It provides conclusive knowledge (because of his divinely guaranteed truthfulness), which is akin to that known necessarily in terms of certainty and proof.

The intellect is also a means to acquire knowledge and what is established by it is of two types: the self-evident, which is attained immediately, without thinking, such as the knowledge that all of something is greater than its parts; and that which is acquired through proof requiring a type of reflection, such as the knowledge of the presence of fire from the sight of smoke.[5] *Ilhām* (inspiration in the heart) is not a means of gaining knowledge of the veracity of something, according to the people of truth.[6]

The Universe is Created

2. The universe (everything other than Allah) with all its constituent parts is created, since it is composed of substances and properties. A substance is something that exists in and of itself,[7] whether it is a compound or a single element that cannot be split up any further. Properties refer to that which cannot exist by itself and occurs in bodies and single elements, like colours, states of being (e.g. movement), flavours and smells.[8]

Belief in Allah

Although the Absolute Reality of Allah Most High is beyond the comprehension of the human intellect, the rightly-guided scholars of Islam have used the faculties with which they have been blessed to compile those statements that can be made about Him. The following beliefs are based on negating that which cannot be ascribed to Him and affirming those Attributes which are known from revelation.

The Attributes of Allah

3. The Creator of the universe is Allah, the One[9], the Eternal, the Ever-Living, the All-Powerful, the Omniscient, the All-Hearing, the All-Seeing, the All-Intending and the All-Willing.
4. Allah is neither a property, a body, nor an element and He does not have a form (like a human being as that is specific to bodies).
5. He is neither limited nor numbered. He does not consist of parts, separated or compounded and is not finite.
6. He cannot be ascribed a nature or a state. He is not located in a place and time does not affect Him. Nothing resembles Him and nothing escapes His Knowledge and Power. He has Eternal Attributes that are established with His Being. These are neither Him nor other than Him. They are: Knowledge, Power, Life, Might, Hearing, Sight, Will and Desire, Action and Creating, Sustaining and Speech.[10]
7. Allah speaks, which is an Eternal Attribute that is neither formed of letters or sounds. This attribute is incompatible with silence and defect and has no organs of sound. Allah Most High is the Speaker. Through His speech He commands, forbids and informs (His creation).
8. The Qur'an is the Speech of Allah and not a creation. It is written down in our books, safe in our hearts (memorised in our minds), recited by our tongues, and listened to by our ears without being incarnated.[11]
9. Originating is an Eternal Attribute of Allah. He creates each thing from its constituent parts at the time that it is to enter into existence according to His Knowledge and Will. He Himself is not a created being. And the Divine Will is Allah's Eternal Attribute established with His Being.

The Believers will see Allah

10. The seeing of Allah by the believers in the Hereafter is possible for the intellect to affirm and necessary to believe in due to the evidences established by the Qurʾān and *Sunnah*.[12] Allah will not be seen in a particular place, direction or by rays of light. Nor will there be distance between the onlooker and the Almighty.

The Decree of Allah (Al-Qaḍāʾ)

11. Allah Almighty is the Creator of all the actions of humanity, whether it is disbelief or faith, obedience or disobedience. All these actions occur by His Will, Desire, Command, Decree and Measure.
12. Humanity have the free choice (to be an obedient servant of the Lord or otherwise) and will be rewarded or punished (accordingly). Their good deeds meet the Almighty's approval while their evil deeds do not have His approval.[13]
13. Capability is integral with action and this is the meaning of the power by which the action is done. This term (capability) is also used to describe the means, the tools and the health that is required for carrying out the action. The following of *sharīʿah* rulings depends on this capability. And humanity is not charged with what they are incapable of doing. The pain suffered in an injury after being struck by a person and the breaking of glass by a person, all these actions are Allah's creation. The creation of actions cannot be ascribed to humanity.
14. The murdered person dies at the time appointed (by Allah). There is only a single appointed time.[14]
15. Each one consumes only their (alloted) portion of sustenance whether it is lawful or unlawful. It is unimaginable that a person will not consume all their assigned sustenance or that someone else will consume it. Unlawful things are also a form of sustenance.
16. Allah allows to go astray whom He wishes and guides whom He wishes.[15] It is not incumbent upon Allah Almighty to give humanity what is best for them.[16]

Belief in *al-Ākhirah* (the Hereafter), its Punishments and its Rewards

Belief in the Hereafter is an essential aspect of Islamic belief, without which the true meaning of existence, the successful return to Allah, is not realised. The descriptions of the various places and states of the next world must be accepted as they are found in the Qur'ān and authentic aḥādīth, *even if they seem to be difficult or impossible to conceive, as this only springs from our habituation to the conditions of the* dunyā *(present life).*

Punishment of the Grave

17. The punishment of the grave is for the unbelievers and some disobedient believers. The delights of the grave are for the obedient ones, as Allah Almighty wills, and only He knows what they are.
18. The questions asked in the grave by the angels, Munkar and Nakīr, are established by evidences from the texts.

Events of the Day of Judgement

19. The Resurrection, the Scales, the Book of Deeds, the Reckoning, the Prophet's Basin and the Bridge are all true.
20. Paradise and the Fire are true and both have been created and already exist. They are permanent and will not perish, nor will their inhabitants perish.

Sin and Punishment

21. Major sin does not remove a believer from faith, nor does it enter him into disbelief.
22. Allah Almighty will not forgive the one who associates others with Him in worship.[17] However, He will forgive other than that for anyone whom He wishes, whether they have committed minor or major sins.
23. Punishment is possible for a minor sin and forgiveness for a major sin as long as it is not regarded as being lawful. In fact, regarding a major sin as lawful is disbelief.

Intercession (Shafāʿah)

24. Intercession in favour of major sinners is proven for the prophets and the righteous people.
25. The major sinners will not remain in the Fire forever, even if they had died without repentance.

The Nature of *Īmān* (Faith), Belief in the Messengers, Angels and Revealed Books

The important issue of the definition of faith is taken up by al-Nasafī before presenting the fundamental beliefs regarding prophecy, angels and revealed scripture. His conception of faith, which is seen from the Maturīdī perspective, is that it is a single indivisible state of the heart which an individual either possesses or does not. This explains both his exclusion of deeds from the content of faith, as well as the assertion that it cannot increase or decrease.

Faith

26. Faith is to assent with the heart and profess with the tongue to that which the Prophet brought from Allah.[18]
27. The quantity of deeds a person does may increase, but the faith of a person does not increase or decrease.[19]
28. *Īmān* and Islam are one and the same thing.[20] When a person has assented in the heart and professed verbally (the testimony of faith), then he can say, 'I am a believer' and it is not correct to say, 'I am a believer, *inshā' Allāh* (God willing).'
29. A blessed person can become evil and an evil person can become blessed.[21] Being blessed or being deprived of blessings (occurs) but not in (Allah's attribute of) giving blessings and being deprived of them, which are two Divine Attributes and change never occurs in Allah's Being or in in His Attributes.

The Purpose of sending the Prophets

30. There is divine wisdom in sending prophets. Allah has always sent prophets from amongst their own peoples so as to tell them the good news and to warn them.

SHAHĀDAH

31. They explain to people what they need to know concerning both the sacred and the profane. And He supported them with miracles that break the natural laws of His creation. All the prophets were teachers, deliverers of the message from Allah and honest and sincere advisors.
32. The first prophet was Adam, may peace be upon him, and the last of them was Muḥammad, may Allah bless him and grant him peace. Although some *aḥādīth* have mentioned the number of prophets sent, it is still preferable not to mention a fixed number. Allah Almighty has said:

    And messengers that We have narrated to you before and messengers We have not narrated to you.[22]

    Therefore it is unsafe to mention a fixed number, since some may be included amongst them who were not prophets and it could be that others may be excluded who were prophets.
33. The best of all the prophets is Muḥammad, may Allah bless him and grant him peace.

The Angels

34. The angels are Allah's servants who carry out His orders and are not to be described as having either male or female gender.[23]

The Books

35. Allah revealed Books to the prophets and explained in them His commandments, prohibitions, promises and warnings.[24]

The Ascension

36. The Prophet's Ascension, a bodily journey in a waking state to the heavens and then to the heights that Allah wished him to ascend, is a reality.

The Beliefs and Practices of the Ahl al-Sunnah wa al-Jamāʿah

This section comprises the remainder of Imām al-Nasafī's creed. It consists of a number of beliefs in different categories that tended to be the subject to dispute by sectarian groups in the early centuries of Islam. The scholars of the Ahl al-Sunnah wa al-Jamāʿah (People of the Prophetic Precedent and the Community), or Sunnīs, affirmed the following tenets as being truly derived from the Qurʾān and Sunnah *and characteristic of the beliefs of the overwhelming majority of Muslims. Nevertheless, it can be seen that some of these points, such as numbers 45 and 46, involving the wiping over leather socks and the permissibility of drinking water in which dates have been soaked, are more appropriately placed within the* fiqh *literature. The explanation for this is that these practices became characteristic of the Sunnīs to the point that someone who denied their validity would knowingly be associating themselves with other sects. This is why it is reported that when the famous Companion Anas ibn Mālik was asked about the Ahl al-Sunnah wa al-Jamāʿah, he said, "It is to love the* shaykhayn *[Abū Bakr and ʿUmar], not to revile the* khatanayn *[ʿUthmān and ʿAlī] and to wipe over the* khuffayn *[leather socks]."*[25] *It is also very significant to note that while the points of belief in this section are important, the denial of many of them would not be enough to remove a person from the fold of Islam.*

Saints and their Miracles

37. The miracles of the saints are true. Miracles of the saint are occurrences that break the usual laws of Allah's creation such as travelling great distances in a short time; the appearance of food, drink and clothes when needed; walking on water; flying in the air; the speaking of animate and inanimate things; the diverting of impending calamities; achieving one's purpose from enemies; and other events. The saint's 'miracle' is really the miracle of the prophet who he follows and this is a sign that he is a saint. He cannot be a saint if he is not firm in his religion

(i.e. he must verbally profess and affirm with his heart the message of his prophet, along with obeying his commands and prohibitions.)

38. The best human beings after the prophets are: Abū Bakr al-Ṣiddīq, then ʿUmar al-Fārūq, then ʿUthmān Dhū Nūrayn and then ʿAlī al-Murtaḍā (May Allah be pleased with them all). Their caliphate was in this particular order and it extended over a period of thirty years, then monarchy and governance followed.

Leadership of the Muslim Community

39. Muslims must appoint a leader who rules them; establishes the Islamic legal system; protects them from enemies; maintains their armies; collects (Islamic) taxes; enforces law and order to control the rebellious and the criminals; organises the Friday and ʿĪd prayers, reconciles disputes and conflicts, accepts testimony to establish legal rights, conducts the marriages of young men and maidens who have no guardians; distributes the booty; and similar matters that are not entrusted to the individuals of the community.

40. The leader must be present. He cannot be hidden, nor awaited. He must be from the Quraysh and it is not permissible that the leader should be from any other tribe, although he need not be from the Banū Hāshim or the children of ʿAlī, may Allah be pleased with him.[26]

41. It is not a condition (of leadership) that the leader must be infallible, nor does he have to be the best person in his time. However, it is a condition that he must be a person of responsibility: capable of ruling well; commanding authority; establishing the law; protecting the boundaries of the Muslim country; and able to deliver justice to any victims.

42. The leader cannot be removed from his office due to his corrupt behaviour or tyranny.[27] It is permissible to pray

behind a person, whether he is righteous or immoral, and it is permissible to perform the funeral prayer for any person, righteous or immoral.

The Companions of the Prophet

43. We stop the person who says anything other than good about the Companions of the Prophet, may Allah bless him and grant him peace.
44. We bear witness that the ten companions who have been given the glad tidings of Paradise by the Prophet, may Allah bless him and grant him peace, are indeed present there.[28]

added to emphasis we are different from shi'as

The Practices of Ahl al-Sunnah

45. We regard the wiping of the *khuffayn* (leather socks) permissible either at home or on a journey.
46. We do not regard as unlawful the drinking of water in which dates have been soaked.

The Upper Limits regarding Sainthood, the Obligation to observe the Sharīʿah *and* Ijtihād *(Derivation of Legal Rulings)*

47. No saint can attain the rank of the prophets.
48. No one can acquire a status where he is free from the obligations and the prohibitions of the *Sharīʿah*.
49. It is possible that the *mujtahid* (expert jurist) may be correct or make an error (in judgement).

Prayers

50. The prayers of the living for the deceased are like charity that benefits them.
51. Allah Almighty accepts prayers and fulfils needs.

Beliefs and Practices that lead to Disbelief (Kufr)

52. We take the outward literal meanings of the texts and to misconstrue their meanings like the Ahl al-Bāṭin[29] is regarded as disbelief and rejection of the texts.

53. To regard disobedience (sin) as permissible is disbelief.
54. To regard disobedience lightly is disbelief.
55. Making mockery of the *sharī'ah* is disbelief.
56. To despair of Allah's mercy is disbelief, as is to feel completely secure from Allah's punishment.
57. To accept the divination of fortune-tellers as the truth is disbelief.[30]
58. The non-existent is nothing.[31]

The Prophet Muḥammad's Future Prophecies, may Allah bless him and grant him peace

59. All the Prophet's predictions, may Allah bless him and grant him peace, about the following events are true:
    i. The signs of the Hour.
    ii. The coming of the *Dajjāl* (The False Messiah and Deceiver).
    iii. The coming of *Dābbah al-Arḍ* (The Beast of the Earth).
    iv. The appearance of *Ya'jūj* and *Ma'jūj* (Gog and Magog).
    v. The coming of ʿĪsā, peace be upon him.
    vi. The rising of the sun in the West.

The Ranks of Prophets, Ordinary Humans and Angels

60. The human messengers (and prophets)[32] are superior to the angelic messengers. The angelic messengers are superior to common humans. And common humans are superior to common angels.

Notes

1 For his biography and that of all other major scholars mentioned in this book, see the section starting on p. 261.

2 *ʿAqā'id* (creed) formally sets out the tenets of the faith, as opposed to *fiqh* (Islamic Law), which sets out the *aḥkām* (practical rituals and laws). The Ahl al-Sunnah wa al-Jamāʿah (or the Sunnīs) comprises three *madhāhib* (schools) of theology: Maturīdī, ʿAsh'arī and Ḥanbalī and four *madhāhib* of *fiqh*: Ḥanafī, Mālikī, Shāfiʿī and Ḥanbalī.

3 These philosophers believe that there is no objective reality to things and that everything is merely an illusion.

4 Some scholars have tried to specify a minimum number and have given varying opinions from as low as four to as much as hundreds. The majority view, including al-Ghazālī, is that this depends on the circumstances of the particular report that is being established. The important thing is that the combination of corroborative reports by independent, reliable witnesses is enough to engender certainty; see Kamali, M., *Principles of Islamic Jurisprudence* (The Islamic Texts Society, 2003), p. 93.

5 Part of the original text has here been replaced by appropriate statements from the commentary by Saʿd al-Dīn al-Taftāzānī, in order to clarify this point; see al- Taftazānī, *Sharḥ ʿAqāʾid al-Nasafī* (Maktabah Kulliyāt Azhariyyah, 1988), pp. 21-2.

6 Al-Taftāzānī comments that what is meant is only that *ilhām* is not a permissible means of knowledge for the *generality* of creation, as there are numerous reports related about its efficacy from the *salaf* (predecessors); see Taftazānī, p. 22.

7 This is, of course, taking for granted that it is entirely dependent upon Allah. The distinction being made is highlighted by the definition that follows.

8 This physical theory was developed by Muslim theologians as a coherent way to categorise the universe intellectually. The essential point which must be believed by the Muslim is that this universe is a contingent creation, while Allah is the Self-Subsistent Creator. If this truth is maintained by theories in modern physics, then it is perfectly possible for them to be acceptable to Islam.

9 He is Wājib al-Wujūb (the Necessary Being) as His existence is not dependent on anything else. It is logical that at the end of the chain of cause and effect there must be One whose existence is self-sustained and that is Allah. In philosophy, this is called the Cosmological Argument.

10 There would seem to be twelve Attributes from al-Nasafī's text. However, the commentator, al-Taftazānī, remarks that Might refers to Power; Will and Desire can be identified together; while Action, Creating and Sustaining all refer to a single Attribute called *al-takwīn* (Originating), which al-Nasafī elaborates on further in a following section (no. 9). From al-Taftazānī's analysis, then, eight Eternal Attributes are affirmed, which is in accordance with standard Maturīdī teaching, see al-Taftazānī, *Sharḥ ʿAqāʾid al-Nasafī*, translated as *A Commentary on the Creed of Islam*, by E. E. Elder, pp. 56-7.

11 As the Speech of Allah, the Qurʾān is an Eternal Attribute, yet what we are able to write down, memorise, recite and listen to in the form of Arabic letters and words is a composition that indicates the underlying Reality. This can be compared to saying that fire is a burning substance, which can be brought to mind as an expression, or written with a pen. It does not, however, follow that the reality of

SHAHĀDAH

fire is composed of sounds and letters; see al-Taftazānī, *A Commnetary*, pp. 63-4.]

12 The most important Qur'ānic reference to this is:

> *On that Day faces will be radiant, gazing at their Lord.* (Q75: 22-3).

13 It may be asked how a person can have free choice and accountability in their actions, if they occur by the Will of Allah and are already written in His Decree. The answer is that by His Omniscience he already knows what His servants will do by their free choice. When each moment of action comes, Allah creates the power that is needed to carry out the chosen act. This is why in the next point (no. 13) al-Nasafī states that all actions are created by Allah and must be ascribed to Him.

14 This point is made to distinguish the belief from the one held by the Muʿtazilī of Baghdad, al-Kaʿbī (d. 317 A.H./929 C.E.), that a murdered person had two appointed times: one for his murder and one for his 'natural' death, which he would have lived until, if he had not been killed; al-Taftazānī, *A Commentary*, p. 95.

15 This means that Allah creates guidance or misguidance, as he is the Creator of everything – although this can be delivered through means, such as guiding by the Qur'ān and misguiding through the whisperings of Shayṭān. It should also be understood that this guidance is defined as *the indication of a path leading to what is sought*, so that a guided individual still must choose to take the right path; see al-Taftazānī, *Sharḥ ʿAqā'id al-Nasafī*, pp. 65-6.

16 As with so many points in al-Nasafī's treatise, this must be understood in the context of refuting the Muʿtazilī belief that Allah must always do what is best for humankind at all particular times. As well as failing to account for the suffering that does exist in the world, within this theological view, Allah is deprived of His freedom. The Maturīdī perspective is that Allah's Justice means that He will never be unjust to His creation, while His Wisdom requires that within any particular trial given to an individual, there is an ultimate purpose. However, as we lack knowledge of the reality of this world and the Hereafter, it is not possible for us to always understand His decisions in this matter; see al- Taftazānī, *A Commentary*, p. 98.

17 This refers to major *shirk* (associating partners with Allah). Minor *shirk*, for instance showing off in prayer, is forgivable. It is important to note that someone who sincerely repents of major *shirk* while alive and ceases committing it, will also be liable for forgiveness.

18 In the case of compulsion, it is permissible for there to be no verbal profession of faith. Al-Nasafī thus represents the position that if there is no compulsion, then faith requires profession. The other view within the Maturīdī school, which is the majority position on the matter,

is that, strictly speaking, faith is only assent by the heart. Therefore, someone without an excuse who does not verbally profess faith, is to be treated as a disbeliever in the matters of the worldly life, but remains a believer with Allah; see al- Taftazānī, *A Commentary*, p. 118.

19 This point has been explained at length in footnote 5 above on p. 7.

20 This assertion is based on the fact that a believer must be judged a Muslim and *vice versa*. In this context, the practical aspects of Islam are seen as fruits of the essential faith, just as the acceptability of the remaining four pillars are built upon the foundation of the *shahādah*; see al-Taftazānī, *A Commentary*, pp. 123-4.

21 The reference here is to entering or leaving faith.

22 *Sūrah al-Nisāʾ* (Q4:164).

23 This is in terms of the reality of their being. It is known that angels sometimes assume the appearance of a male human being, such as the famous *ḥadīth* of Jibrīl (Gabriel). Also in Arabic, which always distinguishes between grammatical gender, it is conventional to use the male forms for describing their actions.

24 The four books that every Muslim should be aware of are, in chronological order: al-Taurah (Torah) revealed to Mūsā (Moses); al-Zabūr (Psalms) revealed to Dāwūd (David); al-Injīl (Gospel) revealed to ʿĪsā (Jesus) and al-Qurʾān revealed to Muḥammad. It should be noted that with the exception of the Qurʾān, no revealed book has been preserved entirely intact by the religious communities in the process of transmitting their heritage. The ultimate reason for this difference is Allah's promise to watch over the Qurʾān Himself:

> *Indeed We have revealed the Reminder (Qurʾān) and We, assuredly, will guard it.* (Q15: 9).

25 Al-Taftazānī, *Sharḥ ʿAqāʾid al-Nasafī*, p. 104.

26 This position, which is that of the scholars of *fiqh* generally, is based on the *ḥadīth* in *Ṣaḥīḥ al-Bukhārī*: *"This matter (caliphate) will remain with the Quraysh even if only two of them were still alive."* However, Islamic history has practically recognised *khalīfah*s that are not from the tribe of Quraysh, such as the Ottomans. Ibn Khaldūn, an expert in the subject of history and Islamic governance, as well as a competent jurist, interprets this rule as specifically linked to the capacity that the Quraysh possessed in the deterrence of strife, based on their group-solidarity, that qualified them for rule. He goes on to argue that 'we stipulate for the person of the commander of the Muslims that he be from the people who have group-solidarity above whoever [else] has it in his time so they can make whoever is like them [in having some group-solidarity] subservient [to them] and the people can agree on the best of protection.' See Ibn Khaldūn, *Muqaddimah*, quoted in

al-Qaraḍāwī, Y., *Approaching the Sunnah* (The International Institute of Islamic Thought, 2007), p. 130.

27 This represents the Ḥanafī view. Imām al-Shāfiʿī is reported as ruling that the leader could be removed under these circumstances, as such a person lacks the required responsibility, the argument being that if he cannot look after himself, then how can he look after others? See al- Taftazānī, *A Commentary*, p. 150.

28 The Prophet, may Allah bless him and grant him peace, said that Abū Bakr, ʿUmar, ʿUthmān, ʿAlī, Ṭalḥah, Zubayr, ʿAbd al-Raḥmān ibn ʿAuf, Saʿīd ibn Abī Waqqāṣ, Saʿīd ibn Zayd and Abū ʿUbaydah ibn al-Jarrāḥ were all in Paradise (*Musnad* of Aḥmad ibn Ḥanbal).

29 A heretical sect that believes that the apparent meaning of the Qur'ān and *aḥādīth* is not their real meaning, but that the texts are symbolic and figurative representations of the true and esoteric meaning (*bāṭin*). Therefore they argue that only those initiates who have received special instructions at the hands of a master can understand these symbols.

30 Forecasters or fortune tellers include psychics, palm readers, astrologers as well as the horoscopes that appear in the newspapers in many Western countries. These all must be completely abandoned by the believers.

31 This statement is in refutation of the Muʿtazilī position that non-existence is a thing (*al-maʿdūm shay'*) in the sense of its possibility, which is verified by its happening. Al-Nasafī's statement reaffirms the uncompromising Sunnī understanding of Allah's act of creation as *ex-nihilo* (out of nothing).

32 All messengers are prophets, but not all prophets are messengers. The difference is that messengers bring a new or altered *sharīʿah*, while other prophets follow that of a previous messenger. A good illustration of this is ʿĪsā, may peace be on him, for when he was sent to the Banū Isrāʾīl, it was as a messenger who came with changes to their existing *sharīʿah*, while, when he will return, it will be as a prophet following the *sharīʿah* of Muḥammad, may Allah bless him and grant him peace.

2nd
Pillar

ṢALĀH

(The Prayer)

The deepening of Divine Love through Devotion

CHAPTER 3

Introduction to the *Sharī ͑ah* and the Science of *Fiqh*

The Purpose of this Chapter

The second pillar of Islam, *ṣalāh* (prayer), like the remaining three pillars, is concerned with specific acts of worship that Allah has legislated for the believers. It therefore comes under the category of *sharī͑ah* (sacred law and ethics), rather than *͑aqīdah* (creed), as its subject is the correct practice of Islamic rituals, rather than the content of belief. As *sharī͑ah* is a term that is often misunderstood, it is well worth looking into its meaning in a little more depth, before distinguishing it from *fiqh* (Islamic jurisprudence), which provides the systematic and practical instructions for carrying out worship. After this, we will examine in more detail the most important categories used in *fiqh*, as learning them is essential for understanding the rules to be found in the following chapters.

The *Sharī͑ah*

The word *sharī͑ah* in Arabic initially signified 'a way to water'[1] – obviously a very important concept for people living in a desert environment! The usage of this term in Islamic sacred law and ethics is very profound for it reflects the belief in divine guidance that shapes our lives and will lead us back to an eternal life through seeking the pleasure of our Creator. The *sharīʿah*, then, is the complete way of life that has been approved by Allah for the believers, including not only specified obligations, prohibitions and permitted acts in aspects of life as different as worship and financial transactions, but also comprehensive ethical guidance.[2] While the confidence that Muslims have in the *sharīʿah* is based upon its revealed sources: the Qur'ān and the authentic *Sunnah* of the Prophet, may Allah bless him and grant him peace, its precise application in society has required a process of interpretation ever since the time of the rightly-guided *khalīfah*s. This is where *fiqh* comes in.

Fiqh

Fiqh literally means 'understanding' and in its technical sense 'Islamic jurisprudence', which has had a rich history with its roots in the earliest days of the Muslim community. During the life of the Prophet, may Allah bless him and grant him peace, his example and guidance were sufficient for all legal and ethical matters faced by his Companions. After his passing, however, it was necessary for the leading members of the community to apply their reasoning to derive rulings from the sources of revelation that were appropriate for the new situations that arose. In fact, even during the life of the Prophet, may Allah bless him and grant him peace, this process began, as recorded in the *ḥadīth* that preserves the instructions given by him to the Companion Muʿādh ibn Jabal, whom he sent to the Yemen:

'The Prophet (may Allah bless him and grant him peace) sent one of his Companions, Muʿādh ibn Jabal (may Allah be well pleased with him), to the Yemen on a mission. [Before he left] the Prophet (may Allah bless him and grant him peace) asked him, 'How will you judge the cases [that come to you]?' And he replied:

'I will judge according to the Book of Allah.' 'But if you do not get anything there, what will you do?' the Prophet (peace be upon him) asked. He said, 'I will refer to the *Sunnah* of

the Prophet (peace be upon him).' 'But if you do not get it even there, what will you do?' the Prophet (peace be upon him) asked again. Then Mu'ādh replied, 'I will exercise my judgement.'
Hearing this, the Prophet (may Allah bless him and grant him peace) patted Mu'ādh on the shoulder and said, 'Praise be to Allah Who has guided the messenger of His Messenger to what pleases His Messenger.'"³ → derived from jihad
In the course of the following centuries, *ijtihād* (effort made for the purpose of derivation of rulings) was developed by generations of jurists into a rich and complex methodology embodied in the theoretical works of the schools of law (*madhhab*s), alongside the substantive body of rules that make up the *fiqh* literature. This systemisation of the entire body of Islamic rulings through the creative endeavour of pious and knowledgable jurists developed its own particular terminology and categories, which are intended to facilitate the practice of a life obedient to Allah. The following section explains the eleven most important categories from the perspective of the Ḥanafī *madhhab* (the other *madhhab*s use a less complicated system based on only five categories).⁴

ṢALĀH

→ tool for analysing
The Categories of Rulings in Islamic Jurisprudence *learn these*
These are the <u>eleven</u> categories of rulings in the Ḥanafī *Madhhab* arranged in sets according to their degree of importance: taken from Maulana Ahmed Raza Khan Bralevi

The Five Types of Obligation/Commendation
1. *Al-Farḍ* – The Obligation: This is a ruling that must be carried out and omitting it is a major sin. It is known definitely   to deny makes you from either the Qur'ān or the *Sunnah*, and therefore its denial is an act of *kufr*. Hence it is also known as *farḍ i'tiqādī*, khafar meaning it is a part of the faith to believe and follow it. Examples of *farḍ* rulings are the performance of the daily *ṣalāh*, paying *zakāh* and fasting in the month of Ramaḍān.
2. *Al-Wājib* – The Necessary: This ruling must also be carried out and its omission is a major sin. However it is different

[margin top: amali — act]

THE FIVE PILLARS OF ISLAM

from the *farḍ* since it is not proven by definite evidence, i.e. the proof for it is not conclusive, insofar as there is some doubt as to whether the *sharīʿah* prescribes it as compulsory or as a recommendation. Therefore, its denial is not *kufr*. Hence it is called *farḍ ʿamalī*, i.e. it is compulsory to act upon it. Examples of *wājib* rulings are the *witr* prayer after *ʿishāʾ* and the *ʿĪd* prayers.

3. **Al-Sunnah al-Muʾakkadah** – The Emphatic *Sunnah*: This ruling is based on a regular activity or a habit of the blessed Messenger of Allah or the rightly-guided *khalīfahs*. *[margin: Ali, Uthman, Umar, Abu Bakr]* The *Sunnah* is neither obligatory nor necessary, but is highly recommended. The *sharīʿah* commends this action as being good and acceptable. To habitually miss the Emphatic *Sunnah* is detestable, since it gives the impression of turning away from the Prophet's practice. Examples of *sunnah muʾakkadah* rulings are establishing the *adhān* (call to prayer) and praying in congregation.

[margin: performed regularly by prophet]

4. **Al-Sunnah Ghayr al-Muʾakkadah** – The Unemphatic *Sunnah*: This is a practice of the blessed Messenger or the rightly-guided *khalīfahs*, but unlike the emphatic *sunnah* this was not performed regularly by them. Examples include the four units of *sunnah* prayer before the *ṣalāh* of *ʿaṣr* and *ʿishāʾ*.

[margin: no sin if we don't do]

5. **Al-Mustaḥabb** – The Desirable: This is a ruling that is approved of in the *sharīʿah*. This includes activities and devotions like voluntary fasting and prayers. It is sometimes called *al-Mandūb* (recommended), *al-Taṭawwuʿ* (voluntary) and *al-ʿĀdah* (decent). Performance of any desirable act earns <u>merit</u> and its omission carries <u>no sanction</u>.

[margin: if we don't do at all then no problem]

The Five Types of Prohibition/Disapproval

6. **Al-Ḥarām** – The Unlawful: This is a ruling that forbids something. In other words it must be avoided. This prohibition is proven by a definite text. To regard an unlawful act as lawful is therefore *kufr*. To commit the unlawful is

[margin left: ṢALĀH]

[margin bottom: like fard. Definate command of Allah. Denial is khufr]

a major sin. Examples include drinking alcohol, gambling and adultery. — Compulsory to avoid. Proven from texts to avoid. Allah forbids

7. *Al-Makrūh al-Taḥrīmī* – The Major Offence: This is a prohibition that is not proved by a definite text. To ignore this ruling is a sin that is punishable, but to regard it permissable is not an act of *kufr*. Examples include praying during the three prohibited times: sunrise, noon and sunset.

8. *Al-Isʿāh* – The Offence: This ruling is between *makrūh taḥrīmī* and *tanzīhī* in terms of importance. It concerns acts that are offensive to do and doing it on a regular basis is sinful. Examples of this category are not rinsing the mouth and cleaning the nose during *wuḍūʾ*.

9. *Al-Makrūh al-Tanzīhī* – The Minor Offence: This is a ruling that concerns acts that are minor offenses. It is rewardable to do avoid them, but there is no harm in doing them. Examples include splashing water on the face during *wuḍūʾ*. We should try + strive to be 'likeable' eg splashing might upset someone.

10. *Khilāf al-Awlā* – The Undesirable: This is the opposite of *mustaḥabb*, it is less than optimal in terms of reward, but there is no harm in doing it. An example of this category is leaving off the performance of additional *nafl* (superogatory) prayers.

The Default State of All Acts

11. *Al-Mubāh* – The Permissable: This is something neither prescribed nor prohibited by the Shariah. It carries neither reward nor any punishment in itself (although it will merit reward or punishment respectively if done with a good or evil intention). This ruling is derived from the Islamic principle that everything is permissable unless it is prohibited. Examples of *mubāh* acts include eating, drinking and sleeping.

— relevance of rituals

Islamic Rituals of Worship

Ritual means 'a way of doing something'. Islamic rituals of prayer and meditation, fasting, charity and pilgrimage are specifically done at fixed times, in a particular place and in a particular way. They are performed in a set order as prescribed and demonstrated by the Prophet Muḥammad, may Allah bless him and grant him peace. This is, in fact, part of the *Sunnah* which has been passed down from generation to generation. The Islamic rituals of worship have therefore remained unchanged over the past fourteen centuries.

Thus Islamic rituals link Muslims to their glorious past and is something that is far bigger than the individual. They also connect Muslims all over world; the *Ummah*, whether in the East or West, performs these rituals in the same way, leading to a complete sense of unity and solidarity. Moreover, these rituals even connect people to their deepest selves through the positive effect they have on the mind.

The modern fast-moving lifestyle, our increasingly-busy schedules, as well as the constant bombardment of information and entertainment laeaves us with little time for relaxation and spiritual activities. How can one escape this madding crowd? Where can one find spiritual peace? Where can one find sanctuary?

It is in the daily prayers, fasting, giving *zakāh* and peforming the pilgrimage and other Islamic rituals of worship! They are like natural breaks in the day. The daily prayers provide an ideal way of cleansing ourselves from the noise pollution and our own busy schedules. They allow us to rid ourselves of the aggravations of daily chores and worldly distractions. Furthermore, they give us the opportunity, time and space to escape the heedlessness of our non-spiritual daily routines and to be in an elevated form of consciousness and awareness of God.

The sacred space in which we perform these rituals also provide us with ample 'spiritual support'. This can be the *muṣallā* (prayer mat) or corner of the room reserved for prayer, or in accordance with the *Sunnah* of the Prophet, may Allah bless him and grant him peace, the *masjid* itself. Every time he was faced with a dilemma, he would enter the House of Allah, in order to regain a balanced perspective.

The practice of praying in congregation is a good example of a ritual that helps to ground, align and give us a sense of belonging to a community. This is partly why the Prophet, may Allah bless him and grant him peace, stressed the attendance of the Friday congregation, saying, *"Anyone who misses three consecutive Friday congregations is not from us."*

In *Islam*, Friday should be both a day of relaxation and worship, as well as socialising with other Muslims. This is an intrinsic part of human nature. Every culture and country has some kind of rituals or customs, which they almost religiously adhere to and that become part of the social fabric.

The funeral prayer and paying condolences to the family of the deceased is a powerful ritual, which helps the family to overcome the pain and grief that they are suffering. The presence of others amidst them gives them a real sense of being part of a community larger than their immediate family. Their burden of grief is lightened and they can become energised to continue their lives with hope for the future.

When we are faced with problems and difficulties, we normally resort to ritual as a form of defence. It is for these situations that Allah instructs us:

> *Oh believers! Seek help in patience and prayer. Truly Allah is with the patient.*[5]

The Human Brain loves Rituals

Brain cells work together to lay pathways of incoming signals. When actions are repeated, for instance, prayers are said over and over again and a pathway is created in the brain like a track across a field: the more trodden, the more engrained it gets.

What is a Wird?

Some spiritual teachers will give their students *wird*s to recite daily. *Wird* literally refers to 'a watering place', or anything that returns, or one returns to, again and again. In Islamic spiritual circles it refers to a portion of the Qur'ān, a Prophetic prayer or a Divine Name recited repeatedly at a set time. This is used in meditation either silently or chanted aloud.

The *wird* helps to focus the mind and is very soothing and calming as well as being invigorating. The repetition of Qur'ānic verses, a prophetic prayer or Divine name (for example *'Yā Laṭīf'* (Oh Sublime!), or *'Yā Ḥayyu, Yā Qayyūm'* (Oh Living and Eternal!) clears the mind of intruding thoughts. The result is that it provides peace and leaves you in a calm and serene state.

The spiritual masters recommend that you sit in a quiet spot preferably after *fajr* prayer. Sit in a relaxed and a comfortable position. Begin by breathing deeply and slowly with eyes closed. Concentrate on the *wird*; repeat it slowly or silently or aloud. Don't let your thoughts wander. Focus on the *wird* and gradually the distractions will eventually fade away and you will feel Divine proximity, a sense of closeness, of happiness. Physically you will be relaxed, refreshed and much more alert – ready for a fresh start to a new bright day.

Notes

1 Lane, E. W., *Arabic-English* Lexicon, (Islamic Texts Society, 2003), Vol. 1, p. 1535.

2 See Weiss, B., *The Spirit of Islamic Law*, (University of Georgia Press, 1998) pp. 17-18.

3 Narrated in *Sunan al-Nisā'ī.*

4 All the *fiqh* rulings in this book are given according to this school of thought which remains the most widely practised of the four Sunnī *madhhabs*. The decision to do this was made so as to present a useful and consistent manual of the five pillars of Islam to the general public. The majority of rulings are taken from the reliable *Nūr al-Īḍāḥ* by al-Shurunbulālī, although other Ḥanafī books were also consulted as required. On some rare occasions, mention may be made, by way of comparison, to one of the other schools if it was thought to be particularly important for the issue at hand. We would like to reiterate that we respect all of the four schools and their contributions to Islamic civilisation. In fact, many of the scholars quoted in this volume on matters other than *fiqh* are adherents of one of the other *madhhabs*.

5 *Sūrah al-Baqarah* (Q2: 153)

CHAPTER 4

The Meaning, Wisdom and Benefits of *Ṣalāh*

The Meaning of *Ṣalāh*

Ṣalāh in Arabic means prayer, but refers in Islam to the specific method of praying which was taught by the Prophet Muḥammad, may Allah bless him and grant him peace, to his companions, consisting of particular actions, including standing, bowing, prostrating and sitting. In English 'prayer' usually signifies supplication, which is equivalent to the Arabic word *du'ā'*, literally meaning calling. While supplication is certainly included within the *ṣalāh*, to avoid confusion in what follows the word 'prayer' will always be used to refer to the formal practice of *ṣalāh*. Establishing *ṣalāh*, as the second pillar of Islam, means not only learning the rules to ensure the correct method of prayer, including all the conditions that must be met, but also to be steadfast in praying five times a day within the prescribed hours.[1] Before entering into the details contained within the *fiqh* of *ṣalāh*, it is extremely important to mention the spiritual, moral as well as social benefits and wisdom of this fundamental form of worship.

The Spiritual Benefits and Wisdom of *Ṣalāh*

Although Allah Almighty is sublime and beyond the human reach, He is approachable through devotion. The heart can feel His presence and the soul can sense the warmth of His benevolence. One of the most effective means of gaining nearness to Him is through *ṣalāh*. The blessed Messenger is reported to have said, 'Ṣalāh *is the ascension of the believer.*'[2] We can describe this most oft-repeated exercise of the Muslim as:

1. Demonstration of his deep conviction in his Creator.
2. A constant reminder of the human being's status as both *khalīfah* (vicegerent) and servant (*'abd*) of the Lord.
3. An acknowledgment of God's wondrous favours on humanity, as well as a verbal and physical expression of gratitude.
4. A source of inner peace and security.
5. A spiritual devotion and physical exercise wherein every joint and muscle of the body joins with the soul to make the praises of the Lord.
6. A regular reminder of the presence of Allah.
7. A training program for self-discipline and *jihād*.[3]

In brief, *ṣalāh* is a practical and obvious sign of a person's faith. Only someone who has the humility to engage in devoted worship to Allah will be able to truly establish prayer. For this reason, the Qur'ān describes it as flowing from an individual's internal purity:

> *Successful will be the one who purified himself, and remembered the name of his Lord so he offered* ṣalāh.[4]

At the same time, the prayer is known to purify the believer's heart, acting as a powerful spiritual cleanser and ridding it of contamination by evil. Emphasising this purifying function of the *ṣalāh*, the beloved Messenger asked his companions:

If there was a stream at the door of someone's house and he were to wash in it five times a day, will any filth remain upon him?' They replied, 'No filth would be left.' He said, 'That is the example of the five daily ṣalāhs; *through these prayers Allah removes all sin.*[5]

In another beautiful *ḥadīth*, the significance of *ṣalāh* is mentioned as follows: Abū Dharr says:

One autumn, the blessed Messenger was walking about and the leaves were falling from the trees. He grasped a branch and more leaves fell. He said *'Oh Abū Dharr!'* and I replied, 'Yes Oh Messenger of Allah.' [He said,] *'When a Muslim prays sincerely his sins fall off him like these leaves fall from the trees.'*[6]

In summer the trees are green with foliage, but in autumn they loose their leaves and they look naked without any remaining leaves. This is a very apt analogy of the cleansing effect of *ṣalāh* upon a person.

The excellence of an individual's prayer is also significantly related to the extent that it is used as part of an individual's *tawakkul* (reliance) on God. This means that a believer will turn to Allah, confident that He can assist us in all matters of our lives. He, Most High, has instructed us to do this in his words:

Seek help in patience and ṣalāh, *truly it is hard except for the humble.*[7]

Here prayer is conjoined with *ṣabr* (patience), as we must wait for Allah's help to come, as He, by His Knowledge and Wisdom, is alone aware of the best time for it. Also, it is a sign of arrogance for the servant to expect immediate help from his Master, a point that is expressed in the second half of this verse. Nevertheless, the faithful believer is confident that Allah, by His Benevolence, will relieve him of his troubles and thus is comforted, obtaining a calm and peaceful state of mind. Seeking assistance through prayer in this way is, of course, also a *Sunnah* of the Prophet, may Allah bless him and grant him peace, as Abū Ḥuẓayfah reported that 'whenever the Messenger was in difficulty he would turn to *ṣalāh*.'[8]

Another obvious impact of *ṣalāh* is the deepening of faith. The regular devotion and rememberance of the Almighty strengthens the bond that an individual has with Allah. The standing up before the Majestic Lord, the bowing and prostrating before Him all symbolize one's obedience and submission to Him. Through prayer, the relationship, attachment and nearness to Allah continually grows until he acquires the highest human qualities and obtains the contentment of his kind and generous Lord.

As prayer is the foremost obligatory duty in Islam and at the very core of an individual's relationship with Allah, the spiritual aspects of *ṣalāh* have filled countless manuscripts and yet contain depths that cannot be plumbed by words alone. This is to say that any description can only give a glimpse of the reality of prayer, hopefully by inspiring an individual to obtain its spiritual fruits for his or herself. Abū Naṣr al-Sarrāj has written the following, which summarises the exalted rank of *ṣalāh* within Islam:

> *Ṣalāh* is the pillar of religion; the contentment of the gnostics; the adornment of the veracious; and the crown of those brought near. The station of *ṣalāh* is the station of connection, proximity, reverence, humility, awe, exaltation, gravity, witnessing, mindfulness, secret meanings and salvation with Allah Most High. It is the standing in front of Allah, drawing near to Him, and the relinquishing of what is other than Him Most High.[9]

Can we afford to miss an exercise that is as useful and beneficial as *ṣalāh*? The answer is a resounding no! The unfortunate ones in Hell will be asked:

'What led you into Hell?' They will say, 'We were not of those who prayed.'[10]

A mere pointer to this truth is sufficient for a sane person, but to emphasize the importance of *ṣalāh* and the terrible punishment for missing it some more warnings can be given: The beloved Messenger said, *'Missing* ṣalāh *leads a person into disbelief'*,[11] and he further said, *'The demarcation between faith and* kufr *is* ṣalāh*'*[12] and *'A person who has missed a single prayer is like someone who has lost all his wealth.'*[13]

Developing Concentration (*Khushūʿ*) in *Ṣalāh*

In terms of its outer reality, *ṣalāh* consists of a series of ritual movements and memorised recitations. Once these are repeated many times they can become an almost automatic sequence and the unthinking Muslim can begin to pray as if he is an automaton, or a robot. This is opposite to the purpose of *ṣalāh* which has been legislated for us by Allah to bring remembrance of Him into our lives. We must, therefore, look to bring greater concentration (*khushūʿ*) into our prayers, for them to be the meaningful spiritual experiences that they are meant to be. This is why Muḥammad Mawlūd writes:

> Pray as if it is your last prayer. Fight Khinzib[14] before he gets to your heart so that he cannot play with it and distract you from the prayer. The one who prays gains nothing more than what he was aware of. One may perform the prayer and, due to a number of reasons, he was only rewarded one tenth of the prayer. The prayer has an amazing and vast light that radiates from the hearts of the humble ones.[15]

The Prophet, may Allah bless him and grant him peace, said:

> *Whoever offers all his prayers on time after a perfect ablution, stands with humility and reverence, prostrates and bows calmly, and offers the entire prayer in a good manner – so that prayer becomes a radiating one and prays for him thus: 'Oh the offerer of prayer! May Allah guard you the way you have guarded me.' And as regards the one who offers the prayer poorly – that is without proper ablution, and not even prostrating and bowing correctly – then the prayer curses him thus: 'May Allah ruin you the way you have ruined me.' Then the prayer is folded and thrown back at his face like a used (dirty) cloth.*[16]

So how can we develop the sort of prayer that envelops us and those around us with its luminosity, rather than that which is a darkness, a disgrace and a curse, due to our lack of due attention?

Imām al-Ghazālī writes:

> There are two reasons why one loses focus and concentration in *ṣalāh*: one is due to external factors and the other is internal factors. The external factors are (such things as): a noisy place where one cannot concentrate because of the distractions – therefore select a quiet place. Perhaps that is why some serious people have a separate room reserved for prayer. The inner factors include thoughts, worries, imaginations and doubts. One must work hard at dumping these wrong thoughts before beginning *ṣalāh*. So before praying, free yourself of any task so that it does not come into your mind later on.
>
> The positive thing you must indulge in is to focus on the meanings of what you are reciting. This will leave no room for useless thoughts. One way to achieve this state of mind is to do *dhikr* before the time of *ṣalāh*. Anyone who wants to seriously focus

his mind in *ṣalāh* should first get rid of the worries, needs and distractions. Empty the mind....'[17]

Mawlānā Rūmī lucidly gives an even more comprehensive understanding of the purpose of meaningful prayer in these lines:

> The purpose of ritual prayer is not that you should bow and prostrate yourself all day. Its purpose is that you develop a prayerful attitude, maintaining the spiritual state achieved in the prayer throughout the day. Whether asleep or awake, at work or rest, you should always remember God. You should be one of: *Those who are constantly at their prayers.*[18,19]

→ kindness, care, forgiveness, modesty, generosity

The Moral Benefits and Wisdom of *Ṣalāh*

values + attitudes

Although the moral benefits of *ṣalāh* are closely linked to those found in the spiritual dimension addressed above, there is an important distinction that justifies setting them apart. Instead of focusing on the relationship between the individual and Allah in terms of forgiveness, faith and reliance, here we look instead at how *ṣalāh* trains a person to act morally in their life in relation to themselves and others, particularly in avoiding the forbidden and seeking the rewardable.

There is no doubt that *ṣalāh* has profound effects on a person, as, like a powerful medicine, it uproots the diseases of the heart. Allah says:

> *Indeed* ṣalāh *restrains indecency and evil.*[20]

Its first and foremost effect, therefore, is the purification of the heart and the evil thoughts, ideas, habits and actions. By making a person self-disciplined it helps him to avoid temptations. Once, the companions complained about a young man who prayed, but also did evil things. The beloved Messenger simply said to them, *'Leave him, his prayers will soon turn him away from his bad ways.'* After some time the same people came to the Prophet and said that the young man had now totally reformed himself. The beloved Messenger was pleased and said, *'Didn't I say so.'*

The regular practice of *ṣalāh* throughout the day reaffirms a person's moral strength, by connecting him to Allah, Most High, who is the source of all goodness and justice. This spiritual revitalisation will naturally lead to increased piety and the ability to stay resolute in performing good and avoiding evil, even in the face of challenging situations and temptations.

The Social Benefits and Wisdom of *Ṣalāh*

There is no doubt that *ṣalāh* serves a very important social function within Islamic society aside from its effects on spirituality and the character. This is the role it plays in bringing people together, particularly in congregation at the *masjid* for the five daily prayers, as well as every Friday's *Ṣalāh al-Jumuʿah* and the two annual ʿĪds. We know from the following *ḥadīth* of the Prophet, may Allah bless him and grant him peace, that Allah is pleased by those who join together in prayer:

> *Two people praying together, where one leads the other, is more liked by Allah Most High than four men that pray one after the other (on their own). Four people praying together are more liked than eight people praying individually. Eight people praying together is more liked by Allah, Most High, than one hundred people praying separately.*[21]

This is, amongst other things, because of the unity that it brings to Muslims despite their diversity and the effect it has in bringing the hearts together in mutual worship of their Creator. The Prophet, may Allah bless him and grant him peace, also said:

> *Performing prayer in congregation is twenty-seven times better than performing it alone.*[22]

In fact, prayer in congregation, particularly for men, has the status in *fiqh* as a *sunnah al-hudā* (practice of guidance) which is very close to *wājib* and should not be left off without an acceptable excuse.

The *Masjid* – The Most Blessed Place on Earth

Ibn ʿAbbās, may Allah be pleased with him, relates that:

> *Masjids* are the houses of Allah on the earth. They shine up to the inhabitants of the heavens just as the stars in the sky shine down to the inhabitants of the earth.[23]

The *masjid*, also known as the mosque, is a fundamental Islamic institution which is meant to encompass much more than the daily congregational prayers, although these are the sparkling jewels of its existence. Traditionally, they were also the centres of education in the community, in which the subjects taught ranged from Qur'ānic exegesis and jurisprudence, to astronomy for determining the correct prayer direction and mathematics for the calculation of inheritance shares.

The social benefits of such worship and the acquisition of knowledge which are strengthened through human relationships can be easily apprehended. *Ṣalāh* in the *masjid* can be said to 'quench the thirst which exists in the depths of the soul for interaction with other members of humanity and acting together with them.'[24]

In traditional societies with a great deal of mutual interdependence, this did the job of placing these inevitable relationships on a level of piety, so, at least ideally, the good manners shown in the *masjid* would be transferred to the marketplace. Modern society, which unfortunately tends to weaken community relations and breed a form of uncaring individualism, is thus in even greater need of the beneficial fruits of communal prayer. Despite this, there is the danger that through unwelcoming practices and sectarianism of all shades, the *essential* unifying function that the *masjid* performs will be lost and drive all but a minority of the community away. In his excellent article, 'Flight From the Masjid', Zaid Shakir writes,

> We should consciously work to foster an open atmosphere in the *Masjid*, an atmosphere that is inviting to all: men, women, youth, conservatives, modernists, converts – everyone. All of us committing ourselves to the creation of such an atmosphere will bring it about. It is essential to remind ourselves that the collective 'we' is weightier than the individual 'me' in Islam. On the Day of Judgement when all of the people are concerned with themselves, our Noble Prophet, peace and blessings of Almighty God be upon him, will be concerned with the entire community; he will be crying out, *'ummati, ummati'* (my community, my community).[25]

Women in the *Masjid*

A particular cause for concern in relation to the *masjid*'s proper role at the beating heart of the Islamic community is the potential exclusion of over half the *ummah* – the women – in one fell swoop. It should be asked: how can anyone, in a single breath, affirm the superiority of the *masjid* over all other places on Earth and then deny or limit its accessability to our mothers, our sisters and our daughters? It is certainly true that the later jurists of the Ḥanafī school ruled that it is *makrūh* for young women to attend the congregational prayers, based on the fear of temptation (*fitnah*).[26] This *ijtihād* was made in sincere consideration of the moral protection of the people, as some of the less pious individuals in society began to use the congregational prayers, which were conducted in the same prayer hall, as an excuse to satisfy their desire to socialise and flirt with members of the opposite sex. It is instructive to compare the standard Shāfiʿī position here, for while it shares the general rule with the Ḥanafīs that women's prayer at home is more rewardable than at the *masjid*,[27] it is a more nuanced and flexible interpretation:

> If a woman's going to group prayer or elsewhere will definitely lead to temptation between the sexes, it is unlawful for her to go. If such temptation can be definitely prevented, her going to attend group prayer remains *sunna*, as is attested to by the *ḥadīth*s that have reached us on the subject. If temptation is feared but not certain to occur, her going becomes offensive. Whether such temptation is likely to occur is something that differs with different times, places, and people.[28]

The classical Ḥanafī viewpoint, as put forward by the author of the *Hidāyah*, is that such fear of temptation is generally present, at least for young women, and congregational prayer in the *masjid* is therefore *makrūh*, although permissable. However, the unstated implication was that if this temptation could be avoided by some means, the original ruling would return. The later Ḥanafīs retained this position, but qualified it with 'under any circumstances', which effectively closed discussion on the issue, so Ibn ʿĀbidīn, for instance, does not comment further on it in his encyclopaedic *Radd al-Muḥtār*.[29] The earlier authorities in the school, however, seem to have taken a rather different opinion of the issue. If we are to look at *Kitab al-Aṣl* (also known as *al-Mabsūṭ*) of Imām Muḥammad al-Shaybānī, a companion of Imām Abū Ḥanīfah and one of the most senior *mujtahid*s in the school, we come across the following statement: 'As for when there is a congregation in a *masjid* in which *ṣalāh* is established and he [any man] is the *imām*, so he steps forward to pray, and there is not another man with him, so the women enter into the prayer, then there is no harm in it.'[30]

Three things should be noted here: firstly the women are not qualified as having to be any particular age; secondly there is no mention of temptation; and thirdly this is presented as a special case only because of the exceptional circumstance of a single man attending that particular *jamāʿah*, and even this is declared to be acceptable. This shows the original *Sunnah* of the blessed Prophet and his companions was taken to be the unquestioned norm by Imām Muḥammad.

Imām al-Sarakhsī (died *ca.* 483 A.H./1090 C.E.), in his significant work also called *al-Mabsūṭ*, echoes this ruling and adds, 'because the *masjid* is not a place of seclusion (*khalwah*).'[31] He further mentions congregational *ṣalāh* with a single man and group of women as only *makrūh* due to the fear of temptation, when prayed in private places, such as people's houses, with no *maḥram* (close relative) to one of the women present. Although writing after al-Qudūrī, whose ruling of young women's attendance to the *jamāʿah* of the *masjid* as *makrūh* was to become the standard opinion of the later scholars, al-Sarakhsī kept a place in his *fiqh* for the original practice of the Islamic community. What this shows is that this is an issue on which the scholars have differed and one that must take into account the context of the society in which the ruling is to be applied. In fact, that this is nothing new in the life of the Islamic community can be demonstrated with reference to the narration of Sālim ibn ʿAbd Allāh, who relates on the authority of his father ʿAbd Allāh ibn ʿUmar that the Messenger of Allah, may Allah bless him and grant him peace, said:

> *'Do not prevent your women from going to the masjid when they seek your permission.'* Bilāl ibn ʿAbd Allāh said: 'By Allah we shall certainly prevent them.' On this, ʿAbd Allāh ibn ʿUmar turned towards him and reprimanded him so harshly as I had never heard

> him do before. He ('Abd Allāh ibn 'Umar) said: 'I am narrating to you that which comes from the Messenger of Allah, may Allah bless him and grant him peace, and you (dare) say: "By Allah we shall certainly prevent them."'[32]

There is undoubtedly a tension between the egalitarian spirit of the prophetic *Sunnah* in giving complete freedom to women to attend the congregational prayers at the *masjid* and the legitimate *ijtihād* of later jurists to err on the side of caution in their judgement that social conditions had changed and that this action should be considered *makrūh*. Both positions are a far cry from the exclusionary (and cultural) position of those who argue that the *masjid* is not *their place* at all. Some scholars, no doubt, argue that in our present day, the level of piety is even less and so there is even more reason to uphold the latter ruling. However, it is important that those with knowledge and authority in the area of Islamic *fiqh* are careful to avoid all simplistic understandings of contemporary society, based more on entrenched cultural traditions than on a luminous understanding of the prophetic wisdom. With *masjid* attendance generally at low levels in the UK, and elsewhere, do those steadfast souls that regularly pray in congregation really present such a worry of *fitnah* that it should remain disapproved for women to offer their *ṣalāh* therein? Furthermore, women play an active role in many areas of social life: undertaking education, teaching, caring for children and the elderly, working, shopping and countless others. In nearly all of these, there is the potential for interaction with members of the opposite sex. Again, in these conditions, is it wise for the overall spiritual health of the Muslim community that of all places, women are strangers to the *masjid*?

It might be asked, 'If the reward for women of prayer at home is more than that of the *masjid*, as is mentioned in sound *aḥādīth*, then why would anyone leave a greater prize for a lesser one?' The answer is that there are a whole host of situations in which, whether or not the ruling of *makrūh* is upheld, women require facilities for prayer and other activities in the *masjid*s. For instance: travellers; those who have recently embraced Islam or cannot otherwise gain obligatory religious knowledge; as well as those who are, for whatever reason, isolated from the community. In all these cases and others, it is arguable that the benefit gained from the spiritual atmosphere and company found at the *masjid* far outweighs the possibility of temptation, particularly if reasonable precautionary steps are taken. Furthermore, the alert mind should be able to spot the hypocrisy of those who, ostensibly for the sake of following sound Ḥanafī scholarship and seeking to protect women, will make the best place in the community, the *masjid*, effectively off limits for them, whilst permitting or encouraging their visits to many places with much greater temptations.

As for attendance to the *masjid* for reasons other than the congregational prayers, such as quiet reflection and study programmes, it should go without saying that it is a priority that women are not only given access, but encouraged, in a practical manner appropriate to the condition of each community. In fact, it is precisely if men and women alike can maintain mutually respectful and pious behaviour upon the potential interactions that characterise human social life, that the *Sunnah* of the *masjid* as a place of education and the remembrance of Allah for the whole community can be realised in all its beauty. This is something that should be striven for in emulation of the practice of blessed Messenger, may Allah bless him and grant him peace, and his companions, not automatically banned on the basis of the presumed corruption of our age.

Notes

1 In general, *Ṣalāh* is central among the rituals within Islamic worship in establishing a healthy spiritual life.

2 This *ḥadīth* is not found in the standard collections, but is widely quoted in relation to this subject. The association of the prayer with the

Mi'rāj or Ascension of the Prophet, may Allah bless him and grant him peace, to his Lord, is nonetheless appropriate, because it is at this time that a believer gains closeness to Him, as is supported by many authentic *aḥādīth*.

3 *Jihād* means intense struggle for the sake of Allah and includes both spiritual and physical dimensions. It can take place in terms of individual training to resist the desires of the lower self, participation in social activism, or in martial struggle when required by the community for the sake of its survival, or to establish a just and stable social order.

4 *Sūrah al-A'lā* (Q87: 14-5).

5 On the authority of Abū Hurayrah, may Allah be pleased with him, and agreed upon by Imāms Bukhārī and Muslim.

6 Narrated in the *Musnad* of Aḥmad ibn Ḥanbal.

7 *Sūrah al-Baqarah* (Q2: 45).

8 Narrated in *Sunan Abī Dawūd*.

9 Al-Sarrāj, *Kitāb al-Luma' fī al-Taṣawwuf* (Leiden, 1914), p. 150.

10 *Sūrah al-Muddathir* (Q74: 42-3).

11 Narrated in *Ṣaḥīḥ Muslim*.

12 Narrated in the *Musnad* of Aḥmad ibn Ḥanbal. [This was said to emphasise the great importance of *ṣalāh*, to show how its abandonment is on the path to abandoning faith, or in the context that someone who denies the obligation of *ṣalāh* becomes a disbeliever. It is put forward that these interpretations are better than saying that the person who does not pray entirely loses their faith (see footnote 5, p. 7 above), and Allah knows best.

13 Narrated by Ibn Hibbān.

14 This is a reference to the *ḥadīth* in which the Companion 'Uthmān ibn Abū al-'Ās came to the Prophet, may Allah bless him and grant him peace and said, 'The Shayṭān comes between me and my *ṣalāh*, and causes me to falter in my recitation.' The Messenger of Allah said, *'That is a shayṭān called Khinzib. If you sense his presence, seek refuge with Allah and spit (very little) to your left three times.'* 'Uthmān (later) said, 'I did that, and Allah rid me of him.' (*Ṣaḥīḥ Muslim*).

15 Mawlūd, M., *Ishrāq al-Qarar*.

16 Narrated by al-Ṭabarānī.

17 Al-Ghazālī, *Kimiya-yi Sa'ādat*.

18 *Sūrah al-Ma'ārij* (Q70: 23).

19 Rūmī, *Fīhi Mā Fīhi*.

20 *Sūrah al-'Ankabūt* (Q29: 45).

21 Narrated by al-Ṭabarānī.

22 Narrated in *Miskāt al-Maṣābīḥ*.

23 Narrated by al-Ṭabarānī.

24 Kurāni, 'Alī Muḥammad, *Falsafah al-Ṣalāh*, (Dār al-Zahdā', 1972), p. 240.

[25] Shakir, Z., 'Flight From the Masjid' (*Seasons*, Spring/Summer 2003), p. 68.

[26] Al-Marghinānī, *al-Hidāyah*, (Dār al-Kutub al-'Ilmiyyah, 2000), vol. 1, p. 61.

[27] Narrated in *Sunan Abī Dawūd*.

[28] Al-Miṣrī, Aḥmad ibn Naqīb, *Reliance of the Traveller* (translated with commentary by Nuh Ha Mim Keller, Amana Publications, 1994), p. 171.

[29] Ibn 'Ābidīn, *Radd al-Muḥtār 'alā Durr al-Mukhtār* (Dār al-Kutub al-'Ilmiyyah, 1994) Vol. 2, p. 307.

[30] Al-Shaybānī, *Kitab al-Aṣl (al-Mabsūṭ)* ('Ālam al-Kutub, 1990), Vol. 1, p. 161-2.

[31] Al-Sarakhsi, *al-Mabsūṭ*, (Dār al-Ma'rifah, 1978), Vol. 1, p. 166.

[32] Narrated in *Ṣaḥīḥ Muslim*.

CHAPTER 5

Preparation for *Ṣalāh*: *Ṭahārah*, *Adhān* and *Iqāmah*

cleaniless
ghusl, wudu
+ tayumum

The Importance of preparing for *Ṣalāh*

All really significant undertakings require preparation and *ṣalāh* is no different. This is partly internal, consisting of the cultivation of an appropriately reverent state of mind and partly external, involving both the absolutely necessary and *sunnah* rituals that preceed the prayer itself. In fact, as Imām al-Ghazālī makes clear, these two aspects should be seamlessly integrated and in this regard he narrates that:

> It is said of ʿAlī ibn al-Ḥusayn that he used to turn pale when he made his ablution. When his family asked him what came over him during his ablution, he would say: 'Do you realise before Whom I wish to stand in prayer?'[1]

The following section will concentrate on the comprehensive rules relating to *ṭahārah*, or ritual purity in Islam, which is not only essential for *ṣalāh*, but also for acts such as touching the Qur'ān and performing *ṭawāf* (circumabulation) around the Kaʿbah. Following this, we shall cover the subject of the *adhān* (call to prayer) and *iqāmah* (call made immediately preceding prayer) which are important *sunnahs*, particularly when establishing congregational prayers.

Introduction to *Ṭahārah* (Purity)

The importance of being clean, wearing clean clothes and living in a clean place is not only important for one's health but equally important for one's spiritual development. Allah Most High says:

> *Truly Allah loves the repentant and those who purify themselves.*[2]

The Messenger, May Allah bless him and grant him peace said:

> *Purity is one half of faith.*[3]

He also said:

> *The key to paradise is* ṣalāh *and the key to* ṣalāh *is purification.*[4]

Purification with *Ghusl* (bath) and *Tayammum* (dry ablution)

Objectives of this section to learn:

- The meaning of *ghusl* and *tayammum*
- When they are required
- The *fiqh* rulings for them including the practical way to perform them according to the *Sunnah*

In fiqh*, purification is divided into two types*:

i. Major – Taking a bath (*ghusl*).
ii. Minor – Performing ablution (*wuḍū'*).

As we shall see, *tayammum* is a dry ablution which can be used for either type of purification in certain exceptional circumstances.

Ghusl

The Meaning of Ghusl

Ghusl means taking a bath, which requires the washing of one's whole body with water. Allah Most High says:

> *If you are a* junub *then purify yourself.*[5]

A *junub* is a person in a state of major ceremonial impurity. This state is recognised by Islamic law as having its own regulations pertaining to how it can arise, the actions that it prohibits and the rules for its removal. As an impure state in which many types of worship are prohibited, it is strongly encouraged by the *sharīʿah* for a believer to remain in it for as short a time as is possible.[6] The Messenger, may Allah bless him and grant him peace, said:

> *The angels will not enter a house that contains a dog, picture or (an habitual)* junub.[7]

Actions that give rise to Major Ceremonial Impurity:

1. Lovemaking between husband and wife
2. Ejaculation of sperm, e.g. having a wet dream
3. Menstruation
4. Childbirth

Actions that are prohibited whilst in a State of Major Ceremonial Impurity:

1. Praying *ṣalāh*
2. Touching or reciting the Qur'ān
3. Entering the *masjid*

The Compulsory Elements of Ghusl:

1. *To gargle* – this means to wash thoroughly the inside of the mouth down to the throat. This is achieved with a mouthful of water and swirling it around the mouth such that the water reaches all parts of the mouth, the tongue, around the gums and down to the throat.
2. *To rinse and clean the nostrils* – to wash the inside of both nostrils such that water reaches the top of the nose and to blow out any accumulated mucus.
3. *To wash the entire body* – every part of the body must be washed thoroughly, from head to toe, so that not a single hair remains dry.

How to perform Ghusl *according to the* Sunnah:

1. Make the intention to purify oneself.
2. Say *bismillāh* (in the name of Allah).
3. Begin by washing both hands up to the wrist.
4. Wash the private parts.
5. Remove any filth from the body.
6. Do full *wuḍū'*.[8]
7. Start to wash the body from the right shoulder, then wash the body from the left shoulder. Finally pour water over the head and make sure that water gets to every part by rubbing with hands. Not a hair should remain dry!
8. Wash the feet last and, if standing in slow-draining water, make an effort to do bring them to a place where fresh water can flow over them.

Note: The ghusl should be taken in a secluded place that no-one else can see. There should be no talking, humming, singing or facing the direction of the Ka'bah (*qiblah*) whilst having a bath.

Tayammum

The Meaning of Tayammum: - make an intention

Tayammum is sometimes called 'dry ablution' since it is a substitute for *wuḍū'* (or *ghusl* if required) and is done without using water. It is a special concession given graciously by Allah. He Most High says:

> *If you are ill, or on a journey, or have been to the toilet, or have made love with your wives and you cannot find water then do 'dry ablution' with clean earth, wiping your faces and hands with it.*[9]

Abū Saʿīd al-Khudrī reports: '*Two men were on a journey and when the time for prayer came they could not find any water, so they did* tayyamum *and performed their prayer. However, a little later they found water and one of them did* wuḍū' *and repeated his prayer, but the other did not. When they returned to Madīnah they told the beloved Messenger, may Allah bless him and grant him peace. He said to the man who didn't repeat his prayer, "You practiced the* Sunnah,*" and to the other man he said, "You have been given double reward."*'[10]

When is Tayammum *permissible?*

When a person wants to pray *ṣalāh* and he is unable to do *wuḍū'*, either because he can't find water or he is unable to use water, it is permissible to do *tayammum*. Here is a summary of the acceptable circumstances:

1. An illness that would be aggravated by the use of water, for example burns. This advice must come from a good physician.
2. There is no water for at least a mile around him.
3. If it is so severely cold such that one cannot take a bath and there is no means of heating the water or warming oneself afterwards.
4. If he fears he will miss his (important) rail, bus or flight if he goes to search for water to perform *wuḍū'*.

5. When he fears that he will miss the funeral or ʿĪd *ṣalāh*, if he went to perform *wuḍū'*.[11]

The Compulsory Elements of Tayammum:

There are three compulsory acts in *tayammum:*

1. To make the intention to perform *tayammum.*
2. To wipe the whole face with hands that have touched clean earth.
3. To wipe both hands from tips of the fingers to the elbows.

How to perform Tayammum *according to the Sunnah*:

1. First make the intention, for instance: 'I am doing *tayammum* to be able to offer my *ṣalāh.'*
2. Say 'Bismillāh'.
3. Lay both hands on stone, sand, clay, earth, or anything covered in dust. Then shake off any excess dust by clapping hands together.
4. Wipe the face with both hands.
5. Repeat Step Three.
6. Wipe both the right hand and then the left hand up the arm to the elbow.

Miscellaneous Points:

1. *Tayammum* can be done with anything from the earth. This excludes things that burn like wood, or melt like metals, iron or copper. So this means things like sand, clay, stone and chalk, as well as soil etc. However if there is dust on wooden furniture or a metal object it can be used.
2. All those things that break *wuḍū'* or make *ghusl* compulsory will invalidate *tayammum.*
3. The availability or the ability to use water will also invalidate *tayammum.*

Purification with *Wuḍū'* (Ablution)

Objectives of this section to learn:

- The meaning of *wuḍū'*.
- The times that it is required.
- The *fiqh* rulings for it including the practical way to perform it according to the *Sunnah*.
- Those things which invalidate it.

The Meaning of Wuḍū'*:*

We have already mentioned Qur'ānic verses and prophetic *aḥādīth* that indicate to the importance of physical purification. The most usual form that this takes is the ritual ablution called *wuḍū'*. *Wuḍū'* literally means cleanliness and its essential elements are give in the following verse of the Qur'ān:

> *O believers! When you stand for the prayer wash your faces and your hands to the elbows, wipe your head and wash your feet to the ankles.*[12]

The blessed Prophet, may Allah bless him and grant him peace, said, *'Allah does not accept the prayer of any one of you when he is unclean – until he does* wuḍū'.'[13]

Hadhrat ʿAlī, may Allah be pleased with him, reports that the blessed Prophet, may Allah bless him and grant him peace, said *'Whoever makes* wuḍū' *in extreme cold receives double the reward.*'[14]

The Times that Wuḍū' *is required:*

Wuḍū' is of three types:

1. *Farḍ* (compulsory). This is the *wuḍū'* required for performing the prayer or for touching the Glorious Qur'ān.
2. *Wājib* (necessary). This is the *wuḍū'* required for circumambulating (*ṭawāf*) of the Kaʿbah.

3. *Mustaḥabb* (desirable). This is made on numerous occasions, for example: before studying, before going to sleep and during *ghusl* as explained previously etc.

The Compulsory Elements of Wuḍū':
There are four compulsory (farḍ) *acts in* wuḍū':

1. To wash the whole face once with clean water. The boundaries of the face are lengthwise from the hairline above the forehead to the bottom of the chin and breadthwise from one ear to the other. The hair of the beard that is on the face within these boundaries is also part of the washing of the face. It is desirable to wash the hair that is longer than the periphery of the face and *Sunnah* to wipe it. If the beard is light (i.e. it is sparse and the skin underneath is visible) it is compulsory to wash it thoroughly through the roots. If the beard is thick (i.e. the skin is not visible), then it is only compulsory to wash the outer layer of it.
2. Washing both hands up to and including the elbows.
3. To wipe a quarter of the head by passing wet hands over it.
4. The washing of the feet up to the ankle bones.

Note: If there is something stopping water from reaching the skin like a tight ring or dough in the nails, then it must be removed and the skin underneath washed.

How to perform Wuḍū' *according to the* Sunnah:
There are seventeen sunnah *acts in* wuḍū':

1. Intention: resolving to do *wuḍū'* for the pleasure of Allah and to carry out His command. The way to do this is to silently intend 'to remove filth' or 'purification'

or even better is to intend, 'to make *wuḍū'* for worship seeking the nearness of Allah' (emphatic *Sunnah*).

2. To begin with *bismillāh* (emphatic *Sunnah*).
3. Washing of both hands to the wrist three times (unemphatic *Sunnah*). But if dirt is suspected on the hand then it is an emphatic *Sunnah*.
4. The *miswak/siwāk*: brushing the teeth when rinsing the mouth or, according to another opinion, before the rinsing of the mouth (emphatic *Sunnah*). *Siwāk* is the small stick derived from the arak tree, also known as the peelu tree or *Salvadora persica*. If it is not available, then using something that removes the yellowness of the teeth and cleanses the mouth like a toothbrush still fulfils the *Sunnah*. If even a toothbrush is not available, one should use the index finger of the right hand.
5. Rinsing the mouth three times, even with a single sip of water, although the full mouth should be filled (emphatic *Sunnah*).
6. Cleaning the nose three times, in which the water should reach the top of the nose (emphatic *Sunnah*). It is desirable to rinse the mouth and the nose with the right hand and to clean the nostrils with the left hand.

Note: It is *Sunnah* to exaggerate in rinsing the mouth and the nose except for the fasting person. This means gargling and cleaning the nostrils with the little finger.

7. Combing a thick beard: this is the combing of hair from the bottom to the top by putting the palms of the hands on the neck and moving the fingers through the beard. This is done after washing the face three times (unemphatic *Sunnah*).
8. The combing of the fingers: intertwining the fingers of one hand in the other, left over right then right over left. For the toes use the little finger of the left hand and start from the little toe of the right foot and finish by the little toe of the left foot (emphatic *Sunnah*).

9. Washing three times: to wash all parts once is compulsory and to wash three times is an emphatic *Sunnah*. The head and ears are excluded from this rule as they are wiped.
10. Immediacy: this is washing of a part before the previous part dries (emphatic *Sunnah*).
11. Wiping the whole of the head: to do so once is an emphatic *Sunnah*. The best way to do this is to put the three fingers of each hand at the front of the head and to hold the index finger with the thumb. Then move the fingers backward over the head and put the palms of the hand on the sides of the head and move them towards the front.
12. The wiping of the ears: wiping the inner ears with the index fingers and the outer ear with the the thumbs (unemphatic *Sunnah*).
13. Performing *wuḍū'* in its correct order as mentioned in the Qur'ān, *Sūrah al-Mā'idah* verse 6 (emphatic *Sunnah*).
14. Starting with the right side: to begin washing of hands and the feet with the right one first (unemphatic *Sunnah*).
15. Rubbing: wiping each part during or after pouring water on it (unemphatic *Sunnah*).
16. Not to be wasteful in using water (emphatic *Sunnah*).
17. Not to splash water, particularly on the face (unemphatic *Sunnah*). This is for the respect of the face and to prevent splashing of used water. The best way to wash the face is to pour water on the top of the forehead and then to gently rub it over the face.

The Desirable Acts in Wuḍū'

There are eleven mustaḥabb (*desirable*) *acts in* wuḍū'*:*

1. To face the Kaʿbah: since this is the most hopeful state of acceptance of supplications, which one ought to read whilst doing *wuḍū'* (see below).

2. To be seated in a high place: to ensure that clothes are not splashed by the used water.
3. To do *wuḍū'* in a clean place: for respect of *wuḍū'* and keeping the clothes clean.
4. Not to talk as this will prevent one from reciting the supplications.
5. To wipe the neck: once only with the back of the fingers of both hands after wiping the ears.
6. To say *bismillāh* before every act.
7. To recite the following supplications:

When rinsing the Mouth:

اللَّهُمَّ أَعِنِّىْ عَلَى تِلَاوَةِ كِتَابِكَ وَكَثْرَةِ الذِّكْرِ لَكَ وَالشُّكْرِ لَكَ

Oh Allah! Help me in the recitation of the Qur'ān, your remembrance, your thanksgiving and goodly devotion.

When cleaning the Nostrils:

اللَّهُمَّ أَرِحْنِيْ رَائِحَةَ الْجَنَّةِ وَأَنْتَ عَنِّىْ رَاضٍ

Oh Allah! Give me the scent of Paradise and Your contentment with me.

When washing the Face:

اللَّهُمَّ بَيِّضْ وَجْهِيْ يَوْمَ تَبْيَضُّ وُجُوْهُ أَوْلِيَائِكَ، وَلَا تُسَوِّدْ
وَجْهِيْ يَوْمَ تَسْوَدُّ وُجُوْهُ أَعْدَائِكَ

Oh Allah! Whiten my face on the Day you will whiten and darken faces.

When washing the Right Arm:

> اللَّهُمَّ أَعْطِنِيْ كِتَابِيْ بِيَمِيْنِيْ وَحَاسِبْنِيْ حِسَابًا يَسِيْرًا
>
> Oh Allah! Give my book of deeds in the right hand and make my reckoning easy.

When washing the Left Arm:

> اللَّهُمَّ لَا تُعْطِنِى كِتَابِيْ بِشِمَالِيْ أَوْ مِنْ وَرَاءِ ظَهْرِي
>
> Oh Allah! Do not give me my book of deeds in my left hand nor from behind my back.

When wiping the Head:

> اللَّهُمَّ أَظِلَّنِيْ تَحْتَ ظِلِّ عَرْشِكَ يَوْمَ لَا ظِلَّ إِلَّا ظِلَّ عَرْشِكَ
>
> Oh my Lord! Give me shade under Your Throne on the Day when there will be no other shade except under Your Throne.

When wiping the Ears:

> اللَّهُمَّ اجْعَلْنِيْ مِنَ الَّذِيْنَ يَسْتَمِعُوْنَ الْقَوْلَ فَيَتَّبِعُوْنَ أَحْسَنَهُ
>
> Oh Allah! Make me among those who pay heed to what is said and follow the best of it.

When wiping the Neck:

اللّٰهُمَّ إِعْتِقْ رَقَبَتِيْ مِنَ النَّارِ

Oh Allah! Free my neck from the Hellfire.

When washing the Right Foot:

اللّٰهُمَّ ثَبِّتْ قَدَمَيَّ عَلٰى صِرَاطِكَ الْمُسْتَقِيْمِ

Oh Allah! Make my feet steadfast on Your straight path.

When washing the Left Foot:

اللّٰهُمَّ اجْعَلْ ذَنْبِيْ مَغْفُوْرًا وَسَعْيِيْ مَشْكُوْرًا وَتِجَارَتِيْ لَا تَبُوْر

Oh Allah! Forgive my sins and accept my efforts and make my trade successful.

After completing the Wuḍū':

أَشْهَدُ أَنْ لَآ إِلٰهَ إِلاَّ اللهُ وَحْدَهُ لاَ شَرِيْكَ لَهُ وَأَشْهَدُ أَنَّ مُحَمَّدًا عَبْدُهُ وَرَسُوْلُهُ

I bear witness that there is no god but Allah. He is alone and has no associate and I bear witness that Muḥammad is His slave and Messenger.

ṢALĀH

Then recite:

اللَّهُمَّ اجْعَلْنِيْ مِنَ التَّوَّابِيْنَ وَاجْعَلْنِيْ مِنَ الْمُتَطَهِّرِيْنَ

Oh Allah! Make me amongst those who repent and who purify themselves.

Finally recite *Sūrah al-Qadr three times* and then:

1. To drink the leftover water standing up facing the *qiblah* like the water of Zamzam.
2. Not to splatter water from the hands.
3. To dry wet parts of the body.
4. To pray two units after the *wuḍū'* at times other than those that are prohibited. The Prophet, may Allah bless him and grant him peace, said:

> *Whoever does* wudū' *like my* wudū' *then prays two units (of prayer)...his sins will be forgiven.*[15]

The Makrūh (Undesirable) Acts in Wuḍū':

▶ Leaving out the emphatic *Sunnah*, like rinsing the mouth, is an offense (*is'āh*). [is regular]
▶ Leaving out the unemphatic *Sunnah*, like starting from the right hand, is a minor offense (*makrūh tanzīhī*).
▶ Leaving out the desirable, like the wiping of the neck, is undesirable (*khilāf al-awlā'*).

The Invalidators of Wuḍū':

1. Anything discharged from where one passes urine or stools.
2. A discharge from any part of body like blood and pus if it starts to flow from its origin.
3. Vomiting food or water if it is a mouthful (in parts or all at once).

4. The discharge of blood from ear, nose or mouth. The reliable indicator for blood in the mouth is the colour of the saliva. If its colour is red then the *wuḍū'* is invalidated, however, if the redness is less than the white, or the sputum is merely a yellowish colour, then *wuḍū'* is not broken. If a red colour is found on one's toothbrush, or something bitten or eaten, like an apple, *wuḍū'* is only broken if the saliva has turned red.
5. Sleeping whilst lying on the side or whilst being supported by something such that if it is removed one would fall. The reason that sleep breaks *wuḍū'* is that during sleep the body is relaxed and there is a possibility of discharge of something. However, sleeping whilst standing, sitting, bowing or prostrating does not break *wuḍū'*.
6. Loss of consciousness or becoming insane.
7. Laughter during the prayer, but not outside the prayer. Laughter in *sajdah al-tilāwah* (the prostration of recitation) or in the funeral prayer does not break *wuḍū'*, although it does invalidate those acts.

Note:
- Whoever has illnesses like incontinence, or chronic flatulence, as well as women who are in a state of *istiḥāḍah* (non-menstrual vaginal bleeding) are excused from the normal ruling and may carry out prayer and other acts of worship that require *wuḍū'*. The only thing they have to do is perform *wuḍū'* before each prayer and they may then pray as much as they wish of both *farḍ* and *nafl* prayer etc. When a new prayer time arrives, this *wuḍū'* must be renewed, as is also the case if it is invalidated by anything other than the excused cause.
- If one is convinced of having made *wuḍū'*, but doubts whether he has broken it, he should consider his *wuḍū'* intact. If his doubt is in leaving off an essential part of the *wuḍū'*, for instance wiping his head, he should go back and repeat that act.

ṢALĀH

A Summary of Wuḍū' in Diagrams:

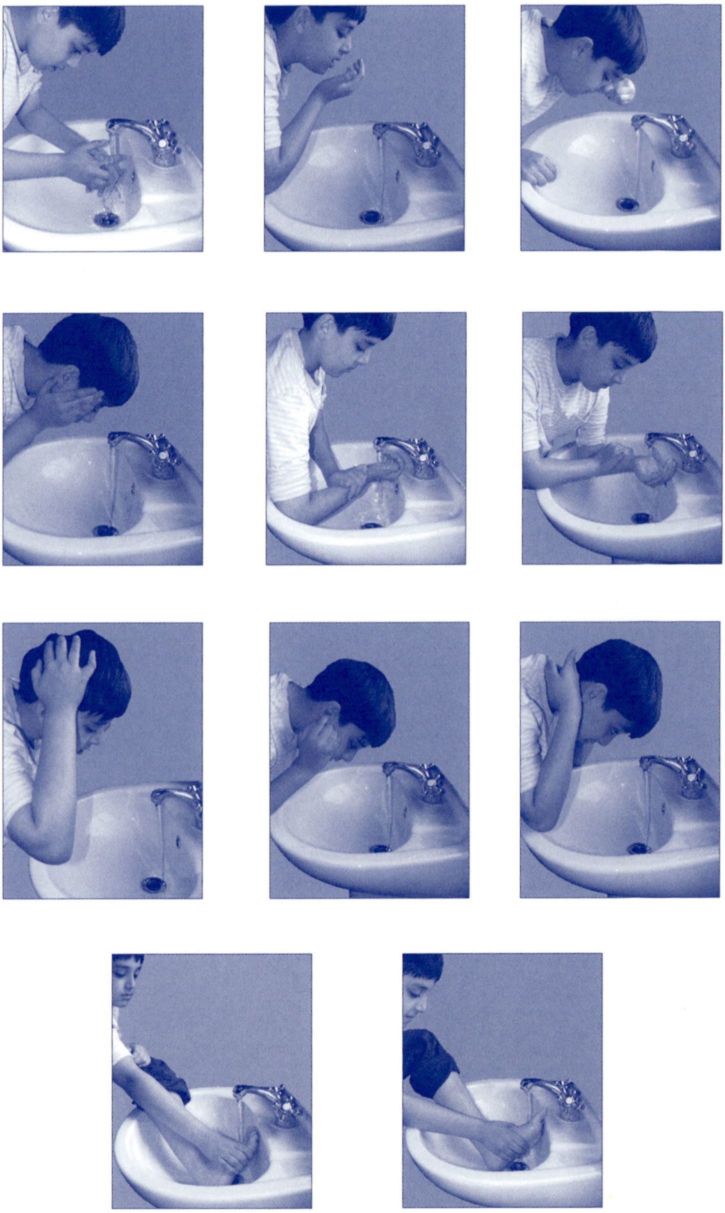

Making the *Adhān* (Call to prayer) and *Iqāmah* (Call made immediately preceding prayer)

Objectives of this section to learn:

- The significance of the *adhān*.
- Its words and meaning.
- The *du'ā'* that should be made after performing or hearing it.

Hadhrat Malik ibn Hawayris, may Allah be pleased with him, narrates that the blessed Prophet, may Allah bless him and grant him peace, said: *'When it is time for the prayer, one of you should call for the prayer and whoever is most pious amongst you should lead the prayers.'*[16]

The *adhān* is one of the special features of the Muslim *ummah* (community) as no other people call to devotion in this particular manner. The spine-tingling sensation of hearing the *adhān* not only informs us of the upcoming congregational prayer, but it strengthens faith in Allah as it resonates in the heart's deepest core. The importance of the *adhān* can be understood from the following *ḥadīth*:

Hadhrat Abū Dardā', may Allah be pleased with him, says that the blessed Prophet said: *'If there are three people in a town or in an open space and they neither call to prayer nor pray in congregation the devil overwhelms them. Therefore pray in congregation for the wolf devours the lost sheep.'*[17]

The *adhān* is a *sunnah mu'akkadah* (emphatic *Sunnah*). Habitually omitting it before praying in congregation is a sin.

The Adhān:

Allah is the Greatest (x4)	اَللهُ أَكْبَرُ (4x)
I bear witness that there is no god but Allah (x2)	أَشْهَدُ أَنْ لآ إِلٰـهَ إِلاَّ اللهُ (2x)
I bear witness that Muḥammad is the Messenger of Allah (x2)	أَشْهَدُ أَنَّ مُـحَمَّدًا رَسُوْلُ اللهِ (2x)
Come to the prayer (x2)	حَيَّ عَلَى الصَّلاَةْ (2x)
Come to success (x2)	حَيَّ عَلَى الْفَلاَحِ (2x)
Allah is the Greatest (x2)	اَللهُ أَكْبَرُ (2x)
There is no god but Allah.	لآ إِلٰـهَ إِلاَّ اللهُ

For the *fajr* (dawn) prayer add the following words after the second *hayya ʿalā al-falāḥ*:

The prayer is better than sleep (x2)	الصَّلاَةُ خَيْرٌ مِنَ النَّومِ (2x)

The Supplication to be made after the Adhān:

اَللّٰهُمَّ رَبَّ هٰـذِهِ الدَّعْوَةِ التَّامَّةِ والصَّلاَةِ الْقَائِمَةِ آتِ مُحَمَّدًا الْوَسِـيلَةَ وَالْفَضِيْلَـةَ وَالدَّرجَـةَالرَّفِيْعَـةَ وَابْعَثْـهُ مَقَامـاً مَّـحْمُوْدًا الَّذِيْ وَعدتَّهْ وَارْزُقْنَا شَفَاعَتَهُ يَوْمَ الْقِيَامَةِ. إِنَّكَ لاَ تُخْلِفُ الْـمِيْعَادِ.

Oh Lord, the Master of this perfect call and of the proper prayer grant our leader Muḥammad (peace be upon him) the rank of wasīlah and of virtue and appoint him to the rank of Maḥmūd, the one that you have promised. Certainly You do not break promises.

The reward for reciting this *duʿā'* is receiving the intercession of the blessed Prophet on the Day of Judgement[18] and for this reason alone we should make sure to commit this supplication to memory.

The Iqāmah

The *iqāmah* is made immediately prior to beginning the five obligitory daily prayers, usually by the *mu'adhdhin* (the person who calls the *adhān*). While it is *sunnah* to recite the *adhān* slowly, the *iqāmah* is to be recited quickly and the following words are added after the second *come to success* (*hayya ʿalā al-falāḥ*):

The prayer is about to begin (2x)	قَدْ قَامَتِ الصَّلاَةُ (2x)

Notes

1 Al-Ghazālī, *Inner Dimensions of Islamic Worship*, translated by Muhtar Holland (The Islamic Foundation, 2000), p. 30.
2 *Sūrah al-Baqarah* (Q2: 222).
3 Narrated in *Ṣaḥīḥ Muslim*.
4 Narrated in the *Musnad* of Aḥmad ibn Ḥanbal.
5 *Sūrah al-Mā'idah* (Q5:6).
6 This is not the case for women's menstruation and post-natal bleeding, as they must wait for a certain period which is not within their control, before taking *ghusl*. It should be remembered that at these times, obedience to Allah and His Contentment come precisely from abstaining from one's usual *ṣalāh*, fasting etc. Of course, other virtuous deeds, including maintaining good character (*akhlāq*), charity

(*ṣadaqah*) and remembrance of Allah (*dhikr*) will be greatly rewarded, particularly considering the adversary being faced.

7 Narrated in Abū Dawūd, Nisāʾī, Aḥmad and al-Dārimī. In this particular version of this *ḥadīth*, in which the term *junub* is added, Imām al-Bukhārī had doubt as to its authenticity and Imām Dhahabī said it was 'unknown' to him. The commentators also explain that *junub* here does not mean one who is in a state of greater ritual impurity and delays the *ghusl* until the prayer time comes, but rather it means here one who habitually neglects to have a *ghusl*. This is because the Prophet, may Allah bless him and grant him peace, on occasion used to sleep in the state of *janābah*, as reported by his wife ʿĀ'ishah. He also used to go to his wives and have one *ghusl* thereafter. Additionally, it is the angels of mercy (*raḥmah*) and blessing (*barakah*) who leave the house in this circumstance but not the recording angels who always remain with us at all times to record everything that we do.

8 It should be noted that any completed *ghusl*, whether consisting of the minimum compulsory (*farḍ*) elements, or the full *Sunnah*, will always include the integrals of *wuḍū'* and completely purify minor impurity.

9 *Sūrah al-Mā'idah* (Q5: 6).

10 Narrated in *Sunan Abī Dawūd*.

11 *Tayammum* is acceptable in this circumstance, because there is no replacement for these prayers if they are missed.

12 *Sūrah al-Mā'idah* (Q5: 6).

13 Narrated in *Ṣaḥīḥ al-Bukhārī*.

14 Narrated by Ṭabarānī.

15 Narrated in *Ṣaḥīḥ al-Bukhārī*.

16 Narrated in *Ṣaḥīḥ al-Bukhārī*.

17 Narrated in the *Musnad* of Aḥmad ibn Ḥanbal.

18 Narrated in *Ṣaḥīḥ al-Bukhārī*.

CHAPTER 6

How to Pray *Ṣalāh*

Objectives of this section to learn:

- The obligation to pray *ṣalāh*.
- The conditions required to begin praying *ṣalāh*.
- The *farḍ*, *wājib* and *sunnah* acts of prayer
- The invalidators of *ṣalāh*.
- How to perform *ṣalāh* correctly.
- To memorize all the relevant passages and *sūrahs*.

The Obligation to pray *Ṣalāh*

One of the most important duties of a Muslim is to pray five times a day. It is one of the five pillars of Islam and the foundation of religion. The Prophet, may Allah bless him and grant him peace, was asked by ʿAbd Allah ibn Masʿūd, "What is the best deed?" His reply was, 'To offer the prayers in their fixed times.'[1] The five prayers are obligatory in their correct time for every sane, adult[2] Muslim, except women while menstruating and during the period of post-natal bleeding.

The Six Conditions for Prayer

Before the prayer can be offered the following six conditions must be fulfilled:

1. To be physically clean, which means to both be free of filth on the body and to be in the state of purity gained by performing *wuḍū'* or *ghusl*.
2. The clothes and the place of prayer must also be clean and free from filth.[3]
3. The body must be covered – the minimum requirement for this covering for men, is from the navel to the knee, and for women, the whole body excluding the face, hands and feet.
4. Time for prayer – The five daily *farḍ* prayers are prescribed at set times during day and night based on the sunrise and sunset. It is important to know the times of prayers since they can only be performed during these times. Allah Most High says:

   > *Surely prayer is prescribed for the believers at fixed times.*[4]

Below we have explained how to find these times in relation to sunrise and sunset. However there are accurate timetables available for every major city in Britain, which are published by local mosques, as well as a range of information available online.[5]

The Time of Fajr

Fajr starts at dawn and ends at sunrise. Dawn is the brightness that spreads from the eastern horizon until it spreads everywhere and rises towards the sky. It is desirable to delay *fajr* until there is light; this is approximately half an hour before sunrise, since the blessed Prophet said, *'The greatest reward for fajr is when it is light.'*[6]

[side tab: ṢALĀH]

The Time of Ẓuhr

Ẓuhr time starts after the sun has began to decline (i.e. afternoon). There are two reports concerning its end:

Firstly, according to Imām Abū Ḥanīfah, may Allah have mercy on him: *ẓuhr* time continues until just before shadows become a length that is double their objects plus their shadow at noon. This is the opinion that has been preferred by the majority of Ḥanafī jurists.[7]

Secondly, according to the Ṣāhibayn, which is the name given to Imāms Abū Yūsuf and Muḥammad, may Allah have mercy on them, *ẓuhr* time continues until just before shadows become a length that is equal to their objects plus their shadow at noon. This opinion agrees with that of the other schools of thought.

A recommended compromise between the two positions is to pray *ẓuhr* according to the earlier end time and then wait until the completion of the later end time until beginning the *ṣalāh* of *ʿaṣr*. Also it should be remembered that it is preferred to delay *ẓuhr* in the summer and to do it early in the winter. Hadhrat Anas, relates:

> The beloved Prophet, may Allah bless him and grant him peace, on hot days used to pray when the day had cooled and when it was cold he would do it early.[8]

The Time of ʿAṣr

ʿAṣr starts when *ẓuhr* time has ended and extends until the beginning of sunset (the disc of the sun touching the horizon). It is best to delay *ʿaṣr* but not so long that the sun changes so that it becomes a reddish-yellow and can be seen without blinding the eyes. The Prophet, may Allah bless him and grant him peace, said:

> *Be quick about the prayer on a cloudy day for whoever misses his* ʿaṣr *has lost his deeds.*[9]

The Time of Maghrib

Maghrib extends from after sunset (the complete disappearance of the disc of the sun from the horizon) until all whiteness disappears from the horizon, in the opinion of Imām Abū Ḥanīfah. According to the opinion of the Ṣāhibayn the end of *maghrib* is marked by the disappearance of the redness on the horizon, which is earlier. The redness disappears approximately 55 minutes after sunset, while the whiteness takes until around an hour and 20 minutes, depending on location and season. It is, however, best to pray *maghrib* at its earliest time, as soon as the sun has set.

The Time of 'Ishā'

The earliest time of *'ishā'* is the disappearance of the redness or the whiteness of the horizon and it continues until the start of dawn. The time for *witr* prayer is after *'ishā'* until dawn.

The desirable time for *'ishā'* is to delay until one third of night has elapsed since the Messenger, may Allah bless him and grant him peace, said:

> *If it wasn't difficult for my* ummah, *I would have ordered them to delay* 'ishā' *to one third or half of the night.*[10]

However for the congregation in the *masjid* to delay *'ishā'* beyond half of the night is *makrūh taḥrīmī*, as there is a fear of low attendance.[11] The desirability of delaying *'ishā'* is only in the winter, as in summer it is best to pray it early due to the shortness of the night.

Makrūh Taḥrīmī *Times for Prayer*

There are three times when prayers are not allowed. They are:

1. From the start of sunrise until the sun is out and bright (approximately 15-20 minutes after sunrise).

2. At noon when the sun is at its zenith (*istiwā'* time). This (and in fact all three of these times) are often mistakenly called *zawāl* times. *Zawāl* properly refers to the time that the sun begins to decline and so marks the beginning of *ẓuhr* when prayer is permissable again. The best way to deal with this time is to find the point of noon (half-way between sunrise and sunset) and then remember not to pray 3-5 minutes before and after this time. Also be careful about some prayer timetables that list *ẓuhr* as starting only one minute after the point of noon, as this is not a safe margin for being sure *ẓuhr* has begun and the prohibited time has ended.
3. Before sunset when the sun is reddish-yellow until sunset. However, if the day's *'aṣr* has not yet been prayed, this must be done along with seeking forgiveness for leaving it so late.

Hadhrat 'Uqbah ibn Amīr reports that 'The Prophet, may Allah bless him and grant him peace, used to forbid us from praying or burying our dead at three times, when the sun is rising until it is high and at noon (when it is at its highest point) and when it begins to set until it has set.'[12]

Two Other Makrūh *Times*

It's not desirable to pray *nafl* (superogatory *ṣalāh*) after *fajr* prayer, even if the sun has not yet risen and likewise after *'aṣr* until the sun has set. It is narrated that 'The blessed Prophet, may Allah bless him and grant him peace, forbid praying after *ṣalāh al-fajr* and *ṣalāh al-'aṣr* until sunset.'[13]

5. The fifth condition of *ṣalāh* is to face the Ka'bah in Makkah. The Glorious Qur'ān tells us:

Turn your face in the direction of the sacred mosque, wherever you all are, turn your faces towards it.[14]

ṢALĀH

Facing the *qiblah* (prayer direction) has become the symbol of Muslim unity. All the mosques are built facing in the direction of the Kaʿbah in Makkah. The direction of the *qiblah* can be easily found using a compass and a map or a special compass with the *qiblah* direction marked on it.

Facing the *qiblah* means that at least some part of the face must be facing in its direction. As shown in Figure 1 a person looking forward from O will be facing the Kaʿbah (Z), then if he turns to X or Y and the angle remains less than 45 degrees it still counts as facing the *qiblah* and his prayer is correct. However if he goes beyond this he will be considered to be facing away from the Kaʿbah and his *ṣalāh* will be invalid.

Figure 1: Facing the *Qiblah*

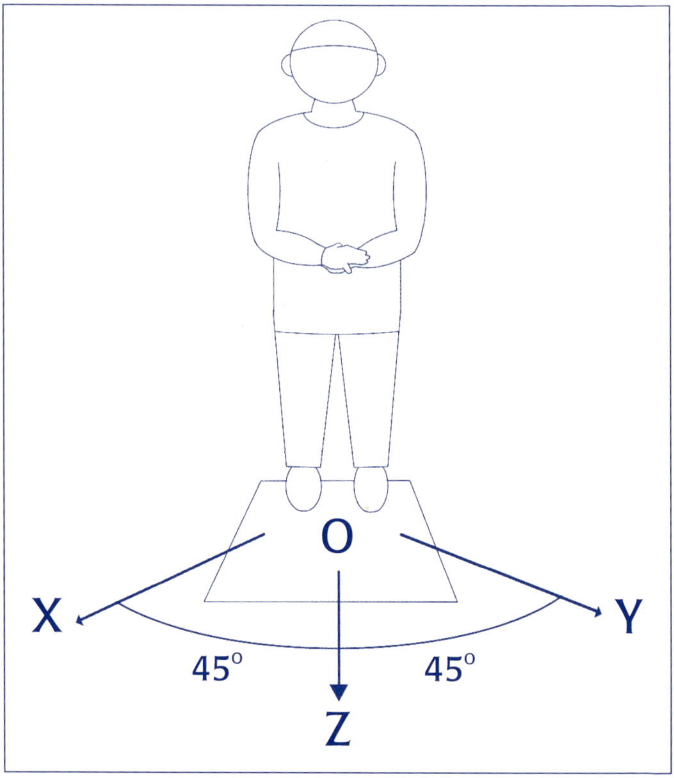

In the event of a person not knowing the prayer direction in a particular location, he should expend effort in determining it, by, for instance, looking towards the direction that the sun is setting (which is westwards) or even the direction that satellite dishes point (which in the UK at least, tends to be close to the *qiblah*), or asking someone. After doing this, he should make his prayer in the direction that he judges to be closest to the *qiblah*. If he later discovers that it was wrong, he does not need to repeat his prayer.

6. To make the intention for the prayer as a means of seeking divine pleasure. It is preferable to make the intention verbally, though silently, in any language. For example:

   I intend to pray two *farḍ rakʿahs* of *fajr* prayer for the pleasure of Allah whilst facing the Kaʿbah.

The minimum that is acceptable is an intention in the heart of praying to Allah, along with awareness of which prayer is being offered including whether it is obligatory. The intention may slightly preceed the opening *takbīr* (saying of *'Allāhu Akbar'*) as long as there is no major movement or action of the type that would invalidate a prayer between them. When praying in congregation one must also intend to follow the *imām* in order to receive the reward of *ṣalāh* in *jamāʿah*.

The Six Compulsory (*Farḍ*) Acts in Prayer

Once the intention for prayer has been made the following acts must be performed in full:

1. *Takbīr al-taḥrīmah*: Saying *'Allāhu Akbar'*. This indicates that the prayer has begun and that speaking, eating and many other actions are forbidden for its duration. The words of *'Allāhu Akbar'* must be audible at least to oneself and this is the definition of 'silent' recitation in the rest of what follows.

2. Standing upright in *farḍ* prayers. However, if someone is severely ill or injured so that he cannot stand up, then it is permissible for him to sit down and pray. Likewise, if a person begins to feel that he can no longer stand in prayer, then they may go into a sitting position and complete it in this way. It is permissible to pray *sunnah* and *nafl* prayers whilst sitting, although the reward is half that of standing up.
3. Recitation of the Glorious Qur'ān. It is compulsory to recite from the Qur'ān in the first two units of *farḍ* prayer and in all the units of *sunnah*, *witr*, and *nafl* prayers. When praying with the congregation it is not permitted to recite from the Qur'ān and the *imām's* recitation is accepted by Allah in its place.
4. Bowing. For men, this is the bending of the back and the neck and grasping the knees with the hands such that the head and the back are level. For women, the back should be inclined at about a 45 degree angle with the hands placed on the thighs.
5. Prostration. This is defined as putting the feet, the knees, the hands, the forehead and the nose on the ground. The prostration must be done on the ground or carpet where the hardness of the ground can be felt. The toes of the feet must also be touching the ground.
6. The last sitting. This is to read the *tashahhud* in the last *rak'ah* (unit) of the prayer.

The Nine Necessary (*Wājib*) Acts in Prayer

The following list of nine things are highly recommended and therefore *wājib* (necessary) since their omission from the prayer makes it invalid unless compensated for by the extra prostrations called (*sajdah al-sahw*):

1. To recite *Sūrah al-Fātiḥah* in the first two *rak'ah* of *farḍ* prayer and in all the *rak'ahs* of *witr, sunnah* and *nafl*. Furthermore this *sūrah* must be read before any other part of the Qur'ān.
2. The major acts of the prayer, bowing and prostration should be properly performed this means to remain in that posture for the minimum time it takes to utter a *tasbīḥ, 'Subḥāna Rabbī al-A'lā'* (*Glory be to my Lord, the Most High*), which takes approximately two seconds.
3. The first sitting. In prayers of three or four units one must also sit at the end of the second unit. In this sitting the *tashahhud* is read and it is important not to read beyond the *tashahhud*, as this will require prostrations of forgetfulness.
4. To end the prayer by saying the *salām* (*al-salāmu 'alaykum wa raḥmatullāh*) twice.
5. To read the *du'ā' al-qunūt* in the third *rak'ah* of *witr* prayer. This *du'ā'* should be read after reciting the *Fātiḥah* and another *sūrah*. A *takbīr* should be said and then the *du'ā'* recited.
6. To make six additional *takbīr*s in the 'Īd prayer (see the specific section on the 'Īd prayer for details).
7. For the *imām* to recite the Qur'ān out loud in the following prayers: *fajr, maghrib, 'ishā', witr* (in Ramaḍan only), *jumu'ah* (Friday prayer) and 'Īd. The Qur'ān is to be recited out loud only in the first two *rak'ahs* with the exception of *witr*, in which he does this for all three. The individual devotee can choose to read aloud or silently in all of these prayers that can be prayed individually. Similarly, both the *imām* and the individual must read silently in *ẓuhr, 'aṣr*, the third *rak'ah* of *maghrib* and the third and fourth *rak'ahs* of *'ishā'*.
8. The *muqtadi'* (follower) should not recite anything whilst standing behind the *imām*.

9. In the prostration the forehead and the hard part of the nose must both be touching the ground.

The *Sunnah* Acts in Prayer

Many of the rituals of the prayer are practices of the beloved Prophet, may Allah bless him and grant him peace, or else the practices of his disciples: these are known as the *sunnah* of the prayer. They are neither *farḍ*, nor *wājib*, but are still very important as they are made in emulation of the prophetic prayer and thus imbue the *ṣalāh* with blessing and light. Furthermore, to omit them habitually is a sin. These *sunnah* actions are:

1. To raise both hands to the ears when saying *takbīr al-taḥrīmah*.
2. To stand straight and upright whilst saying the *takbīr*.
3. To immediately afterwards place the right hand over the left hand such that the palm of the right hand is on the back of the left hand grasping the left wrist with the little finger and the thumb of the right. For women it is sufficient to put the right hand over the left hand on top of the chest.
4. To silently recite the *thanā'*, which begins *'Subḥānaka Allāhumma...'*
5. To silently recite the *taʿawwudh*, which begins *'Aʿūdhu billāh...'*
6. To silently recite the *basmalah*, which begins *'Bismillāh...'*
7. To silently say *'āmīn'* at the end of *al-Fātiḥah*.
8. To say *'Samiʿa Allāhu al-ḥāmidah'* out loud if praying behind the *imām* (silently if praying alone) and then to silently say *'Rabbanā laka al-ḥamd'*.
9. When standing, the distance between the two feet should be the width of a fist.
10. To read the appropriate *tasbīḥ* in the *rukūʿ* (bowing) and the *sajdah* (prostration). See the supplications below for the details.

11. Whilst bowing, the hands should firmly grasp the knees (for men).
12. The back should bend such that it is nearly at a right angle (90 degrees) to the legs. The back and the neck should be so level that a full glass of water would not spill over! (This is also only for men.)
13. To raise the head after the bowing and stand upright.
14. To sit between the two prostrations.
15. When going to the ground for the prostration the knees should touch the ground first then the hands then the nose and finally the forehead. This order should be reversed when rising from the prostration.
16. In prostration the nose and the forehead should be placed on the ground with the two palms flat down at an equal distance on either side, leaving a gap.
17. During the prostration, for men, the belly should be kept clear of the thighs, the elbows away from touching the sides and the forearms well clear off the ground. However, women should be more compact and modest in their prostration, such that their belly and thighs are touching each other and their elbows are resting against the sides and their forearms are laid on the ground.
18. To put the hands on the middle of the thighs whilst sitting in the *tashahhud*.
19. In the sitting position, for men, the left foot should be sat on with its upper side flat on the floor on its side and the right foot propped up with the heel vertical and the toes bent, pointing in the direction of the *qiblah*. Women should sit on their left buttock and rest one thigh against the other with their legs together to their right side.
20. When reciting the negation (*lā ilāha...*) during the *tashahhud* the index finger should be raised and then dropped on reading the affirmation (*illa'llāh*). The way to do this is by making a circle with the middle finger and the thumb and raising the index finger.

21. To read *al-Fātiḥah* in the third and the fourth rakat of *farḍ* prayers.
22. To send blessings on the beloved Prophet, may Allah bless him and grant him peace, after the final *tashahhud*.
23. To make a *du'ā'* derived from the words of the Glorious Qur'ān or *Sunnah*.
24. To say *'al-salāmu 'alaykum wa raḥmatullāh'* twice and turn the head to the right and then to the left.
25. The intention should be to salute the congregation, the guardian angels and the righteous jinns. The members of the congregation should intend to salute the *imām*.

The Special *Sunnah*s for Congregation

1. The devotees in the congregation should do their first *takbīr* along with the *imām* (or slightly after him) and not before him.
2. The *imām* should do all the *takbīr*s and *salām* aloud so that the congregation can hear him. The individual does theirs silently.
3. The second *salām* should be said in a lower voice than the first.
4. The latecomer to congregation should wait slightly after the first *salām* to ensure that the *imām* is not going to do the *sajdah al-sahw*.

The Desirable (*Mustaḥabb*) Acts in Prayer

Mustaḥabb is any action that is preferred by the *sharī'ah*; it is neither compulsory, *wājib* nor *sunnah*. Its performance earns reward and its omission is not blameworthy. The following are desirable in prayer:

1. When doing the first *takbīr* the hands should be outside the sleeves.
2. The devotee should keep his gaze on his place of prostration when standing, on his feet whilst bowing, on

his nose whilst prostrating, on his laps whilst sitting and on his shoulders when ending with *salām*.

3. The *tasbīḥ*s in bowing and prostration should be read more than thrice and in odd numbers.
4. Effort should be made to avoid yawning and if that isn't possible then the mouth should be covered with the hand.
5. Every effort should be made not to cough.
6. The *imām* and the congregation should stand up when the words *'ḥayya 'alā al-ṣalāh'* are read during the *iqāmah* since these words are commanding one to come to the prayer and when the congregation stands up it is as though they are responding positively to it!

The Undesirable (*Makrūh*) Acts in Prayer

Makrūh acts are the opposites of the necessary and recommended actions. If it results in the omission of a *wājib* it is *makrūh taḥrīmī* (a major offense), the omission of a *mu'akaddah* (emphatic) *sunnah* is termed *is'āh* (an offense) and the omission of an unemphatic *sunnah* is called *makrūh tanzīhī* (a minor offense). The following things are undesirable in the prayer:

1. To engage in a useless activity done absent-mindedly, for instance, playing with the beard or ones clothes or cracking fingers (*makrūh taḥrīmī*). ← Not liked · Don't do
2. To look at something by turning the head around.
3. To pray with sleeves rolled up.
4. To pray just in trousers without wearing a shirt (*makrūh taḥrīmī*).
5. To recite the Qur'ān in any posture other than standing up (unless having an excuse to sit down in prayer).
6. To repeat the recitation of the same *sūrah* of the Qur'ān (after *al-Fātiḥah*) in two consecutive *rak'ah*s.
7. To recite one *sūrah* of the Qur'ān in the first *rak'ah* of prayer and then recite the *sūrah* which precedes it in the second *rak'ah*.

ṢALĀH

don't shut eyes

8. To read two different *sūrah*s in two consecutive *rak'ah*s such that the *sūrah* inbetween them is missed out. Example: in the first *rak'ah al-Ikhlāṣ* and in the second *al-Nās* thus omitting *al-Falaq*.
9. To smell scent intentionally.
10. To shut the eyes without good reason (*makrūh tanzīhī*).
11. To lift the eyes skywards (*makrūh taḥrīmī*).
12. For men to cover the mouth and the nose with a scarf.
13. To prostrate on the nose only without putting down the forehead (*m. taḥrīmī*).
14. For men to lay their forearms on the ground in prostration (*makrūh taḥrīmī).*
15. To prostrate with the forehead covered with a turban or anything else (*makrūh taḥrīmī*).
16. To prostrate on something with an animal picture on it.
17. To perform the prayer in the graveyard such that whilst standing in the prayer a grave is seen in front of one. However if it is the blessed grave of the Prophet, may Allah bless him and grant him peace, it is not *makrūh*.
18. To pray when there is an urgent need to go to the toilet (*makrūh taḥrīmī*). It is preferable to break the prayer, relieve oneself, and make fresh *wuḍū'*.
19. To pray when one is hungry or thirsty with available food and drink present, if one will be distracted in prayer. If there is a fear that the prayer time will end if one were to eat then it is not *makrūh*.
20. To pray with the head uncovered without an excuse, unless uncovering of the head adds to humility and greater concentration in *ṣalāh*.
21. To pray in a place where people are sleeping.
22. To pray in front of a fire since it resembles the Zoroastrians.
23. To pray in front of someone facing you (*makrūh taḥrīmī*).
24. To pray in a public place where people are passing to and fro without a barrier (*makrūh tanzīhī*).

> *Note*: A barrier is anything placed in front of the devotee like a chair, stick or a wall. It must be at least a foot high and of any thickness. The distance between the devotee and the barrier must be at least three feet.

The Invalidating (*Mufsid*) Acts in Prayer

The following is a list of acts that render one's prayer null and void i.e. non-existent and expressionless.

1. To intentionally speak anything audibly.
2. To ask Allah for worldly things.
3. To reply to *salām* or any other form of greeting.
4. To do something in the prayer that would make the onlooker think that one is not praying. This is defined as *ʿamal kathīr* (major action), as distinct from *ʿamal qalīl* (insignificant action).
5. To turn away the face and the chest from the *qiblah*.
6. To eat or drink. Even if a morsel the size of a sesame seed is put into the mouth, that will invalidate the prayer as will picking a piece of food stuck in the teeth.
7. To grunt and to make low-level noises which are gestures of pain or to cry with pain.
8. To respond to:

    i. A sneeze by saying *'God bless you'*.
    ii. Good news by saying *'thanks be to Allah'*.
    iii. Amazing news by saying *'glory to Allah'*.
    iv. Anything by using a Qur'ānic verse or a phrase.

9. The expiry of the time limit for leather socks or if they slip off by themselves.
10. To giggle or laugh audibly.
11. To omit any of the *farḍ* actions or to omit any of the *wājib* acts without compensating with a *sajdah al-sahw*.

ṢALĀH

How to Perform the *Ṣalāh*

In order to perform the prayer the following words and passages of the Qur'ān and *Sunnah* must also be memorised:

Takbīr

> اَللهُ أَكْبَرُ
>
> *Allah is the Greatest.*

Thanā'

> سُبْحٰنَكَ اللّٰهُمَّ وَبِحَمْدِكَ وَتَبَارَكَ اسْمُكَ وَتَعَالٰى جَدُّكَ وَلَآ إِلٰهَ غَيْرُكَ.
>
> *Glory be to You Oh Allah, all praise is for You, blessed is Your Name and exalted is Your Majesty. There is no god other than You.*

Ta'awwudh

> أَعُوْذُ بِاللهِ مِنَ الشَّيْطٰنِ الرَّجِيْمِ.
>
> *I seek refuge in Allah from the accursed Satan.*

Basmalah

> بِسْمِ اللهِ الرَّحْمٰنِ الرَّحِيْمِ.
>
> *I begin with the name of Allah, the Most Merciful, the Most Benevolent.*

ṢALĀH

Al-Fātiḥah

ٱلْحَمْدُ لِلَّهِ رَبِّ ٱلْعَـٰلَمِينَ، ٱلرَّحْمَـٰنِ، ٱلرَّحِيمِ، مَـٰلِكِ يَوْمِ ٱلدِّينِ. إِيَّاكَ نَعْبُدُ وَإِيَّاكَ نَسْتَعِينُ. ٱهْدِنَا ٱلصِّرَٰطَ ٱلْمُسْتَقِيمَ، صِرَٰطَ ٱلَّذِينَ أَنْعَمْتَ عَلَيْهِمْ، غَيْرِ ٱلْمَغْضُوبِ عَلَيْهِمْ وَلَا ٱلضَّآلِّينَ. (آمِينْ)

All praise is for Allah the Lord of the universe. The Most Merciful, the Most Gracious, Owner of the Day of Judgement. You alone we worship and from You alone we seek help. Guide us on the straight path, the path of those whom You have favoured, those whom have neither earned Your anger nor have gone astray. (Amīn)

Tasbīḥ (in *rukūʿ*)

سُبْحَانَ رَبِّيَ الْعَظِيْمِ

Glorified is my Lord the Almighty.

Ḥamd

سَمِعَ اللهُ لِمَنْ حَمِدَهْ. رَبَّنَا لَكَ الْحَمْدُ

Allah has heard him who praises Him. Oh our Lord! All praise is for You.

Tasbīḥ (in *sajdah*)

سُبْحَانَ رَبِّيَ الأَعْلَىٰ

Glorified is my Lord the Most High.

Tashahhud

التَّحِيَّاتُ لِلّٰهِ وَالصَّلَوٰتُ وَالطَّيِّبٰتُ اَلسَّلَامُ عَلَيْكَ أَيُّهَا النَّبِيُّ
وَرَحْمَةُ اللهِ وَبَرَكَاتُهُ اَلسَّلَامُ عَلَيْنَا وَعَلٰى عِبَادِ اللهِ الصَّالِحِيْنَ
أَشْهَدُ أَنْ لَآ إِلٰهَ إِلَّا اللهُ وَأَشْهَدُ أَنَّ مُحَمَّدًا عَبْدُهُ وَرَسُوْلُهُ.

All verbal praises, bodily devotions and charity are for Allah. Peace be upon you Oh Prophet and Allah's mercy and his blessings. Peace be on us all and the righteous servants of Allah. I bear witness that there is no god other than Allah and I bear witness that Muḥammad is His servant and messenger.

Ṣalawāt (Darūd Sharīf)

اَللّٰهُمَّ صَلِّ عَلٰى مُحَمَّدٍ وَعَلٰى آلِ مُحَمَّدٍ كَمَا صَلَّيْتَ عَلٰى
إِبْرٰهِيْمَ وَعَلٰى آلِ إِبْرٰهِيْمَ إِنَّكَ حَمِيْدٌ مَّجِيْدٌ. اَللّٰهُمَّ بَارِكْ عَلٰى
مُحَمَّدٍ وَعَلٰى آلِ مُحَمَّدٍ كَمَا بَارَكْتَ عَلٰى إِبْرٰهِيْمَ وَعَلٰى
آلِ إِبْرٰهِيْمَ إِنَّكَ حَمِيْدٌ مَّجِيْدٌ.

Oh Allah! Exalt Muḥammad and exalt the family of Muḥammad as you exalted Ibrāhīm and the family of Ibrāhīm. Indeed you are the Praiseworthy and Most Glorious. Oh Allah! Bless Muḥammad and bless the family of Muḥammad as you blessed Ibrāhīm and the family of Ibrāhīm. Indeed you are the Praiseworthy and the Most Glorious.

Du'ā' *of Ibrāhīm (any supplication from the Qur'ān and* Sunnah *can be made)*

رَبِّ ٱجْعَلْنِى مُقِيمَ ٱلصَّلَوٰةِ وَمِن ذُرِّيَّتِى رَبَّنَا وَتَقَبَّلْ دُعَآءِ. رَبَّنَا ٱغْفِرْ لِى وَلِوَٰلِدَىَّ
وَلِلْمُؤْمِنِينَ يَوْمَ يَقُومُ ٱلْحِسَابُ.

Oh my Lord! Make me and my children regular in prayer. Our Lord accept our supplication. Our Lord forgive me, my parents and all the believers on the Day of Judgement.

Taslīm

السَّلَامُ عَلَيْكُمْ وَرَحْمَةُ اللهِ وَبَرَكَاتُهُ

May peace and Allah's mercy be upon you.

Witr *Prayer*

After praying four *farḍ*, two *sunnah* and two *nafl* units of *'ishā'* prayer, it is *wājib* (necessary) that one should pray three units of *witr* (or at any time before *fajr* begins). *Witr* is similar to other prayers except that in the third unit after reading *Sūrah al-Fātiḥah* and any other *sūrah*, one raises the hands and makes a *takbīr* and then recites the following *du'ā'*:

اَللَّهُمَّ إِنَّا نَسْتَعِينُكَ، وَنَسْتَغْفِرُكَ، وَنُؤْمِنُ بِكَ، وَنَتَوَكَّلُ عَلَيْكَ،
وَنُثْنِي عَلَيْكَ الْخَيْرَ، وَنَشْكُرُكَ وَلَا نَكْفُرُكَ، وَنَخْلَعُ وَنَتْرُكُ
مَنْ يَفْجُرُكَ، اللَّهُمَّ إِيَّاكَ نَعْبُدُ وَلَكَ نُصَلِّيْ، وَنَسْجُدُ وَإِلَيْكَ
نَسْعَىٰ، وَنَحْفِدُ وَنَرْجُوا رَحْمَتَكَ، وَنَخْشَىٰ عَذَابَكَ إِنَّ عَذَابَكَ
بِالْكُفَّارِ مُلْحِقٌ.

Oh Allah! We seek Your help and forgiveness. We believe in You and rely upon You. We praise and thank You. We are not unthankful to You. We reject and leave him who disobeys You. Oh Allah! We worship You alone and pray and prostrate before You and we hasten eagerly towards You. We hope for Your Mercy and we fear Your Punishment as surely Your Punishment is to be meted out to the unbelievers.

Some Dhikr *(Remembrance) and* Duʿā*'s after* Ṣalāh

Ṣalāh is itself the best form of *dhikr* that we can make to remember Allah, however, once the prayer is over we are told to continue to remain in that state. The Messenger of Allah, may Allah bless him and grant him peace, taught his beloved daughter Fāṭimah, may Allah be pleased with her, to do the following *dhikr* every night before bed:

> Subḥānallāh *thirty-three times,* al-ḥamduli'llāh *thirty three-times and* Allāhu Akbar *thirty-four times.*[15]

For this reason, this particular *dhikr* is known as *'Taṣbīh Fāṭimah'*. It is a highly recommended practice to be performed after each *farḍ* prayer.

Again, although the entire *ṣalāh* should be a humble and longing petition for Allah's forgiveness, blessings and favour, it is the *Sunnah* of the blessed Prophet, may Allah bless him and grant him peace, to continue to make supplication following the formal prayer. Hadhrat Sawbān, may Allah be pleased with him, says 'Whenever the blessed Prophet, may Allah bless him and grant him peace, finished his *ṣalāh* he would do *istighfār* (seeking forgiveness) thrice and then make his *duʿā's.'* During these times he used to raise both his hands up to his chest as though begging for Allah's mercy. The following are well-attested *duʿā*'s from the Qur'ān and *Sunnah* that the Prophet used to regularly make.

Prayer for Peace and Security

اَللّٰهُمَّ أَنْتَ السَّلَامُ وَمِنْكَ السَّلَامُ وَإِلَيْكَ يَرْجِعُ السَّلَامُ
حَيِّنَا رَبَّنَا بِالسَّلَامِ وَأَدْخِلْنَا دَارَ السَّلَامِ تَبَارَكْتَ يَاذَا
الْجَلَالِ وَالْإِكْرَامِ.

Oh Lord! You are the Granter of peace and security, from You comes all peace, and to You returns all peace. Keep us alive in peace and enter us into the House of Peace. Blessed and Exalted are You, Oh Lord of Majesty and Nobility.

Prayer for Goodness in Both Worlds

رَبَّنَآ ءَاتِنَا فِى ٱلدُّنْيَا حَسَنَةً وَفِى ٱلْءَاخِرَةِ حَسَنَةً وَقِنَا عَذَابَ ٱلنَّارِ.

Oh our Lord! Give us goodness in this world and in the Hereafter and protect us from the punishment of Hellfire.

Prayer for Firmness in Faith

رَبَّنَا لَا تُزِغْ قُلُوبَنَا بَعْدَ إِذْ هَدَيْتَنَا وَهَبْ لَنَا مِن لَّدُنكَ رَحْمَةً إِنَّكَ أَنتَ ٱلْوَهَّابُ.

Oh our Lord! Do not allow our hearts to deviate after You have given us guidance and grant us mercy from Your presence; truly You are the Granter of all bounties.

Prayer for Forgiveness

Hadhrat Abū Bakr, may Allah be pleased with him, says:

> I asked my beloved master to teach me a prayer which I could read in my *ṣalāh*, the Prophet, may Allah bless him and grant him peace, taught me.

اَللَّهُمَّ إِنِّيْ ظَلَمْتُ نَفْسِيْ ظُلْماً كَثِيْراً وَلاَيَغْفِرُ الذُّنُوبَ إِلاَّ أَنْتَ فَاغْفِرْ لِيْ مَغْفِرَةً مِنْ عِنْدِكَ وَارْحَمْنِيْ، إِنَّكَ أَنْتَ الْغَفُورُ الرَّحِيْمُ.

Oh Lord! I have enormously wronged myself and only You can forgive my sins, forgive me and have mercy on me; truly You are the Forgiving, the Merciful.

Prayer For seeking help in Devotion

Hadhrat Muʿādh ibn Jabal, may Allah be pleased with him, says that once the blessed Prophet, may Allah bless him and grant him peace, held his hand and said, *'Oh Muʿādh, I swear by Allah that I love you, I advise you after each* ṣalāh *to never forget to say these words:*

اَللَّهُمَّ أَعِنِّىْ عَلىٰ ذِكْرِكَ وَشُكْرِكَ وَحُسْنِ عِبَادَتِكَ.

Oh Lord! Help me to remember you, to thank you and to worship you properly.'[16]

Prayer for seeking Allah's Refuge

Hadhrat Abū Hurayrah, may Allah be pleased with him, says that the blessed Prophet, may Allah bless him and grant him peace, used to pray in these words:

اَللَّهُمَّ إِنِّيْ أَعُوذُ بِكَ مِنْ عَذَابِ النَّارِ، وَعَذَابِ الْقَبْرِ، وَفِتْنَةِ الْمَحْيَا وَالْمَمَاتِ، وَفِتْنَةِ الدَّجَّالِ.

Oh Lord! Protect me from the punishment of Hell, from the punishment of the grave, from the trials of life and death and from the mischief of the Dajjal.[17]

Prayer for the Heart

Hadhrat ʿAbd Allah ibn ʿAmr ibn al-ʿĀṣ, may Allah be pleased with him, says the Prophet, may Allah bless him and grant him peace, used to pray:

يَا مُقَلِّبَ الْقُلُوْبِ ثَبِّتْ قَلْبِيْ عَلٰى دِيْنِكَ.

Oh Turner of the hearts, turn my heart to Your worship.

Prayer for the Love of Allah

Hadhrat Abū Dardā', may Allah be pleased with him, reports that the Prophet, may Allah bless him and grant him peace, said, *'One of the prayers of Dawūd was:*

اَللّٰهُمَّ إِنِّيْ أَسْأَلُكَ حُبَّكَ وَحُبَّ مَنْ يُحِبُّكَ وَالْعَمَلَ الَّذِيْ يُبَلِّغُنِيْ حُبَّكَ، اَللّٰهُمَّ اجْعَلْ حُبَّكَ أَحَبَّ إِلَيَّ مِنْ نَفْسِيْ وَأَهْلِيْ وَمِنَ الْمَاءِ الْبَارِدِ.

Oh Lord! I seek your Love and the love of your beloved. I seek deeds that will bring me to Your love. Oh Lord! Make Your love more dear to me than myself, my family and cold water.

Prayer for Protection from Evil

Hadhrat Ziyād ibn ʿAlāqah, may Allah be pleased with him, said that the beloved Messenger, may Allah bless him and grant him peace, used to pray:

اَللّٰهُمَّ إِنِّيْ أَعُوذُ بِكَ مِنْ مُنْكَرَاتِ الأَخْلَاقِ وَالأَعْمَالِ وَالأَهْوَاءِ.

Oh Lord! Protect me from evil morals, evil deeds and evil desires.

Summary of the Procedure for *Ṣalāh*

(1) Make the intention. Raise the hands, saying the *takbīr*.

(2) Fold the hands together. Recite the *thanā'*, *taʿawwudh*, *basmalah*, *Sūrah al-Fātiḥah* and another *sūrah*.

(3) Now say a *takbīr* and bend down into *rukūʿ*. Read the *tasbīh* of *rukūʿ* three, five or seven times.

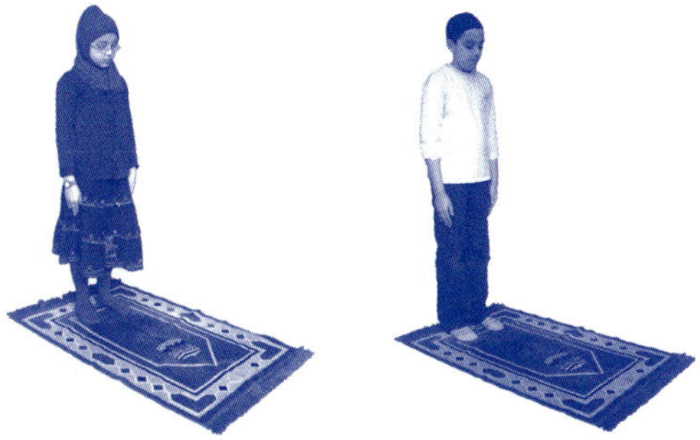

(4) Now rise and stand up straight and read the *ḥamd*.

(5) Say a *takbīr* and go into prostration. Read the *tasbīḥ* of *sajdah* three, five or seven times.

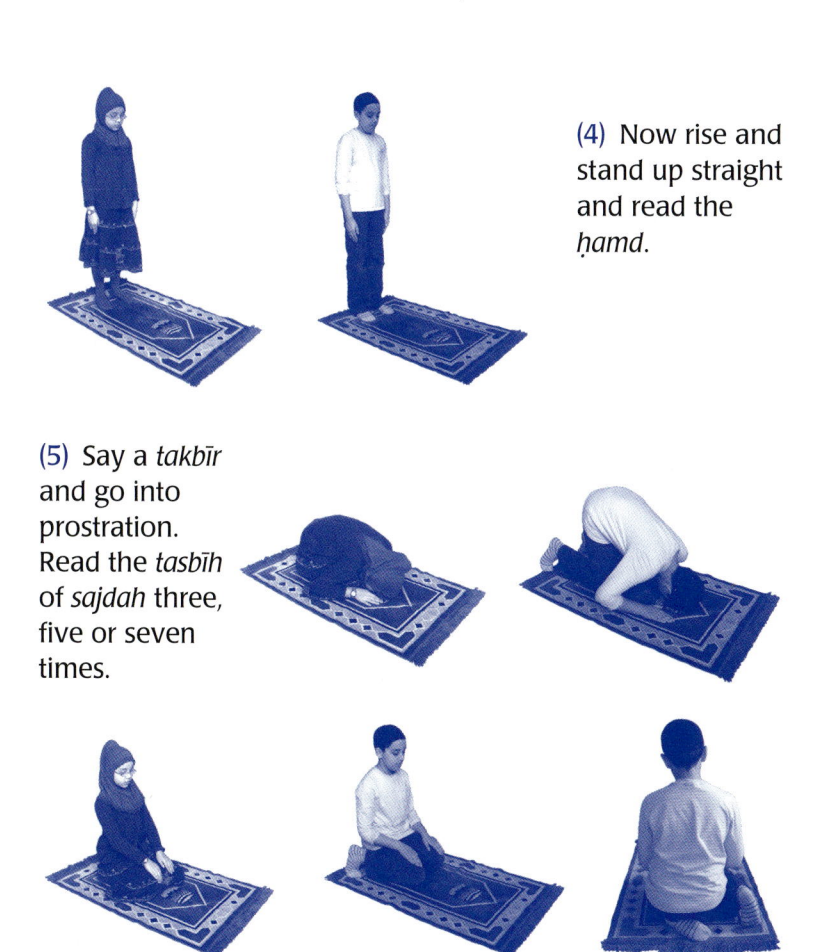

(6) Then saying *takbīr* sit up.

(7) Then prostrate again to complete one *rakʿah*. Stand up and begin a second one with the *basmalah*, repeating steps (2) to (7).

(8) Sit and read the *tashahhud*, *ṣalawāt* and *du'ā'*, if performing only two units of prayer.

If performing three or four units, stand up after the *tashahhud* and complete the additional unit(s) before sitting again and reciting *tashahhud, ṣalawāt* and *du'ā'*.

(9) Now do the *salām*.

The *Nafl* Prayers (Voluntary *Ṣalāh*s)

Apart from the daily five *ṣalāh*s there are other times for offering voluntary *ṣalāhs*, which are categorised as *nafl*. The five daily prayers are a duty upon every Muslim, and whilst the *nafl ṣalāh* is optional, its merit is enormous. This is expressed beautifully in Allah's own words:

> *Whoever has enmity towards My friend, I declare a war against him. The thing that brings My devotee closer to Me is the performance of acts I have made compulsory and My devotee continues to draw nearer to Me through nafl until I love him. When I love him I become his ear with which he hears and I become his eye with which he sees and his hand with which he grasps and his feet with which he walks, and if he asks Me for anything I will grant it and if he seeks My protection I will indeed give it.*[18]

The compulsory duties of the *sharīʿah* are the foundations, which save a person from the wrath and the anger of the Almighty, whilst the *nafl* activities (of *ṣalāh*, charity, *ʿumrah* etc.) are done from love and service to Allah. The metaphor in the *ḥadīth* means that Allah helps His servants by protecting them from committing evil, and the *nafl* activities deepen his faith and strengthen his conviction.

The daily lives of the best true believers are punctuated with voluntary *ṣalāhs*. Some of these are:

Tahajjud

This is the *ṣalāh* performed in the darkness of night after waking up. The blessed Prophet, may Allah bless him and grant him peace, performed it regularly and encouraged his companions likewise. In the *ḥadīth* it is also called *qiyām al-layl* (night vigil). The Messenger, may Allah bless him and grant him peace, said:

> *Pray* tahajjud *like the righteous devotees of the past since it takes you closer to Allah, blots out your sins and stops you from evil.*[19]

The minimum number of *rakʿahs* of *tahajjud* is two and maximum is twelve.

ṢALĀH

Ishrāq

This carries a great reward, as the Prophet, may Allah bless him and grant him peace, said:

> *Whoever performs* ishrāq *has the reward of* ḥajj *and* ʿumrah.

The way to perform this prayer is to remain in the *masjid* after praying *fajr* and wait until the sun has risen (15 to 20 minutes after sunrise) and then pray two or four *rakʿah*s.

Ḍuḥā

The blessed Messenger, may Allah bless him and grant him peace, said:

> *Every joint of your body should do an act of goodness each morning. Every* tasbīh *is an act of goodness, enjoining good and forbidding evil is also goodness and the two* rakʿats *of* ḍuhā *are equal to these.*[20]

The minimum amount of *ḍuḥā* is two *rakʿah*s and the maximum is twelve. Its time is from the time the sun is high (approximately 45 minutes after sunrise) until noon.

> *Note:* Some scholars have held that *ishrāq* and *ḍuḥā* are really the same *nafl ṣalāh*, but given each name based on the time that they are prayed. In any case, there is immense reward and spiritual well-being available for incorporating these practices within one's ritual life.

Awwabīn

Literally this means those who turn away from forgetfulness to the rememberance of their Lord and from sin to goodness. The Prophet, may Allah bless him and grant him peace, said:

> *Whoever prays six* rakʿahs *after* maghrib *and does not talk in between them gets the reward of twelve years worship and his sins forgiven even if they are like the froth on the surface of the sea.*[21]

Combining Two Prayers

In Ḥanafī *fiqh*, combining two prayers and praying them together is not permissible in any situation whether at home or on a journey, except for two:

1. It is permissible for the pilgrims to combine *ẓuhr* and *ʿaṣr* at ʿArafah.
2. It is permissible for the pilgrims to combine *maghrib* and *ʿishāʾ* at Muzdalifah. Hadhrat ʿAbd Allāh ibn Masʿūd, may Allah be pleased with him, says the blessed Prophet, may Allah bless him and grant him peace, used to pray the *ṣalāh*s at their fixed times except for combining at Muzdalifah and ʿArafah.[22]

The permissible way to combine two prayers (*ẓuhr* with *ʿaṣr* and *maghrib* with *ʿishāʾ*) is to delay the first to near its end time and pray the second in its earliest time. In this case it is only an apparent combining, as in reality each *ṣalāh* is still offered within its own time. This, at least from the Ḥanafī perspective, best explains the *ḥadīth* that mention the combining of prayers in other than the two exceptional situations mentioned above.

Making Up for Missed *Ṣalāh* (*Qaḍāʾ*)

It is very important to perform the five daily prayers within their fixed times and it is a grievous sin to delay or miss them without an excuse. Anyone who finds it a hardship to fit them all into his or her daily routine should make a sincere *duʿāʾ*, as Allah has made nothing obligatory that is beyond the capacity of His servants and He is, without doubt, ready to assist those who wish to act in obedience to Him. In certain situations, such as menstruation and post-natal bleeding in women, the *ṣalāh* is actually prohibited with no need for making it up. There are also other situations in which, although one does not commit a sin, one should make up the missed prayers as soon as possible. These can range from oversleeping and genuinely forgetting (as long as not stemming from willful neglect), to unconsciousness and a fit of insanity (if it is for less than a day). This delayed offering of *ṣalāh* is called *qaḍā'*.

Rules for the Performance of Qaḍā'

1. It is important to pray the missed *ṣalāh* in their order, for example, the *fajr qaḍā'* should be before *ẓuhr*, *ẓuhr qaḍā'* before *'aṣr* and so on. However if more than six prayers are missed then the order is no longer necessary.
2. *Qaḍā'*, like all *ṣalāh*, is not permissible at sunrise, sunset and noon. Apart from these three times, *qaḍā'* is permissible even after *fajr* and *'aṣr ṣalāh*.
3. *Ṣalāh* missed whilst traveling has to be made up by doing *qaḍā* of two *rak'ah*s and not four *rak'ah*s for *ẓuhr*, *'aṣr* and *'ishā'*.[23]

Guidelines for Those who Owe Many Qaḍā'

Sometimes a person may find themselves with many weeks, or even years of missed or improperly performed *ṣalāh*. Such a case often requires a more systematic approach than someone with only a few *qaḍā'* to perform, particularly if it is to be prevented from overwhelming them and leading them into despair; and as it is essential that they still maintain their current schedule of prayers.

We shall take a hypoethetical case of twenty-year-old Karim, who only recently began to perform his daily *ṣalāh*. He is required to make up for all the *ṣalāh* missed from his puberty, which here we will take to have started at 14. In other words he has to do *qaḍā'* for six years *ṣalāh*. *Qaḍā'* is only of *farḍ* and *wājib* (i.e. *witr*) prayers. The best way to do the *qaḍā'* of one's life is, in the case of Karim, to pray with each daily *ṣalāh* the equivalent missed *ṣalāh*. For example, before praying *fajr* everyday, he should also do the *qaḍā'* of *fajr*. This must be made clear when making the intention i.e. he should say he is doing *qaḍā'* of his earliest missed *fajr*. Similarly, after *ẓuhr* he does *qaḍā'* of *ẓuhr* and the same after *'aṣr* and so on. In this example, Karim will take six years to fully make up for his missed prayers. If Karim wanted, he could read two *qaḍā's* with every *ṣalāh*, which would lead to him completing them all in three years.

On special nights such as *Laylat al-Qadr* in Ramaḍān and *Laylat al-Bara'a* (also known as *Shab-i-Barāt*), which is the 15th Sha'bān, it is suggested that one reads *qaḍā' ṣalāh* instead of *nafl*.

To facilitate and quicken the performance of *qaḍā'*, the following concessions are permissible:

1. In the 3rd and 4th *rak'ah* of the *farḍ* prayer, *Sūrah al-Fātiḥah* can be missed and instead one may recite *"ṣubhānallāh"* three times.
2. In the *rukū'* and *sujūd* do the *tasbīḥ* once only.
3. One can also miss out the *ṣalawāt (darūd sharīf)* and the *du'ā'* after *tashahhud*.
4. In *witr*, instead of reciting the *du'ā'* of *qunūt* read *"rabighfirlī"* (رَبِّ اغْفِرْ لِي) three times.

Notes

[1] Narrated in *Ṣaḥīḥ al-Bukhārī*.

[2] Maturity, known as *bulūgh*, or becoming *bāligh*, is a very important concept in Islamic law. This is defined as occuring upon the first menstruation of a female (minimum age 9), or seminal emission of a male, or upon reaching the age of 15. Each of the action-orientated four pillars of Islam only becomes an obligation for an individual upon reaching maturity by this definition and *not* the cultural or legal standards of one's society.

[3] Filth (*najāsah*) refers to specific substances that are judged impure based on *sharī'ah* evidences and is of two types: heavy and light. Heavy filth includes blood, excrement, urine of non-*ḥalāl* (to eat) animals, sexual fluids, alcohol and pork. Any of these present on a garment amounting to more than the size of a *dirham* (about a 2p coin) makes prayer impermissable. Light filth is principally the urine of *halāl* animals and invalidates prayer if present in quantities greater than a quarter of the garment.

[4] *Sūrah al-Nisā'* (Q4: 103).

5 The website *www.Islamicfinder.org* is generally reliable and includes a number of options for those wishing to observe a particular criterion for calculation, or juristic opinion.

6 Narrated in *Sunan al-Tirmidhī*.

7 ʿAbd al-Ghanī al-Maydānī, *Al-Lubāb*, (Maktabah al-ʿIlm al-Ḥadīth, 2002), p. 57-8.

8 Narrated in *Sunan al-Nisāʿī.*

9 Narrated in *Sunan Ibn Mājah*.

10 Narrated in *Sunan al-Tirmidhī*.

11 Al-Marghinānī, *Al-Hidāyah*, v. 1, p. 43.

12 Narrated in *Ṣahīḥ Muslim*.

13 Narrated in *Sunan al-Tirmidhī*.

14 *Sūrah al-Baqarah* (Q2: 144).

15 Narrated in *Ṣaḥīḥ al-Bukhārī.*

16 Narrated in *Sunan Abī Dawūd*.

17 Narrated in *Ṣahīḥ Muslim*.

18 Narrated in *Ṣaḥīḥ al-Bukhārī.*

19 Narrated in *Sunan al-Tirmidhī*.

20 Narrated in *Ṣahīḥ Muslim*.

21 Narrated in *Sunan al-Tirmidhī* and by al-Tabaranī.

22 Narrated in *Sunan al-Nisāʿī.*

23 This is because travellers must shorten these prayers, which is called *qaṣr*. Originally, the journey that one had to be on to qualify for this dispensation was one of three days and nights. The Ḥanafī jurists have taken this prophetic injunction to refer to three days and nights riding and walking a camel (the standard method of travel in Arabia at the time) and have given an average distance of about 50 miles (77km, which is rounded to 48 miles), with which the rule is generally applied today, regardless of the method of transport used.

CHAPTER 7

Special Congregational *Ṣalāh*: The Friday, *ʿĪd* and Funeral Prayer

The Friday Prayer

Objectives of this section to learn:

- The importance of Friday Prayer (*Ṣalāh al-Jumuʿah*) and its rulings.
- The merits of Friday Prayer.
- The conditions for it to be correctly established.

The Importance of Friday Prayer

The name *al-Jumuʿah* is derived from the verb *ijtaʿama* which means the gathering together of people. Allah Most High says:

> *O believers! When you are called to the prayer on Friday, then hurry to Allah's remembrance and leave trading.*[1]

Jabīr ibn ʿAbd Allāh says the blessed Prophet, may Allah bless him and grant him peace, gave us a sermon and said, *'Oh people! Seek forgiveness from Allah before you die and rush to do good deeds before you become busy...and know that Allah has made Friday compulsory in this place of mine, in this month of mine, from this year until the Day of Judgement. Whoever misses it in my life or after me and he has a just or cruel ruler who wants to reduce it or stand against it, Allah will not unite his gathering, nor bless his work. Listen! There is no prayer for him, no* zakāh *for him, no* ḥajj *for him, no fasting for him and no righteousness until he repents and Allah turns to him in kind.'*[2]

Jabīr narrates the Prophet, may Allah bless him and grant him peace, said: *'The Friday Prayer is compulsory upon whoever believes in Allah and the Day of Judgement, except for the sick, the traveler, the child and the slave.Whoever neglects it because of business or sport, Allah neglects him and Allah is the Independent the Praiseworthy.'*[3]

The Nature of the Friday Prayer

It is *farḍ ʿayn* (i.e. compulsory for every individual who fulfils its conditions.) It consists of two units of prayer that are a substitute of *ẓuhr* and if it is missed the four units of *ẓuhr* still have to be performed.

It is narrated from ʿUmar that the Prophet, may Allah bless him and grant him peace, said: *'The prayer during a journey is two units, ʿĪd al-Aḍḥā is two units, ʿĪd al-Fitr is two units and the Friday prayer is two units.'*[4]

The compulsory nature of the Friday prayer is established from the Qur'ān and *Sunnah*, as we have seen, as well as consensus (*ijmā'*). Its denial, therefore, is an act of *kufr*.

For Whom is Friday Prayer Compulsory?

Friday prayer is only compulsory for the following people:

- On men not on women.
- On freemen who are at liberty.

- On adults not on children.
- On the healthy not on the sick.
- On settled residents not on travelers.
- On the sane not on the insane.

The Merits of Friday Prayer

Abū Hurayrah reports that the blessed Prophet, may Allah bless him and grant him peace, said: *'Whoever takes a bath on Friday and wears his best clothes and puts on perfume (if he has it); then comes for the prayer and does not trample over people; then prays what Allah has made compulsory for him; then remained silent when the* imām *appeared until he finished his prayer: It will be an atonement for (his sins) from Friday to Friday.'*[5]

Abū Hurayrah reports from the blessed Prophet, may Allah bless him and grant him peace, that on Friday there are angels at every door of the mosque and write down the names of people, upon the order of their entry. When the *imām* comes out they close their books and listen to the sermon. The reward of the first is like giving a she-camel, then like giving a cow, then like giving a ram, until he even mentioned a hen and an egg. The one who comes after that, only comes with a duty towards the prayer.[6]

Abū Hurayrah reports from the Prophet, may Allah bless him and grant him peace, that he said: *'Oh group of Muslims! God has made this day a festival for you so take a bath and use the* miswak.'[7]

Abū Lubābah said that the blessed Prophet said: *'Friday is the best of all days and greatest of them all in the sight of Allah.'*[8]

Aws ibn Aws relates that the blessed Prophet, may Allah bless him and grant him peace, said: *'"The best of your days is Friday, in it Adam was created and on this day the Trumpet will be blown and on it (the people) will become unconscious, therefore send more blessings upon me on this day, as your blessings are presented to me."* A man asked "Oh Messenger! How are our blessings conveyed to you, when you will be decayed." He replied, *"Allah has forbidden the earth to eat the bodies of the prophets."'*[9]

Warnings against missing the Friday Prayer

Abū Hurayrah said he heard the Messenger, may Allah bless him and grant him peace, saying on the steps of the *minbar*, *'People should stop their trading on Fridays or else Allah will seal their hearts and they will become amongst the forgetful.'*[10]

Abū Ja'd reports from the Prophet that he said, *'Whoever misses three Fridays consecutively due to laziness, Allah seals his heart.'*[11]

ʿAbd Allāh reports that the blessed Prophet said about people who remain behind in (i.e miss) Friday prayer, *'I thought of telling someone to lead the congregation and then I would go and burn the houses of those who remain behind on Friday.'*[12]

Sumūra ibn Jundab reports that the Prophet, may Allah bless him and grant him peace, said, *'Whoever misses Friday without a good excuse should give a* dinār *(in charity), and if he doesn't have that, a half* dinār.'[13]

The Conditions for establishing the Friday Prayer

These are six:

1. *Praying in a Town*: The Friday prayer must take place in a town or larger settlement. According to Imām Abū Hanīfah: 'It is a large town with markets and a governor who is able to do justice to the oppressed people.'[14] It is permissible to do Friday prayer in several places in one town and it is permissible in a single place like open ground.

   Those people for whom Friday is not compulsory as they live in villages or hamlets should pray *ẓuhr* with *adhān* and *iqāmah*. Travellers, if they are in a town on Friday, may pray *ẓuhr* individually, and similarly, people of the town if they have missed the Friday prayer, may do likewise, as can prisoners and sick people. Friday prayer is permissible in Minā but not in ʿArafah.

> *Note:* In all those places in which there is doubt about whether it is a township, the people should pray *jumuʿah* and then pray four units of *ẓuhr* as a precautionary measure.

2. *The Sultan*: Friday prayer should be established only with the permission of the Muslims' ruler, who should choose the *imām* to lead. This is to ensure there is no civil commotion or breach of law and order. The sermon should only be given by the permission of this leader.

   If it is not possible to obtain the sultan's decree for the establishment of Friday prayer due to his death or turmoil then the people can choose their own *imām*. If non-Muslims rule the country, Muslims should appoint their own *qāḍī* (judge) and establish Friday and ʿĪd prayers and so on, and they should work towards having a religious authority.
3. *The Time of Ẓuhr*: Friday prayer is not permissible before or after *ẓuhr* time. Anas ibn Mālik reports the Prophet, may Allah bless him and grant him peace, used to pray the Friday prayer when the sun began declining (from its zenith).[15]
4. *Admission Open to Everyone*: There should be no hindrance to anyone wishing to enter the place of prayer.
5. *The Congregation*: It is a condition that there should be at least three people other than the *imām*.
6. *The Khuṭbah (sermon)*.

The Conditions for the Khuṭbah

i. It must be before the prayer not after it. It is not permissible to do the *khuṭbah* (sermon) afterwards.
ii. There should be at least one person listening.
iii. There should be no talking between the *khuṭbah* and the prayer.
iv. It should be loud so that the audience can hear.

Note: It is not a condition for the *khuṭbah* to be in Arabic apart from the *āyahs* of the Qur'ān even if the *khaṭīb* (*imām* giving the *khuṭbah*) is capable of delivering it in Arabic (according to Imām Abū Hanīfah) and it is a condition according to the Ṣāḥibayn (Imāms Abū Yūsuf and Muḥammad). When the *imām* appears for the sermon then there should be no talking, no praying, or replying to the sneeze or returning the *salām* or sending blessings on the Prophet, may Allah bless him and grant him peace. If someone is praying *nafl* and the *khaṭīb* begins, he should break his prayer before the prostration. One can sit as one likes for the *khuṭbah*, however the best way to sit is as if performing *tashahhud*.

The Sunnahs of the Khuṭbah

These are seven:

i. *Ṭahārah*: The *khaṭīb* should be clean and in ritual purity.
ii. Sitting on the pulpit before starting the sermon.
iii. The *adhān* should be said in front of him. The people hearing the second *adhān* should not respond to it, but the *imām* may.
iv. Standing up whilst giving the two sermons.
v. The congregation should turn towards the *khaṭīb*. However, al-Sarakhsī notes that the custom has become to face towards the *qiblah* and not the *khaṭīb* directly, as this would disturb the rows needed for *ṣalāh* after the *khuṭbah* is completed, particularly as the congregations are very large. He, therefore, approves this custom for its reduction of hardship on the people.[16]
vi. Performing the *khuṭbah* according to the *Sunnah*: The *khuṭbah* is split into two parts, separated by a brief sitting.

    The first *khuṭbah* starts with *taʿawwudh* silently and then *ḥamd* and *thanā'* loudly, followed by the declaration of blessings upon the Prophet (may Allah bless him and grant him peace), and then warning against sins and reminders of things that would lead to to Allah's pleasure here and salvation in the Hereafter, as well as recitation of verses of the Qur'ān.

    The second *khuṭbah* begins with *ḥamd, thanā'* and blessings upon the Prophet, may Allah bless him and grant him peace, and then prayer for the welfare of the Muslims, in which forgiveness is sought for them, the ruler is prayed for and God's help is asked for him as appropriate to the political circumstances. An example from the early Muslims is Abū Mūsā al-Ashʿarī, who used to pray for ʿUmar in his *khuṭbah* and no one amongst the companions of the Prophet criticised him. It is also desirable to make mention of the four caliphs and the two uncles of the Prophet, may Allah bless him and grant him peace.

vii. Sitting down between the two parts of the *khuṭbah*: To sit between the two sermons for a short period, as long as it takes to read three verses of the Glorious Qur'ān.

ʿAbd Allāh ibn ʿUmar said, 'The Prophet, may Allah bless him and grant him peace, used to make two *khuṭbahs* and sit in between them.'[17]

The ʿĪd Prayer

Objectives of this section to learn:

- About ʿĪd and its importance.
- How to perform the ʿĪd prayer.

ʿĪd means "the returning" since it comes again and again as the favours of Allah are showered on us repeatedly and thus ʿĪd refers to all happy occasions. However, there are two famous ʿĪds: ʿĪd al-Fiṭr, celebrated at the end of Ramaḍān, and ʿĪd al-Aḍḥā, which is celebrated on the 10th of the month Dhū al-Ḥijjah.

The ʿĪd was instituted in the first year of the *Hijrah* (emigration to Madīnah). Anas reports the blessed Prophet, may Allah bless him and grant him peace, arrived in Madīnah and the people used to celebrate two festivals, so he asked them, '*What are these two days?*' They said, 'We used to celebrate them in the days of ignorance', so he said, '*Allah has substituted two better ones for you: the Day of Sacrifice and the Day of* Fiṭr.'[18]

The Rulings of ʿĪd Prayer

ʿĪd prayer is *wājib* (necessary), since the blessed Prophet, may Allah bless him and grant him peace, performed it regularly and never missed it, so did the rightly-guided caliphs and the great *imāms* and jurists. It is *wājib* on whomever the Friday prayer is *wājib* upon, since the conditions for both are the same with one exception: the *khuṭbah* is *wājib* for Friday prayer, but only a *sunnah* for ʿĪd. ʿĪd al-Aḍḥā is not *wājib* on the pilgrims staying in Minā.

> *Note*: ʿĪd al-Fiṭr can be delayed by one day and ʿĪd al-Aḍḥā by three days if required.

Time for ʿĪd Prayer

The time of ʿĪd prayer is from approximately 35 minutes after sunrise until noon. It is best to pray ʿĪd al-Aḍḥā early so the people can sacrifice their animals. However ʿĪd al-Fiṭr can be delayed so that people can pay their charity.

Jundab reports that the Prophet, may Allah bless him and grant him peace, used to pray ʿĪd al-Fiṭr when the sun was two *ramḥayn* above the horizon and ʿĪd al- Aḍḥā when it was one *ramḥayn*.[19] A *ramḥayn* is a length of thirteen metres and here refers to a measure of time taken by the sun to rise above the horizon by approximately five degrees. It's equivalent to about 35 minutes.

Sunnahs of ʿĪd

1. It is *sunnah* for the *imām* to deliver two sermons after the ʿĪd prayers and teach people the rules about either the charity of *fiṭr*, or the sacrifice.
2. It is *sunnah* to hold the ʿĪd prayer in a vast open place. It is undesirable to pray ʿĪd in the *masjid* without a good cause.
3. To take a *ghusl* (bath).

Desirable Practices on ʿĪd

1. It is desirable to eat at least 3, 5 or 7 dates (an odd number) before leaving for the ʿĪd al-Fiṭr prayer. If dates are not available other things can be eaten, preferably sweet. This is because the beloved Prophet, may Allah bless him and grant him peace, did not have dinner on ʿĪd al-Fiṭr until after he had eaten dates.[20] On ʿĪd al-Aḍḥā, he didn't eat until he had prayed ʿĪd. It is desirable to eat the meat of the sacrificed animal first since it is a blessing from Allah.
2. To clean the teeth (i.e. with the *miswak*).
3. To put on perfume.
4. To wear best clothes, whether new or washed.
5. To pay *ṣadaqah al-fiṭr* (sometimes called *fiṭrānah*) *before* the ʿĪd prayer. The payment itself is *wājib* for those eligible for *zakāh* (the details can be found in the appropriate section relating to the fourth pillar).
6. To give donations and be generous.
7. To express happiness and cheerfulness.
8. Greetings: the companions of the Prophet, may Allah bless him and grant him peace, used to meet one another by saying 'May Allah accept it from us and from you.' In Syria, Egypt and Pakistan, the custom is to say 'ʿĪd mubārak laka' or 'Kullu ʿamin wa antum bikhayr' or 'ʿĪd Saʿīd'. The Companions also used to shake hands, which is in fact, a *sunnah* after each prayer and at every meeting.
9. Going to the prayer early to guarantee a place in the first row, which gives extra reward.
10. Morning Prayer: the morning prayer is compulsory, however, on ʿĪd day it is even more meritorious than usual to pray it in the local *masjid* with the congregation.
11. Reading the *takbīr* on the way to pray:

    i. For ʿĪd al-Fiṭr, according to Imām Abū Hanīfah, the *takbīr* should not be read loudly when going to the ʿĪd prayer. It is instead desirable to read it quietly.

However, according to the Ṣāḥibayn, it's desirable to read the *takbīr* loudly on the way to the ʿĪd prayer until one reaches the place of prayer.

ii. For ʿĪd al-Aḍḥā: it's desirable to read the *takbīr* aloud according to all the Imāms.

12. Route to and from prayer: one should come to the place of prayer walking by one route and to return home by another route.
13. Beautifying oneself: to wear the best clothes, perfume, clip nails, trim hair, beard and moustache. In brief, to look smart and clean as an expression of thanksgiving.

How to perform the ʿĪd Prayer

The performance of the ʿĪd prayer is similar to other prayers except in two ways. First, in there is no *adhān* or *iqāmah* and secondly, there are six extra *takbīr*s. It has two units and to begin one makes the intention by saying, 'I intend to pray two units of ʿĪd prayer with six extra *wājib takbīrs* behind the *imām*.'

After the *imām* opens the prayer with *takbīr* say the usual *takbīr al-taḥrīmah* and raise the hands parallel to the ear lobes. Then fold the hands and read the *thanā'*. The *imām* will say the first extra *takbīr* loudly and lift the hands to the ears and then lower them, which the follower should copy. This is repeated twice more, then fold the hands and quietly listen to the *imām*'s recitation of *al-Fātiḥah* and a *sūrah*. The first unit is completed as in other prayers.

In the second unit the *imām* starts by reciting *al-Fātiḥah* and a *sūrah*. He then says the three remaining extra *takbīr*s, raising his hands each time, which the follower should copy. He does not raise his hands for the fourth *takbīr*, which is the usual signal for bowing. The second unit is then completed as in normal prayer. After the prayer it is *sunnah* to remain sitting and to listen to the *khuṭbah*.

Takbīr al-Tashrīq

It is *wājib* to say the *takbīr al-tashrīq* loudly once (thrice is better) after each *farḍ* prayer starting from *fajr* on the Day of ʿArafah (9th of Dhū al-Ḥijjah) and finishing after the *ʿaṣr* prayer on the third day after ʿĪd (13th of Dhū al-Ḥijjah) inclusive. There is no harm in reading the *takbīr* after ʿĪd prayer.

Allah is the Greatest (x3)	اَللهُ أَكْبَرُ (3x)
There is no god except Allah.	لَا إِلٰهَ إِلَّا اللهُ
Allah is the Greatest (x2)	اَللهُ أَكْبَرُ (2x)
and for Allah is all praise.	وللهِ الْحَمْدُ

The *takbīr* should be said immediately after the *salām* and should not be delayed. It is sinful to talk intentionally after the *salām* thus missing the *takbīr*. If the *imām* forgets the *takbīr*, the congregants should nevertheless start reading it out aloud.

The Funeral Prayer

Objectives of this section: to learn:

- The conditions, *farḍ* and *sunnah* elements of the funeral prayer.
- To memorise the relevent *duʿā's*.
- To learn how to perform the funeral prayer correctly.

Funeral prayer is a communal obligation (*farḍ kifāyah*), which means that if at least a few people perform it in a locality, everyone else is relieved of the burden. However, if it is omitted by everyone, then they all are accounted the sin of neglecting the obligatory.

The Conditions of Funeral Prayer

The conditions for the devotee are exactly the same as those for a normal *ṣalāh*.

In order to perform the prayer over a dead body, it must be:

1. Of a Muslim, as there is no funeral prayer over a non-believer. Allah Most High says *'And do not ever pray over one from them who has died and do not stand over his grave. Indeed they disbelieved in Allah and his Messenger and died whilst they were transgressors.'*[21]
2. Present wholly, half or at least its head remaining. The *ṣalāh* on the absent body is not permissible. The Prophet's *ṣalāh* for the Negus of Ethiopia was his special privilege.
3. Clean, i.e. it must be washed or given *tayammum* if there is no water.
4. Placed in front of the *imām*. It is not permissible to have it at the back.

The Farḍ *Elements of Funeral Prayer*

Funeral prayer has the same *farḍ* elements of normal *ṣalāh*, except:

1. There is no *rukūʿ* (bowing), *sujūd* (prostrating), or sitting.
2. The prayer must be performed standing up straight and is not permissable to be performed in a sitting position.
3. There are four *takbīrs*. Each *takbīr* is equivalent to one *rakʿah* and, therefore, the prayer is invalid if even one *takbīr* is missed.

The Sunnah *Elements of Funeral Prayer*

1. To read the *thanā'* after the first *takbīr*:

> سُبْحـٰنَكَ اللّٰهُمَّ وَبِحَمْدِكَ وَتَبَارَكَ اسْـمُكَ وَتَعَالٰى
> جَدُّكَ وَلآ إِلـٰهَ غَيْرُكَ.
>
> *Glory be to You Oh Allah, all praise is for You, blessed is Your Name and exalted is Your Majesty. There is no god other than You.*

2. To read the *ṣalawāt* (*darūd sharīf*) upon the blessed Prophet after the second *takbīr*.
3. To read the *duʿā'* for the deceased after the third *takbīr*.

   i. The following *duʿā'* is for men and woman:

> اَللّٰهُمَّ اغْفِرْ لِحَيِّنَا وَمَيِّتِنَا وَشَاهِدِنَا وَغَائِبِنَا وَصَغِيْرِنَا
> وَكَبِيْرِنَا وَذَكَرِنَا وَأُنْثَانَا، اَللّٰهُمَّ مَنْ أَحْيَيْتَهُ مِنَّا فَأَحْيِهِ
> عَلٰى الإِسْلَامِ وَمَنْ تَوَفَّيْتَهُ مِنَّا فَتَوَفَّهُ عَلٰى الإِيْمَـانِ.
>
> *Oh my Lord! Forgive our living, our dead, those who are present and then are absent and our young ones and our adults, our men and our women. Oh Lord! Whosoever you keep alive amongst us keep him alive upon Islam. And whosoever you cause to die let him die with faith.*[22]

   ii. The *duʿā'* for male children and insane people is as follows:

اَللّٰهُمَّ اجْعَلْهُ لَنَا فَرَطًا وَاجْعَلْهُ لَنَا أَجْرًا وَذُخْرًا وَاجْعَلْهُ لَنَا شَافِعًا وَمُشَفَّعًا.

Oh Lord! Make him a provision, reward and a treasure for us in the Hereafter. Make him our intercessor whose intercession is acceptable.

For female children and insane people use the following *duʿā'*:

اَللّٰهُمَّ اجْعَلْهَا لَنَا فَرَطًا وَاجْعَلْهَا لَنَا أَجْرًا وَذُخْرًا وَاجْعَلْهَا لَنَا شَافِعَةً وَمُشَفَّعَةً.

Oh Lord! Make her a provision, reward and a treasure for us in the Hereafter. Make her our intercessor whose intercession is acceptable.

If these *duʿā'*s are not known then any other *masnūn* (known from the *Sunnah*) *duʿā'*s can be read.

4. It is recommended that the *imām* stands in line with the chest of the dead or in line with his head or middle.
5. It is recommended to have three rows, as the blessed Prophet, may Allah bless him and grant him peace, said: *'If three rows have prayed upon him, then he has been forgiven.'*[23] However if the number of people is very large then seven rows should be formed.

The Procedure for the Funeral Prayer

Funeral prayer is offered standing and there is no bowing or prostration. It is comprised of four *takbīrs*. After the intention, and always following the *imām*'s lead, say the first *takbīr* and raise the hands to the ears and fold them. Read the *thanā'* and then say the second *takbīr*, without raising the hands. Read the *ṣalawāt* upon the Prophet, may Allah bless him and grant him peace, then make the third *takbīr*. Now read the *duʿā'* and then say the fourth *takbīr*. Then turning right say the *salām* and then to the left.

Note: 1. Remember to not raise the hands, except when saying the first *takbīr*.
2. If the *imām* says five *takbīr*s by mistake then the *muqtadiʿ* (follower) should not follow him in this, but wait for him to do the *salām*.
3. The Glorious Qur'ān should not, on this occasion, be read for *duʿā'*. However, it is permissible to read *Sūrah al-Fātiḥah* as a *duʿā'*.
4. If the body is presented at the time of *maghrib* prayer, then the funeral prayer should proceed the *maghrib sunnah* prayers.
5. If someone joins the funeral prayer late and has missed one or more *takbīr*, then he should make up for his omissed *takbīr*s after the *imām* has done the *salām*.
6. If a child is born and dies without making a movement or a sound then he will be buried without the funeral prayer. However, if he makes any kind of noise or shows signs of life before dying, he will be washed and the funeral prayer performed.
7. If someone is buried without the funeral prayer, then the prayer should be said at his grave.
8. If someone dies at sea and the land is inaccessible, then he will be washed and the funeral prayer offered and he will be cast into the sea.
9. Funeral prayer in the *masjid* is *makrūh*, but permissible in the case of rain or for any other valid excuse.

The Traveller's Prayer

Allah Most High said in the Qur'ān, *'When you are travelling in the land, then you are allowed to shorten the prayer.'* (Q4: 101) ʿAbd Allāh bin ʿAbbās said that the Messenger, may Allah be well pleased with him, used to pray four units of *ẓuhr*, *ʿaṣr* and *'ishā'*, but when he was travelling he used to shorten them to two units.[24] 'Abd Allāh bin 'Umar narrated that the Prophet, may Allah bless him and grant him peace, would pray two units when travelling and would say *'these are full and not diminished'*, meaning that one gets the full reward of four units.[25]

The definition of a traveller is a person who intends to travel a distance of 57 miles from his home for a period of 15 days or less, and one becomes a traveller when the boundaries of a town are crossed, and the shortening of the prayers begins from this point until re-entering the town boundaries. It is a major sin for the traveller to pray full four units except when praying behind a resident *imām*, in which case all four units should be prayed. A traveller should not neglect to pray the *Sunnah* prayers.

There are two types of home: an original home and a second residence. An original home is where one has been born, or his parents or his family are living there. A second residence is a place where one lives temporarily for more than fifteen days. If one sets up a home in another place where he works then this too will be considered as his original home. Similarly if one moves to another place and buys or leaves a house these as well, then both will be considered as original homes, and so he or she will not be considered a traveller there.

How to pray whilst travelling on an Airplane, Train or Coach

The easiest way is to remain seated and offer the prayer siting down by gestures, so one would bow slightly for *rukū'* and bit more for the prostration. It is highly recommended that one repeat these prayers on arrival at one's destination. One of the reasons for this is that one will have missed out two conditions of prayer, namely facing the *qiblah* and not standing up during the prayer.

Notes

1 *Sūrah al-Jumuʿah* (Q62: 9).
2 Narrated in *Sunan Ibn Mājah*.
3 Narrated by al-Dāraquṭnī.
4 Narrated in the *Musnad* of Aḥmad ibn Ḥanbal.
5 Narrated in *Sunan Abī Dawūd*.
6 Narrated in *Sunan Ibn Mājah*.
7 Narrated by al-Ṭabarānī.
8 Narrated in *Sunan Ibn Mājah*.
9 Narrated in *Sunan Ibn Mājah*.
10 Narrated in *Ṣaḥīḥ Muslim*.
11 Narrated in *Sunan al-Nisāʾī*.
12 Narrated in *Sunan al-Nisāʾī*.
13 Narrated in *Sunan Abī Dawūd*.
14 Mentioned in *Radd al-Muḥtār*.
15 Narrated in *Ṣaḥīḥ al-Bukhārī*.
16 Al-Sarakhsī, *al-Mabsūṭ*, (Dār al-Maʿrifah, 1978), v.2, p. 30.
17 Narrated in *Ṣaḥīḥ al-Bukhārī*.
18 Narrated in *Sunan Abī Dawūd*.
19 Narrated in *Ṣaḥīḥ Muslim*.
20 Narrated in *Ṣaḥīḥ al-Bukhārī*.
21 *Sūrah al-Tawbah* (Q9: 84).
22 Narrated in *Sunan al-Tirmidhī*.
23 Narrated in *Sunan al-Tirmidhī*.
24 Narrated in Muslim.
25 Narrated in Ibn Mājah

3rd Pillar

ZAKĀH

(The Almsgiving)

The Growth of Divine Love through the Purification of Wealth

CHAPTER 8

The Meaning and Wisdom of *Zakāh*

Allah, Almighty, says:

> *Establish the prayer and pay the zakāh.*[1]

The root of the Arabic word *zakāh* has two different meanings: growth and purification. In the Qur'ān, *zakāh* refers to a specific obligatory almsgiving that Allah has commanded the believers to establish, although most of its details are to be found in the *Sunnah* of the Prophet, may Allah bless him and grant him peace. We can see that both the concept of growth and that of purification are to be found within this duty that comprises the third pillar of *Islam*. Spiritually, giving *zakāh* leads to closeness with Allah and earns much merit. This growth in one's relationship with Allah results in the purification of the heart and mind, while morally, the giving of *zakāh* pulls out the roots of greed and selfishness. Also in terms of the wealth itself, sacrificing a small portion acts as a purification for the rest and signifies Allah's permission for it to lawfully grow further.

Allah tells the Messenger, may He bless him and grant him peace:

> *Take alms from their wealth, cleansing them and purifying them through it.*[2]

Here the payment of *zakāh* is the cause of purification. Moreover, the Messenger said, 'Zakāh *is a proof*', meaning proof of one's faith in Allah, the Messenger and the Hereafter. Indeed one of the demands of Islam is to make sacrifice of ones wealth, *zakāh* is the minimum amount required to fulfill this obligation.

In the Qur'ān, there are three pairs of commandments that are repeated many times: faith and good deeds; worship of Allah and kindness to parents; and *ṣalāh* and *zakāh*. Their structure suggests they are linked as though one without the other is meaningless and incomplete. Thus, prayer is not complete without paying *zakāh*.

The Spiritual Benefits and Wisdom of *Zakāh*

Imām al-Ghazālī explains in more detail why *zakāh*, as the purification of wealth, is the third most important pillar of *Islam*.[3] He says that a true Muslim must love God more than anything else, the rule being that love does not admit a partner. The mere utterance of the words of the *shahādah* is not enough, until one is willing to sacrifice other objects of love. In this way one is openly saying, 'I love God more than my wealth: that is why I am giving it away.'

Al-Ghazālī divides people into three groups with regard to love of wealth and love of God:

1. The first group of people are the most pious and God-loving people who sacrifice everything they have. They do not keep anything for themselves. An excellent example is Abū Bakr, may Allah be pleased with him, who donated all he had for the cause of Islam.

2. The second group are righteous people who spend their wealth for others' needs. They spend the excess and surplus money that they have for the Divine Pleasure and give more than the obligatory amount of *zakāh*. In fact, they help anyone whom they find in need.
3. The third group of people are those who are satisfied with paying their *zakāh* only and neither pay more nor less. This is the lowest rank of a Muslim who still remains in obedience to God's obligation.

The Importance of Zakāh *in the* Sunnah

The *ḥadīth* literature vividly describes the virtues of *zakāh*, enthusiastically praising its benefits in order to motivate people. Here are few beautiful gems from the Messenger, may Allah bless him and grant him peace:

- ʿAbd Allāh ibn ʿUmar narreated that the Messenger, may Allah bless him and grant him peace, said, *'Islam is built on five pillars: bearing witness that there is no god but Allah, establishing regular worship, paying* zakāh, *pilgrimage and fasting in* Ramaḍān.'[4]
- Ṭalhah ibn ʿUbaydah narrates that a man from Najd came to the Messenger, may Allah bless him and grant him peace and asked about his duties in Islam. The Messenger said, *'Performing the five daily* ṣalāh.' He then said, 'Anything else?' The Messenger said, *'No, except what you want to do voluntarily and the fasting in Ramaḍān.'* He again said, 'Anything else?', so the Messenger said, *'No, except what you can do voluntarily and paying* zakāh.' 'Is there anything else?', the man asked once more. The man turned around and said, 'By God I will not do more or less than this.' Upon hearing this, the Messenger said, *'He will be successful if he keeps his word.'*[5]
- Abū Hurayrah said, 'When the Messenger died and Abū Bakr became the *Khalīfah*, some people turned to *kufr* and others refused to pay *zakāh*. Abū Bakr decided to fight those

who refused to pay *zakāt* and said, "I will fight anyone who distinguishes between *ṣalāh* and the paying of *zakāh*. If they refuse to pay a rope's worth of *zakāh*, I will fight them until they pay it." 'Umar said, "By God, I know that Allah has opened Abū Bakr's heart and mind and that he is right!"'[6]

- Abū Ayyub al-Ansārī said that a man asked the Messenger, 'Tell me a deed that will take me into Paradise?' He said, '*Worship God alone without associating anyone with Him, establish the prayer, pay* zakāh *and always be kind to relatives.*'[7]
- Abū Hurayrah said that the Messenger, may Allah bless him and grant him peace, said, '"*For the wealthy man who had gold and silver, but does not pay* zakāh, *these precious metals will be heated in the fire of Hell and put on his side, back and face. When they get cold they will be reheated and put on again.*" He then mentioned livestock and how it will hurt its owner if he had not paid *zakāh* on it.'[8]

The Moral Benefits and Wisdom of *Zakāh*

There are four major moral vices: greed, arrogance , jealousy and anger. The giving of *zakāh* from one's wealth is designed to remove these negative qualities in particular greed, arrogance and jealousy. Al-Ghazālī mentions a person's unwillingness to share wealth with others as being a wretched moral disease. Allah Most High says:

> *Whosoever is saved from their own greed, it is they who are the successful ones.*[9]

The legislation of the payment of *zakāh* as one of the foremost duties of *Islam* is designed to remove greed and to thereby purify the individual from this despicable trait. Just as the fasting of Ramaḍān provides a yearly detoxification of the body and the desires, the *zakāh* should do the same for the soul's tendency for avarice and the hoarding of material things. It is with the deepest understanding of the potential for weakness in the human being that Allah created that He tells us:

> *Beautified for mankind is the love of the joys that come from women and children, heaped-up hordes of gold and silver, branded horses, cattle and well-tilled land. Those are the comforts of the wordly life, but with Allah is a more excellent abode.*[10]

As we will see, with the obvious exception of one's family and (for most jurists) horses, all the other desired things mentioned in this verse will require payment of *zakāh*, which acts as an acknowledgment of Allah's favours – a crucial reminder that others are not as fortunate – and allows us to realise that the spiritual and moral excellence of sacrifice for Allah is worth so much more than these wordly goods, despite their outward attraction.

It is important also to mention that *zakāh*, as an institution of Islam, avoids the danger of the rich becoming arrogant and patronising in their giving, because it is actually a 'right' of the poor, a concept which applies, although to a lesser extent, to *ṣadaqah* in the sense of voluntary charity. Allah Most High says in identification of the successful believers:

> *And those who in their wealth is an acknowledged right – for the beggar and the destitute.*[11]

This certainly does not mean that Islam approves of the practice of begging as a way of life. The Prophet, may Allah bless him and grant him peace, would seek to show people how they could take up a trade and would say, *'It is better for any one of you to tie a bundle of firewood and carry it on his back and sell it than to beg from a person. He* [the person asked] *may give or may refuse.'*[12] He also said, *'A person would continue begging from people until he would come on the Day of Resurrection and there would be no flesh on his face.'*[13]

Overall, this shows the balanced approach that Islam takes to the moral questions that are thrown up by the existence of wealth and poverty in society. A person in dire straits does have a 'right' to receive help from others and ideally this should be facillitated through *zakāh* and *ṣadaqah* without the need for begging. If the situation does get so desperate for an individual that he is forced to beg, then he is permitted, but it should only be a temporary measure.

The Social Benefits and Wisdom of *Zakāh*

Zakāh functions within the Islamic community as a fundamental mechanism of redistributing wealth. The more wealthy that any individual becomes, the greater the amount that he must return to benefit the poorer members of society. Along with the prohibition of *ribā* (usury/interest) this ensures that no wealth can stay hoarded in the possession of the rich, as over time it will slowly but inevitably be transformed into *zakāh*. This demonstrates an altogether more just paradigm than the currently dominant economic model, in which rather than hoarding or making exploitative interest-based loans, the wealthy are encouraged to invest in social projects and to provide interest-free loans. The following verse of the Qur'ān was revealed in the context of booty gained in the course of the Prophet's campaigns, may Allah bless him and grant him peace, but the principle that is elaborated is applicable to wealth in general within Islamic society and achievable through a well-ordered system of *zakāh*:

> *It is for Allah, the Messenger, the near of kin, the orphans, the needy and the wayfarer, so that it does not become something which revolves between the rich amongst you.*[14]

The function of *zakāh* on the social level then, is to make sure that there is a safety net for people who fall into hard times – marking a bare minimum of poverty beyond which the community allows no-one to go – as well as giving much needed assistance to certain underprivileged and needy groups. It is a sorry fact, therefore, that despite there being much wealth in the Muslim *ummah* as a whole, terrible, biting poverty severely afflicts so much of humanity around the world. This is something that urgently needs to be addressed by the most senior of our *'ulamā'*, as the forms in which wealth is manifested in the current age is vastly different to that of the classical Islamic civilisation in which the rulings for *zakāh* were derived. There is a grave danger that through neglect of the principle and spirit of Allah's command, made all the worse for being clothed in a superficial adherence to the outer form of the *Sunnah*, immense amounts of rightful *zakāh* will not be collected and distributed to those who need it most. Yūsuf al-Qaraḍāwī summarised the problem facing us as follows:

> There are new matters that did not exist in the past and were not known to the ancient jurists. These new matters require new religious injunctions. Today, Muslims ask many questions about *zakāh* that must not be left without answers. Questions such as how to consider new forms of wealth other than livestock, agricultural produce and fruits. These new forms of wealth include huge buildings for rent, enormous factories and plants, machines and equipment, and all kinds of fixed and circulating capital that provide tremendous flow of income out of their production lines and rental proceeds such as ships, cars, planes and hotels. There are new trading and industrial corporations, the new forms of income of professionals like physicians, engineers, and lawyers and huge numbers of employees receiving wages and salaries. Are all these zakātable or not, and if they are zakātable, what is the percentage of *zakāh* on them? When is it due? And on what basis in *Sharī'ah* is it founded?'[15]

This issue is obviously not a simple one and is potentially contentious, as *zakāh* is rightly seen as falling under the category of *ʿibādah* (worship). Thus some will argue that our only job as Muslims is to act in obedience to Allah's commands in the Qur'an and through the *Sunnah* of his Messenger, may Allah bless him and grant him peace, in the form they have been given, without inquiring further into their deeper purpose and underlying rationale. In response to this, two things should be made clear: firstly, despite being a form of worship, *zakāh* clearly has aspects in common with *muʿāmalāt* (transactions between people) and thus to be implemented at all must take account of the prevailing social conditions. Secondly, one of the great scholars of the latter centuries of Islam, Shāh Walī Allāh al-Dihlawī, chose to address this very issue at the start of his book *Ḥujjat Allāh al-Bālighah*, in which he writes:

> Perhaps it is thought that the *sharīʿah* rulings do not comprise anything beneficial, and that there is not a correspondence between actions and what Allah has made as recompense for them. Therefore, the likeness of responsibility under the *sharīʿah* is that of a master that wants to test the obedience of his servant. So he orders him with lifting a stone, or touching a tree, with no benefit to it other than the test. Then when he obeys, or disobeys, he is requited for his act. This is a rotten conjecture which is refuted by the *Sunnah* and the consensus of the generations that are witnessed as good.'[16]

The implication of this is that whilst the payment of *zakāh* is an act of obedience, it also comprises distinct objectives at the social level. It is the job of the *ijtihād* of qualified jurists to analyse these matters and to come with solutions that are rooted in the very essence of the Islamic ethos, yet responsive to the needs of the present. For the purposes of this book, however, the classical rulings as found in the *fiqh* books of the Ḥanafī school will be used, as they represent a widely accepted formulation of the law concerning *zakāh* and an excellent introduction to this fascinating area of study.

Notes

1 *Sūrah al-Baqarah* (Q2: 43).
2 *Sūrah al-Tawbah* (Q9: 103).
3 This and the passages attributed to al-Ghazālī in Chapter 9 are based on the section on *zakāh* in his *Ihyā' 'Ulūm al-Dīn*.
4 Narrated in *Saḥīḥ al-Bukhārī* and *Saḥīḥ Muslim.*
5 Narrated in *Saḥīḥ al-Bukhārī* and *Saḥīḥ Muslim.*
6 Narrated in *Saḥīḥ al-Bukhārī* and *Saḥīḥ Muslim.*
7 Narrated in *Saḥīḥ al-Bukhārī* and *Saḥīḥ Muslim.*
8 Narrated in *Saḥīḥ al-Bukhārī* and *Saḥīḥ Muslim.*
9 *Sūrah al-Ḥashr* (Q59: 9).
10 *Sūrah Āl 'Imrān* (Q3: 14).
11 *Sūrah al-Ma'ārij* (Q70: 24-5).
12 Narrated in *Saḥīḥ Muslim.*
13 Narrated in *Saḥīḥ Muslim.*
14 *Sūrah al-Hashr* (Q59: 7).
15 Qaraḍāwī, Y, *Fiqh al-Zakāh*, translated by Monzer Kahf, (King Abdulaziz University), v. 1, p. xxi.
16 Al-Dihlawī, Shāh Walī Allāh, *Ḥujjat Allāh al-Bālighah*, (Dār al-Kutub al-'Ilmiyyah, 1995), p. 9.

CHAPTER 9

The Payment of *Zakāh*

Objectives of this section to learn:

- Who must pay *zakāh*.
- What types of wealth necessitate *zakāh* and how to calculate the amount due.
- Who deserves to receive *zakāh*.
- How to pay *zakāh*.
- The correct manners to observe whilst paying *zakāh*.

Who must pay *Zakāh*?

It is *farḍ* upon every adult sane Muslim who has as much wealth, after subtracting debts, as the *niṣāb* (specific minimum amount), which varies depending on the type of wealth (see Table 1 below) after he has been in possession of the *niṣāb* for a full lunar year.[1] As the Islamic calendar uses the lunar year, the easiest way to keep track of *zakāh* payment is to make a note of the Islamic date when one reaches the *niṣāb*. *Zakāh* will be due on this date in one year's time, as long as the amount of wealth in the category still is as least as much as the *niṣāb*.

Note: 1. It must be paid, or at least be separated from one's wealth (if another person is to actually give it), with the intention of *zakāh*, as it is a type of worship. Someone who gives all their wealth away without intending *zakāh* is relinquished of the obligation.

2. Whatever wealth is gained throughout the year will be added to the *niṣāb* and the *zakāh* due will be on the amount owned at the end of the year-long period.
3. If someone comes into possession of the *niṣāb* amount, but then drops below it during the course of the year, they still must check their wealth exactly a year on. If it is back up to the *niṣāb*, or higher, they must pay *zakāh*.
4. If someone's wealth drops to nothing, or they go into net debt, any previously reached *niṣāb* becomes irrelevant, cancelling rule 2 above.
5. It is permissable to pay *zakāh* in advance (i.e. for two years), if possessing *niṣāb*.

What Types of Wealth necessitate *Zakāh*?

Zakāh is due upon money, gold, silver, camels, goats, sheep, cows, buffaloes and crops, as well as all goods possessed for trade. It is *not* due upon one's residence, clothes, household furnishings, transport and armaments.

Table 1 - How Much *Zakāh* is to be Paid?

Type of wealth	***Niṣāb*** (Minimum Amount)	Rate of ***Zakāh***
Money in cash or bank	Value equal to 85g of gold or 600g silver.[2]	2.5%
Gold	85g	2.5%
Silver	600g	2.5%
Goats or sheep	40	1
Cows	30	1
Crops	Per harvest	▸ 5% from irrigated farm land ▸ 10% from rain-watered land

> *Note:* 1. The table above gives a simplified version of the *zakāh* due on animals by only showing the amounts due upon exactly reaching *niṣāb* and omitting camels, due to their rarity in the UK. The *Sunnah* specifies the ages of animal to be given (e.g. 2 year old) for various herd sizes above the *niṣāb* and the details of these, if required, can be found in books of *fiqh* such as *al-Hidāyah*, or upon consulting an *ʿālim* (religious scholar).
>
> 2. *Zakāh* is also due on all gold and silver jewellery that is for personal use or adornment. The *zakāh* to be paid will be based on its valuation.
>
> 3. There is no *zakāh* on diamonds, pearls, or other precious stones, unless they are for business and, in that case, they must be valued and *zakāh* is paid at a rate of 2.5%.

Who deserves to receive *Zakāh*?

Allah the Almighty says:

> *Almsgiving is only for the poor; the destitute; those who administer it [zakāh]; those whose hearts are to be won over; the freeing of slaves; those in the way of Allah; the indebted; and travellers in need. This is ordained by Allah, and Allah is All-Knowing and Wise.*[3]

Thus, the eight categories of people who are entitled to receive *zakāh* are:

1. The *fuqarāʾ* (the poor) – those who do not have wealth that reaches the minimum level of *niṣāb*.
2. The *masākīn* (the destitute) – those entirely without wealth.
3. *Zakāh* collectors and administrators – people who work for the collection, administration and distribution of *zakāh* can be paid from what is collected.
4. Those whose hearts are to be won over – this is of three types of people that were present at the time of the Prophet, may Allah bless him and grant him peace, and to which he gave *zakāh*:

i. Those that he wanted to treat well so that they entered into Islam, and their people with them.
ii. Those that had recently entered into Islam, but were weak, so he wanted to help them to become established in it.
iii. Those that he gave *zakāh*, in order to fend off their evil.

It is mentioned by al-Marghinānī, the author of *al-Hidāyah*, that this category (4) is no longer applicable due to Allah's honouring and enriching Islam and he cites an *ijmā*ʿ (consensus) on this.[4]

5. Purchasing freedom for slaves – *Zakāh* funds can be used to help slaves purchase their freedom from their masters.[5]
6. People in debt – *zakāh* may be used to clear a person's debt, if he has no means to do so.
7. Those in Allah's way – This is specifically for people who have not otherwise been paid for their military service, although it is potentially wider than this and could include the support of social and educational projects.
8. Travellers – anyone who is away from home and is in need of money can receive *zakāh*, even if he is very wealthy there. He is given enough for his transportation and personal expenses to get back home.

How is *Zakāh* Paid?

In classical Islamic civilisation, *zakāh* was partly administered as a tax that was assessed and collected by the government, before being appropriately distributed to those in need. The great scholar Abū al-Ḥasan al-Māwardī, in his famous *al-Aḥkām al-Sulṭāniyyah* (*The Laws of Islamic Governance*), makes an important distinction between two types of wealth in terms of how they should be paid as *zakāh*:

> Zakātable wealth is of two kinds: manifest and hidden. The first refers to that which cannot be

concealed, like crops, fruit and cattle; the second to that which can be concealed, like gold and silver and merchandise.

The person in charge of tax collection does not concern himself with the *zakāh* of concealed goods and wealth, as their owners are more entitled to pay the *zakāh* thereof, unless they hand it over to him of their own free will, in which case he accepts it and distributes it by way of being of assistance to them. His assessment of the *zakāh* of wealth is restricted to what is manifest.'[6]

For Muslims living in countries such as the UK, there is obviously no government-level organised *zakāh* collection, which by its nature is something that must have some power of enforcement. However, as the vast majority of people only have the 'concealed' type of wealth, in the form of money, gold, silver and tradeable goods etc., this issue does not usually come up. What has happened instead is that social and charitable organisations, as well as local *masjid*s, have taken up the role of voluntarily taking *zakāh* payments and distributing them to needy people. Strictly speaking, however, it is entirely valid for a Muslim to give his own *zakāh* as he sees fit, as long as he stays within the rules of *fiqh*.

Zakāh can be paid to all the eight (seven according to Ḥanafī *fiqh*) categories, or to anyone of them, however it is best to give an amount that will help the recipient to meet their needs and to take them out of poverty.

It is not permissible to pay *zakāh* to a non-Muslim, a wealthy person who has the *niṣāb*, a wealthy child, or members of Banī Ḥāshim (the family of the Messenger, may Allah bless him and grant him peace), nor is it correct to pay *zakāh* to one's parents, children, or wife. All other relatives can be paid *zakāh* – in fact it is more virtuous to pay them than other people, if they are needy. The closer the relatives the more deserving they become, followed by one's neighbours, people from the locality and then the city etc. Shaykh Abū Hafs al-Kabīr said a person's *zakāh* is not accepted if his relatives and near ones are needy.

Imām Ghazālī gives terse and candid advice with regards to the payment of *zakāh*. He said: 'Always intend to pay *zakāh*, without delay, at the time it is due on all the wealth on which it is compulsory.'

The Manners of paying *Zakāh*

Imām Ghazālī also gives the following advice:

1. Pay the *zakāh* quietly, preferably in secret, and certainly do not make a show of it. The Messenger, may Allah bless him and grant him peace, praised such people when he said, '*There are seven whom Allah will give shade on the Day when there is no shade except His shade...*[and he went on to mention] *a man who gives in charity so secretly that the left hand does not know what the right hand has given.*'[7]
2. It is better to give *zakāh* openly, however, when it is going to motivate and spur others to give as well. Allah Most High says:

   > *They spend from what we have provided them, secretly and openly, and they hope for a commerce that will never fail. For He will pay them their wages and increase them from his bounty. Indeed he is Forgiving, Responsive.*[8]

3. It is despicable and sinful to boast about one's *zakāh*, or to remind the recipient and humiliate him, and one should never think of oneself as the benefactor or as superior. The Qur'ān forbids any kind of condescending attitude towards the beneficiary. Rather the giver of *zakāh* should think that he has done him a favour by accepting his *zakāh* and helped to purify him. He should not hope for honour,

ZAKĀH

service or gratitude from the recipient. He should forget about it and only look for reward from Allah.

4. Do not seek to please your own self from giving *zakāh* and think of your charity as a small act of kindness rather than as a great act. Remember the rule with regards to a religious act: if considered small, it becomes great and if considered great, it becomes small.
5. When giving charity, search for the best recipient. These are:

   i. God-fearing, pious and prayerful people.
   ii. Students, scholars and people who have dedicated themselves to learning Islamic sciences. This way you will be helping to spread the message of the *dīn* (religion).
   iii. People who hide their needs and do not complain, they are shy and honourable people. Search for them and help them. Allah the Almighty says:

   > *(Alms are) for the poor, who are restricted in the cause of Allah, and cannot travel in the earth (to seek work). The ignorant person thinks they are wealthy, because of their modesty. You will know them by their mark: they do not beg all and sundry with importunity. And whatever good thing you spend, indeed Allah knows it well.*[9]

   iv. Close relatives, excepting one's own parents and children, are the most deserving of a person's *zakāh*. The Prophet, may Allah bless him and grant him peace said, '*Payment of* ṣadaqah [*zakāh*, or voluntary almsgiving] *to the destitute gives its reward, and to the close relative it gives two: the reward of* ṣadaqah *and that of joining the ties of kinship.*'[10]

Notes

1 The lunar year is counted by the twelve monthly cycles of the moon and comes to 355-6 days, which is 10 days shorter than the solar year.

2 As the price of gold and silver in pounds sterling or other currencies varies, ask your jeweller, find out from the newspaper, or go to a website (e.g. *www.24hgold.com/english*) and follow the links. If, for instance, 1.0g of gold is £19, then the nisāb of 85g would be £1615 (price in June 2009). Some scholars argue that rather than always using gold to determine the *niṣāb* for money, which has normally been the case, it is better to use silver if this results in a lower number and so is more beneficial for the poor. For example if 1.0g of silver costs £0.30, then the *niṣāb* of 600g would be £180, which would result in considerably more *zakāh* being paid.

3 *Sūrah al-Tawbah*, (Q9: 60).

4 The point here is that during the *khilāfah*s (caliphates) of Abū Bakr and then ʿUmar, may Allah be pleased with them both, the Muslim community became increasingly dominant and wealthy in the entire Arabian peninsula and beyond. It was, therefore, no longer necessary to allocate *zakāh* funds for winning the hearts, as entering into Islam had become more attractive on the worldly, as well as spiritual, level. As for the claim of *ʿijmā'*, al-Lakhnawī points out that it must be 'silent' (i.e. put forward by one of the *mujtahid*s of the community – here the early *khalīfah*s – and not contradicted by the others) as he lists a number of major scholars that have accepted the continued applicability of this category, including al-Ḥasan al-Baṣrī, Aḥmad ibn Ḥanbal and al-Shāfiʿī, may Allah have mercy on them. Al-Marghinānī, *Al-Hidāyāh* with commentary by al-Lakhnawī, *al-Miṣbāḥ*, v. 1, p. 204, note. 13.

5 Slavery as an institution is now formally outlawed in Muslim countries and of course in international law in the line with the United Nations' 1948 Universal Decleration of Human Rights, and its supplementary Anti-Slavery Convention of 1956.

6 Al-Māwardī, *al-Aḥkām al-Sulṭāniyyah* , translated as *The Laws of Islamic Governance*, by Asadullah Yate, (Ta-Ha Publishers, 2005), p. 168.

7 Narrated in *Saḥīḥ al-Bukhārī* and *Saḥīḥ Muslim.*

8 *Sūrah al-Fāṭir*, (Q35: 29-30).

9 *Sūrah al-Baqarah*, (Q2: 273).

10 Narrated in *Sunan Ibn Mājah*.

ZAKĀH

4th
Pillar

ṢAWM

(The Fasting in Ramaḍān)

The Expression of Divine Love through Self-Discipline

CHAPTER 10

The Blessings of Ramaḍān and Fasting

Ramaḍān is the Spring of Righteousness

In spring, new vegetation appears and the gardens begin to bloom, winter gloom is overcome and the earth expands to let heaven enter into its midst. Similarly, in the month of Ramaḍān, there is a sudden burst of spiritual activity. Mosques are crowded and there is a feeling of warmth and compassion and joy in the air, an ardent desire to worship. Muslims look forward to the coming of Ramaḍān, as it has brought and continues to bring with it the manifold blessings of Allah, the foremost of which is the Qur'ān itself. He Most High says:

> *The month of Ramaḍān is that in which the Qur'ān was sent down as a guide for humankind and as (providing) clear evidences of guidance and the criterion (between right and wrong). Whosoever of you witnesses the month, fast within it.*[1]

Describing this prosperous time of worship, Abū Hurayrah, may Allah be pleased with him, narrated that the Messenger, may peace and blessings be upon him, said:

Ramaḍān has come to you as a blessed month. During this month Allah has prescribed fasting for you, the gates of Heaven are opened and the gates of Hell are closed. The rebellious devils are chained. There is a night in this month that is better than a thousand months, whoever misses it is indeed deprived of enormous blessings.[2]

The Messenger, peace and blessings be upon him, variously encouraged and spurred people to value this blessed month. He once said, *'If Muslims knew the greatness of Ramaḍān then they would wish that the whole year was Ramaḍān.'*
Abū Hurayrah, may Allah be pleased with him, reports that the blessed Messenger, peace and blessings be upon him, as having said:

My people have been blessed with five special favours in Ramaḍān: (1) the breath of the fasting person is better that the smell of musk; (2) the angels pray for them; (3) Paradise is prepared for them; (4) the mischievous devils are chained; and (5) the fasting people are forgiven.[3]

God is most Generous. He gives without asking and gives so abundantly, *subḥānallāh*. The Prophet, peace and blessings be upon him, in telling us about the five special favours of Allah in this month, first mentions that the bad breath coming from the mouth of the fasting person is better than musk, a valuable perfume. This 'bad breath' is the result of the changed metabolism of the body. As blood sugar levels fall during fasting, the body begins to use stored fats. A by-product of fat metabolism are ketone bodies, which are volatile and smelly substances and they appear in the breath of the fasting person.

But what does it mean to say *'this bad breath is dearer to God than musk'*? The scholars have explained this in several ways. It could mean one of the following: (1) in the Hereafter, Allah will grant him a perfume which will be better than musk;

(2) on the Day of Judgement, as people will rise from the dead, they will smell of perfume; and (3) it could mean that the smell of their breath is better in the sight of Allah than that of musk, simply because God loves his obedient and fasting slave. What a beautiful way to express love. Fasting is the gate to all other devotions, as the heart is illuminated as the desire to serve and worship Allah grows.

Since fasting is no ordinary act of worship, Allah says in a *ḥadīth qudsī*:

> *All the deeds of the son of Adam are increased in value from ten to seven hundred times except for fasting, since it is for Me alone; I shall reward my servant as I please.*[4]

The second blessing for the fasting person is the prayer of the angels. *Aḥādīth* tell us that when Allah loves one of His servants, He tells Jibrīl that so and so is beloved, so Jibrīl loves him too and he proclaims to all the angels that so and so is Allah's beloved. They too begin to love him until his love is implanted in the heart of all the people.[5]

Another interesting feature of Ramaḍān is that *'mischievous devils are chained'*. It is a common experience that even in the most Islamic society, sins and crimes are still committed in Ramaḍān, although somewhat less than usual – so the question is what is this *ḥadīth* getting at?

This apparent dilemma has been variously addressed by the scholars. The first thing is that the *ḥadīth* specifies that only mischievous and rebellious devils are chained, suggesting that the 'minor devils' who are numerous remain free to do as they like. Another interesting explanation for some of the evil we see in Ramaḍān is that the devils are indeed chained but men who have acquired the characteristics of the devil, by living a life full of sins, are free to roam amongst us. In the following *ḥadīth*, the Prophet, may peace and blessings be upon him, explains the process whereby a man becomes devil-like:

When a person commits a sin a black spot appears on his heart, if he repents sincerely then it is wiped off – otherwise it remains there, and when he sins again a second black spot appears and if he persists in sinning, the entire heart becomes covered with black spots. Nay their hearts have become rusted.[6]

The *ḥadīth* graphically describes such a heart in this way. Those people who are accustomed to sins will continue their habits even in Ramaḍān, although the blessings of the month and the general increased piety of the community lead many to rethink. Abū Hurayrah, may Allah be pleased with him, narrates that the Messenger of Allah, peace and blessings be upon him, said:

God does not refuse the prayers of three people; the fasting person until he opens it, the just ruler and the oppressed. The prayer is raised above the clouds and a door in the sky is opened for it.

In Ramaḍān, the habit of the Prophet, may Allah bless him and grant him peace, the companions and the saints, was to spend more time in prayer and supplication. A tradition says that the angels of the Mighty Throne are told to leave and say *'amīn'* for the prayers of the devotee. This is an indication that the prayer will be accepted, however, despite this Divine promise, our faith sometimes falters and we do not put our trust in Allah as we should, and demand to see our prayer fulfilled immediately there and then. This is the hasty and rash nature of man. The next *ḥadīth* explains the Divine wisdom that operates in delaying the fulfilment of our prayers. The Prophet, peace and blessings be upon him, said:

When a Muslim asks for something, as long as it is not severing a relationship or a sin, one of the following three things happen: either he gets what he asked for, or an impending calamity is diverted from him, or he is credited with reward for the Hereafter.

Another *ḥadīth* says that:

On the Day of Judgement, a person will be reminded about all his prayers and how they were accepted or a calamity was diverted from him and some prayers which were not fulfilled in his life time, he will be given enormous reward for them. When he sees the reward for his unfulfilled prayer he will wish that none of his prayers were ever fulfilled in the world so that he could reap their reward!

A Month of Mercy, Forgiveness and Deliverance

It was narrated by Salmān, may Allah be pleased with him, that the Messenger of Allah, peace and blessings be upon him, delivered a sermon on the last day of Shaʿbān:

Oh People! There comes upon you now a great and most blessed month, wherein lies a night greater in worth than a thousand months. The fasting during this month is made compulsory and the extra prayers by night are optional. Whosoever tries drawing near to Allah by performing any virtuous deed in this month, for him shall be such reward as if he had performed any obligatory duty at any other time of the year. And whosoever performs any obligatory duty, for him shall be the reward of 70 times such duty at any other time of the year.

This is indeed the month of patience and the reward for true patience is Paradise. It is the month of sympathy with one's fellow men. It is a month wherein a true believer's livelihood is increased. Whosoever feeds a fasting person in order to break the fast at iftār, *for him there will be forgiveness of his sins and emancipation from the fire of*

> *Hell and he will receive the reward equal to the fasting person, without that person's reward being diminished in the least.*

Some of the companions then said:

> Not all of us possess the means whereby we can provide enough for a fasting person to break his fast.

The Prophet, peace and blessings be upon him, replied:

> *Allah grants the same reward to him who gives a fasting person a single date or a sip of milk or drink of water to break the fast.*
>
> *This is a month the first part of which brings Allah's mercy, the middle of which brings His forgiveness and the last part of which brings freedom from the fire of Hell. Whosoever lessens the burdens of his servants in this month, Allah will forgive him and free him from Hell. And there are four things you should endeavour to perform in great number, two of which shall be to please your Lord, while the other two shall be those without which you cannot make do.*
>
> *The first two qualities are to bear witness that there is none worthy of worship except Allah and to ask for forgiveness. And as for the two you cannot do without: ask Allah for Paradise and seek refuge from the Hellfire.*
>
> *And whosoever gives a fasting Muslim water to drink at* iftār*, Allah will grant him a drink during the Day of Judgement from the fountain of Muḥammed after which he shall never again feel thirsty until he enters Paradise.*[7]

A Commentary:

This sermon succinctly outlines the brilliance of the sacred month. Some of the outstanding features of this month are:

- One of its nights, the Night of Power, is more valuable than a thousand months.
- Fasting during the day is compulsory, whilst praying *tarāwīḥ* at night and listening to the Qur'ān is *sunnah*.
- This is a month of patience, in which believers should learn to gladly accept the hardships of fasting, its hunger and thirst.
- Fasting helps develop compassion and willingness to help the needy and the poor and the goodness of feeding others at *iftār* time is described.
- The holy month is divided into three parts: mercy, forgiveness and salvation. First the mercy of Allah engulfs everything, followed by His forgiveness thus the Muslims achieve salvation from Hellfire.
- The Messenger, may peace and blessings be upon him, then advises employers to be kind to their workers. To lighten their work and to allow them time for devotion during this month.
- Finally he tells us to do four things:

    1. To recite the *kalimah*.
    2. To seek forgiveness.
    3. To ask for Paradise.
    4. To seek refuge from Hell.

There are many more *aḥādīth*, which mention vividly the benefits and virtues of fasting in Ramaḍān. We will here pick a few more of these fragrant flowers from the delightful meadow of the Prophet. The beloved Muṣtafā, peace and blessings be upon him, said:

On the Day of Judgement the Glorious Qur'ān and the fast will intercede (on your behalf). The fast will say 'Oh

Lord! I stopped him from eating, drinking and sexual activity throughout the day', then the Qur'ān will say, 'Oh Mighty Lord! I stopped him from rest and sleep at night so I will intercede for him.'[8]

All the scholars accept the reality of these intercessions. The value of good deeds are also greatly inflated in Ramaḍān and forgiveness is close at hand, as is witnessed by the following prophetic narrations:

An 'umrah performed in Ramaḍān has the value of ḥajj.[9]

The five prayers, from one Friday to the next and from one Ramaḍān to the next, are an atonement for a man's sins as long as he avoids the major ones.[10]

Notes

1 *Sūrah al-Baqarah* (Q2: 185).
2 Narrated in *Saḥīḥ al-Bukhārī.*
3 Narrated in the *Musnad* of Aḥmad ibn Ḥanbal.
4 Narrated in *Saḥīḥ Muslim.*
5 Narrated in *Saḥīḥ al-Bukhārī.*
6 Narrated in *Saḥīḥ al-Bukhārī.*
7 Narrated by Ibn al-Khuzaymah.
8 Narrated in *Saḥīḥ Muslim.*
9 Narrated in *Sunan al-Tirmidhī.*
10 Narrated in *Saḥīḥ Muslim.*

CHAPTER 11

Fasting: A Means of Moral and Spiritual Growth for the Individual and Community

Fasting was prescribed for Us to develop *Taqwā*

Allah the Most Wise says:

> *Oh you who believe! Fasting is prescribed for you as it was prescribed to those before you, so that you may develop* taqwā *(awareness of God).*[1]

Fasting during the month of Ramaḍān is a difficult exercise. Amongst all the Islamic forms of worship it is the one that most tests man's endurance and ability to control his appetites. To go without food, drink or sexual pleasure for 11-18 hours (in winter the fast is short and in summer long) may appear as self-torture to the outsider, but the believer sees this as self-denial which trains him to fulfil his purpose in life. When God, the All-Wise tells the believers to fast, He explains to them that it was *'prescribed to those before you'*. Furthermore, He gives the reason for demanding this act of worship in these words: *'so that you may develop* taqwā (*awareness of God*)'. Allah need not explain the reasons for His commandments, but He is Benevolent and Most Generous, so in order to comfort us and to satisfy our inquisitive nature, He explains that previous peoples have fasted and found it beneficial. They were capable of doing it – *and so will you*. Moreover, it will lead to becoming a *muttaqī*, a God-aware or pious person.

What is *taqwā*? Some people translate the term as 'fear of God'. *Taqwā* literally means 'to protect oneself from those things that may cause harm', so perhaps it can be best understood as a sense of awareness, being on one's guard, vigilant and attentive lest one falls into the temptations of the ego and the *Shayṭān*. We must aim to show this high level of alertness in our everyday life.This is why some scholars say that *taqwā* is simply to obey Allah and to avoid the forbidden things. As Ibrāhīm ibn Adhām says, '*Taqwā* is that people do not find a fault in your speech, and the angels do not find a fault in your actions whilst the angels of the Throne see no fault in your inner motives.'

How does fasting develop *taqwā*? Imagine it is a hot day and you are extremely thirsty, with your stomach grumbling with pangs of hunger due to the fast. There is sweet cold water in a jug and delicious food on the table and suddenly you realise that *no-one is watching you!* It is only because of one's *taqwā* that he refuses to lift his hands towards the drink and the food in obedience to the Lord's command. Also, if he is able to abstain from the usually permissable things, do you not think that he will be able to avoid all those things that Allah has forbidden? One of the objectives of this month-long exercise is that one becomes able to avoid sins in the other eleven months of the year.

Fasting carries with it many spiritual benefits and is an effective means for spiritual growth, moral development, improvement of bodily health and social good. We shall discuss these benefits of fasting one by one to understand this wonderful programme of personal development.

Spiritual Growth

What do we mean by spirituality? Spirituality refers to a man's relationship with his Creator, faith in Him, reliance upon Him and a sense of attachment to Him. This spiritual link cannot be felt through the five physical senses nor easily expressed through everyday language. Experienced through the heart it is nonetheless more real to the truly devoted servant than anything else in his life. This relationship with the Lord of all the Worlds gives the believer a sense of identity, realising the Majesty and Grandeur of Allah and at the same time recognises his own weakness and dependence on Him, he submits himself and declares, 'There is no god but Allah', he becomes aware of the reality that 'I am the servant and He is the Master' and is filled with awe and a sense of wonder and mystery when he looks around him, gaining certainty that his purpose in life is to worship and adore Allah! This is an enlightening experience of transcendence, arousing in the humble man the desire to become closer to God and achieve His nearness, so where does he begin? He looks for a role model, in the universal man, the mercy to the universe, Allah's beloved Messenger Muḥammad, may peace and blessings be upon him, and in him he finds 'a beautiful example'. He familiarises himself with his teaching and follows his example in every aspect of his life. Practicing the *Sunnah*, the life pattern of the 'Holy Prophet' in its totality leads to a heightened awareness of the presence of Allah and one of the key acts in this is *ṣawm* (fasting).

Marmaduke Pickthall makes the following comments in an article calling Muslims to the proper observance of fasting:

> 'The whole purpose of Islam, and all its rites and observances, is nothing but the training to perfection of energetic, righteous men and women. Not those who dream of angels in an easy-chair, not those who wish well to everybody without doing anything, but those who actually do good works, with zeal and

> earnest purpose, in their sphere of influence, and who guard themselves against things evil.'[2]

Just as the world of consumerism diverts man's attention away from spirituality, fasting helps to connect man with his Lord. It is a powerful means of disengaging us from the material world and reinforcing spirituality. The purpose of fasting is to remind the believer of his spiritual reality over and above his immediate concerns of eating, drinking and sexual pleasure. Fasting restrains carnal desires: those cravings that, if left uncontrolled, will weaken the soul and eventually destroy it. Fasting, by overriding these desires, brings man closer to Allah and the power of the soul is then unleashed upon temporal cravings. This important place of fasting in developing spirituality is universally recognised by all religions: 'Its modes and motives vary considerably according to climate, race and civilisation; but it would be difficult to name any religion in which it is not wholly recognised.'[3]

Using Ramaḍān as a Programme for Spiritual Growth

Most of the time the human being feels imprisoned and bound, restricted by his circumstances, work and, above all, his physical needs. Humans need food, drink, mental rest, socialisation with others and leisure for physical well-being. For many people, the fulfillment of these needs is the focus of their entire life – meeting these bodily needs is the be all and end all of life as they continually work to earn enough money to satisfy these needs. This cycle of earning and consuming results in a positive feedback loop, the more is earnt, the more is consumed in a vicious cycle, a hallmark of this modern Western consumerist society.

Fasting, or abstinence from food, drink and worldly pleasures, is a perfect antidote to this excessive lifestyle. Through fasting, man moves towards the non-physical and non-material world – the spiritual world. By fasting, one temporarily becomes free of one's physical needs. You can escape the prison of the senses, control food and drink intake, regulate speech and sleep and experience the flavours of the spiritual realm.

Just as the obsessive quest to fulfill the physical needs is a veil between a soul and its Creator, so fasting is a means to remove that veil. Whilst fasting, there is the sense of closeness to God, peace of mind, a feeling of freedom and a state of relaxation. Reducing social contact and pleasures, coupled with more devotion, prayer and utterance of Divine Names all help to deepen the spiritual experience and leads away from the temporal world.

The whole month of Ramaḍān is a programme, which enables man to become acquainted with the spiritual world. The soul yearns to be near its Creator and fasting is a means of achieving this, as Allah says:

> *We are closer to him than his jugular vein.*[4]

Fasting is the light of the spirit. Through it, during the month of Ramaḍān, the believer is obliged to make every moment of the day a time of worship. He should also go beyond this in other acts of devotion in seeking the pleasure of his Almighty Lord.

In order to fully benefit from this 'spring of righteousness', we should strictly adhere to a programme that develops our spirituality gradually throughout this blessed month. The following is a well-tested programme that can be followed by the Muslim who yearns to make the most of the opportunity that Ramaḍān offers:

Preparation

In the preceding month of Shaʿbān, begin fasting on the *sunnah* days of Mondays and Thursdays. Prepare yourself mentally and physically for the great month to come, which is also a *sunnah* of the Messenger, may peace and blessings be upon him.

Days 1–5 of Ramaḍān

As the holy month dawns, change your daily routines such that you can easily pray five times in the day, preferably with the congregation in the *masjid* (in the case of men). You should listen to the Glorious Qur'ān in the daily *tarāwīḥ* after *'ishā'*; recite *"Yā Ḥayyu yā Qayyūm" (Oh Ever-Living One! Oh Self-Sufficient One!)* whenever possible; and resolve to read the complete Qur'an at least once during the month. Remember to reduce your food intake at *seḥrī/suḥūr* (pre-dawn meal) and *iftār* (sunset meal upon completing fasting). From Day One, start praying the voluntary (*nafl*) prayers (see Chapter 6), like *ishrāq* after *fajr*. Women can do this at home by remaining on the *muṣallā* (prayer mat). You must also get into the habit of praying *awwābīn*. As this takes place after *maghrib*, it is sometimes missed due to preoccupation with eating – a real pity and absolutely contrary to the true spirit of the month.

Days 6–10

The effects of abstinence from pleasure and food begin to show effect. You are more attentive and alert in your prayer and increasingly moved by the verses of the Qur'ān as you listen to them. You are already feeling much better and lighter physically and mentally. You sleep less: perhaps about 7.5 hours a day (for a person who usually averages 8 hours), the aim is to reduce this further as the month progresses. The time saved is spent in recitation and devotion.

Days 11–16

For the last ten days you have reduced your desires for food, drink, pleasures, and sleep. The frequent recitation and constant worship help to control the senses and physical needs. Giving up all these solely for the pleasure of the Lord brings the soul closer to its Creator. Your heart by now is soft and your mind calm and generous. You are inclined toward your Lord and desire to be close to Him. So get up early for *seḥrī* (30-45 minutes) and pray *tahajjud*, also called the night vigil, which one should hate to miss at this time of the year. Food consumption should be low too, as this helps the soul to grow and escape the clutches of the temporal world. Avoid too much meat and oily foods, eat more salads and fruit as well as drinking more fruit juice. Already, both physical stamina and mental alertness have improved enormously and you must continue to build on this.

Days 17–20

By now you should be able to reduce your sleep time to seven hours (or one hour less than is usual outside Ramaḍān). With low food consumption and healthy spiritual habits, you can concentrate more on recitation and devotion. Reduce social meetings, this is a time to be with your Lord. Your prayer routine will consist of five daily prayers as well as regular *ishrāq* after *fajr*, *awwābīn* after *maghrib* and *tahajjud* at night.

Days 21–25

Only a maximum of 10 days left (including these five) so guard them and value every sweet moment. You may be fortunate enough to take the 10 days off work and stay in the *masjid* to do *iʿtikāf*. This spiritual retreat is a must for the serious devotee. Many have climbed the heights of spirituality in these 10 days, sitting alone or in the company of the righteous, in the house of Allah at the most blessed time of year, reading, learning or teaching the Divine Book. What a splendid time it is: far from the world of work, abstaining from food, away from lowly pleasures, in the serene atmosphere of the *masjid*, you can now experience the delights of the spiritual world. The sleeping period has been reduced to six and a half hours per night, leaving more time for devotion, contemplation and study.

Days 26-29/30

In just a few days this righteous month leaves. Cherish every moment. Constant recitation of *'Yā Ḥayyu yā Qayyūm'*, blessings upon the beloved Messenger, may Allah bless him and grant him peace, as well supplications for salvation from the Hellfire, are now the habit of the tongue. Periods of deep contemplation are becoming longer and longer and the heart feels at peace. Allah, Almighty says:

> *Truly, in the remembrance of Allah do the hearts find rest.*[5]

Coming in the last portion of Ramaḍān, the Night of Power is the crowning feature of this most special of months. This night is honoured in the Qur'ān as follows:

> *The Night of Power is better than a thousand months.*[6]

Keep a night vigil throughout this night to experience the nearness of Allah, the beauty of the Qur'ān, and feel around you the presence of the angels as they descend to embrace you. It is said that even the noble Archangel Jibrīl will be there.

Using Fasting as a Means for Moral Development

For our peaceful and successful existence we must be able to distinguish between right and wrong, good and bad. This sense of knowing what is right and what is wrong is known as morality. The moral sense is expressed through personal traits such as truthfulness, honesty, respecting others, sacrifice, generosity and patience. It is about abandoning blind whims. The aim of moral development is to improve behaviour and enrich human relationships with one another. Fasting is an effective means of developing morality, as it teaches the principle of self-denial and therefore encouraging sacrifice for others. It is about becoming more aware of others, their rights and our responsibilities, as well as developing patience (calm endurance of hardship). In contemporary society, moral confusion reigns supreme and there is a need to develop a genuine moral sense. The Messenger, may peace and blessings be upon him, whilst commenting on the moral benefits of fasting said, *'Whoever does not give up lying and cheating then God does not require him to give up eating and drinking.'*[7] – thus making it absolutely clear that fasting is not merely giving up food and drink but giving up bad habits too! Another *ḥadīth* describes fasting as a shield until it is broken and some inquisitive soul asked him what will break it and he said, *'Lying and backbiting.'*

Certain rules have to be observed to derive the full moral benefit and impact of fasting:

1. The eyes have to be controlled, with no lustful and sensual gazes. The Messenger, peace and blessings be upon him, said, *'A lustful gaze is the arrow of the devil and whoever avoids it receives the Divine Light which illuminates their heart and mind.'* In our sex-ridden and obsessed society where the *Shayṭān* prompts us constantly, it is vital that we control our eyes.
2. The tongue should be controlled so that it does not gossip, lie or backbite. It should not hurt anyone's feelings.
3. The ears should not listen to bad words, such as swearing, gossip or backbiting.
4. All the limbs should be guarded lest they fall into temptation.
5. One must ensure that he breaks his fast with *ḥalāl* food and eats and drinks in moderation. To stuff oneself with delicious food at dawn and dusk really defeats the whole object of fasting which includes experiencing the pangs of hunger and seeing for oneself what it means to be poor and deprived of food. If we make up for the missed meal, but just at a later time, then we will not learn these valuable lessons.
6. Finally, humility. At the end of the day we must hope and pray that Allah accepts our efforts and be apprehensive that they could be rejected.

The Social Benefits and Wisdom of the Obligatory Fast in Ramaḍān

In Ramaḍān, the whole community fasts: young and old; rich and poor; employer and the employee. This creates an atmosphere of unity, as everyone is doing the same things: fasting, praying and reciting the Qur'ān. There is a sense of brotherhood and sisterhood, a sense of belonging to a community of believers, where one is valued. Fasting is an experience through which one can empathise with the needy and hungry of the world; in other words, it develops the ability to associate with the deprived and to help alleviate their suffering throughout the year. The Messenger, peace and blessings be upon him, invited Muslims to share their food with others, saying, *'Anyone who feeds a fasting person will be given an equal reward to his.'*[8]

Also, during this most luminous month, it is possible to witness charitable collections springing up nightly in every *masjid* like green shoots after the rainfall. Individuals who ordinarily find it hard to give up their wealth to help others are stimulated by the spirit of sacrifice and blessings of the month to do just that. In fact, this is in entirely accordance with the *Sunnah*, as it is narrated by Ibn ʿAbbās:

> The Prophet, may Allah bless him and grant him peace, was the most generous amongst the people and he used to be more so in the month of Ramaḍān when Jibrīl visited him, and Jibrīl used to meet him every night of Ramaḍān until the end of the month. The Prophet used to recite the Holy Qur'ān to Jibrīl, and when Jibrīl met him, he used to be more generous than a fast wind (which causes rain and welfare).[9]

The Health Benefits of Fasting

Although the primary purpose of fasting is *'so that you may develop* taqwā', it carries health benefits as well. The obvious

ṢAWM

is weight loss, for thirty days a whole meal and a snack or two are taken away from our daily food intake. This is equivalent to about 1,000 calories per day, 30,000 calories in a month, roughly the amount needed to burn off eight pounds (3kg). Fasting brings about a complete physiological change, giving rest to the digestive tract and the central nervous system. The trouble is what we miss during fasting we often more than make up for at *ifṭār*. *Ifṭār* is no longer a glass of water and some dates: it has become a sumptuous festival which is incomplete without several courses, including fried snacks, cooked meats and juices of the most exotic fruits. This kind of *iftār* diminishes the health benefits of fasting, for which the rule is simplicity and moderation. *Ifṭār*, and indeed *suḥūr*, should consist of meals low in fat and high in carbohydrates, to sustain one for worship and help to trim the waistline. Also increase vegetable intake and lower meat consumption (which sadly goes up in *Ramaḍān*, as one can see from the long lines at the *ḥalāl* butchers).

Some people have a large meal at *suḥūr*, usually with rich, fatty foods, such as bread fried in butter, with the hope that it will keep them going throughout the day. The problem with this strategy is that the fat is absorbed by the blood and safely stored in fat deposits around the body. As the day passes, the body first uses the carbohydrates and as soon as the body senses an 'impending starvation', it slows down the metabolism and conserves energy by functioning on fewer calories. This natural 'fuel efficiency mode' makes it harder for you to lose weight. Only a small portion of the fat consumed at breakfast will be used, the rest becomes flab!

If you want to really benefit from the fast then try this strategy at *ifṭār*: open the fast with dates and water or juice and eat slowly. It has been shown that it takes about 20 minutes for the stomach to fully signal to the brain that the body is full. This is why quickly wolfing down a meal in a few minutes leads to overeating. Then pray *maghrib* (and *awwabīn*) before going back to eat a moderate portion of your evening meal. You'll eat much less, *inshā' Allāh*, and will be protected from excessive lethargy during the evening's devotion which should include *tarāwīḥ* and *tahajjud*. Follow the other *sunnah*s too: eating slowly, taking small bites, chewing well and thanking Allah for the food.

Fasting in the month of Ramaḍān is a great blessing for the overweight and can be used as a way to lose weight healthily. Nibbling biscuits and chocolate between meals are amongst the two main reasons for obesity – by fasting, one easily rids oneself of such compulsions. In fact, the practice of fasting should really help all of us to develop the good habits of moderation, simplicity and attentiveness, which will ensure that we do not over indulge in eating. As Allah Most High says:

> *Eat and drink but do not squander. Indeed, Allah does not love the squanderers.*[10]

Another practice which not only earns us spiritual reward but also ensures we keep fit and healthy in Ramaḍān is *tarāwīḥ* (additional congregational prayers after *'ishā'*). This is both an important social gathering in the *masjid* and an illuminating opportunity to allow the Glorious Qur'ān to penetrate the heart. This is the longest form of congregational worship lasting well over an hour depending on the speed of the *imām*'s recitation. The repeated cycles of sitting and standing (twenty for *tarāwīḥ* itself and another nine for the *farḍ 'ishā'*, *sunnah* and congregational *witr* prayers) is equivalent to walking a good three miles. According to Dr. Shahid Ather, a professor of medicine at Indiana University in America, 20 *rak'ah*s of *tarāwīḥ* burns 200 calories and is considered a mild form of exercise.

Notes

1. *Sūrah al-Baqarah* (Q2: 183).
2. Pickthall, M., 'Fasting in Islam' (*Islamic Review and Muslim India*, vol. 8, December 1920).

[3] Article 'Fasting' in *The Encylopaedia Brittanica.*
[4] *Sūrah Qāf* (Q50: 16).
[5] *Sūrah al-Ra'd* (Q13: 28).
[6] *Sūrah al-Qadr* (Q97: 3).
[7] Narrated in *Ṣaḥīḥ Muslim.*
[8] Narrated in *Ṣaḥīḥ Muslim.*
[9] Narrated in *Ṣaḥīḥ al-Bukhārī.*
[10] *Sūrah al-A'rāf* (Q7: 31).

CHAPTER 12

The *Fiqh* Rulings for Ramaḍān

Objectives of this section to learn:

- When Ramaḍān begins and ends.
- The obligatory nature of fasting in Ramaḍān.
- Who must fast and who is exempt.
- Under what circumstances a diabetic should fast.
- What the fast is and when it begins and ends.
- The actions that nullify the fast.
- What is to be done when a fast is nullified and whether atonement (*kaffārah*) is required.
- The actions that do not nullify the fast.
- The actions that are undesirable (*makrūh*) while fasting.
- The meaning and practice of *tarāwīḥ* prayer.
- How the Messenger, may Allah bless him and grant him peace, used to fast in Ramaḍān.

Beginning and ending Ramaḍān

When Sha'bān, the eighth month of the Islamic calendar approaches its end, people should look out for the crescent of the new moon at sunset on the 29th day. If the moon is sighted, then the fasting will begin the next day and if it is cloudy and the moon is not visible then thirty days of Sha'bān will be completed. The blessed Messenger, may peace and blessings be upon him, said, *'Fast after sighting the moon and end the fasting by sighting it and if it is cloudy then complete thirty days of Sha'bān.'*[1] This should be a simple formula for beginning Ramaḍān and celebrating 'Īd, although unfortunately differences in its application have resulted in some controversy in modern times (see Appendix for more details). The Ḥanafī jurists say that if the weather is cloudy, or obscured by dust or the like, then, in determining the start of Ramaḍān, the *imām* should accept evidence of sighting the crescent from even a single honest witness. As for beginning Shawwāl (and therefore 'Īd al-Fiṭr), under the same conditions, there should be at least two witnesses. However, in both cases, if the sky is clear there should be numerous witnesses (i.e. enough to convince the *imām* as to the credibility of the report).

The Day of Doubt

This is the 30th day of Sha'bān when, due to cloudy weather, the crescent has not been seen despite people searching for it. Therefore there is some doubt as to whether it is the 30th of Sha'bān or the 1st of Ramaḍān. Fasting on this day is *makrūh*, except for someone who regularly fasts it, for instance a person who follows the *sunnah* fasts of Mondays and Thursdays.

The Obligation to fast the Month of Ramaḍān

As the third pillar of Islam, fasting the month of Ramaḍān is an obligation upon every adult, sane Muslim who is capable of doing it and does not possess a reason to be exempt (see below). It was first prescribed in the second year of the *hijrah* and we have already quoted the passage in *Sūrah al-Baqarah* in which this is announced (Q2: 183-5). Hence anyone who denies that fasting is obligatory falls into disbelief (*kufr*).

Who is exempt from Fasting?

The following groups of people do not have to fast, or cannot fast, during Ramaḍān: the insane; children; the sick; travellers; the elderly; pregnant women; nursing women; and women menstruating or in the period of post-natal bleeding. These groups are further described below:

Children

Fasting is not obligatory on children, until they reach maturity (in the technical sense used by *fiqh*[2]). Parents, however, should encourage children to fast occasionally, or partly (i.e. until lunchtime!), so they get into the habit of fasting. If done with due regard to the child's health, this can be an excellent way to introduce them to the spirit of Ramaḍān, as well as helping them not to be greedy and selfish.

The Sick

A person who is ill and worried that the illness will get worse if he fasts should not fast until he fully recovers. However, he will have to make up for the missed fasts after Ramaḍān. When there is no hope of ever getting better from the illness (as in diabetes Type 1) then he can make up for his fasts by feeding a needy person. Allah Most High says:

> *The ransom* (fidyah) *on those who can afford it is the feeding of the needy.*[3]

The amount of food to be given for each missed fast is 1 kilogram of wheat or two kilos of dates. Alternatively, enough food for two meals can be supplied or the amount of money with which two average meals can be bought (approx. £2.00/meal). So a chronically-sick person who cannot make up missed fasts can pay £4 a day or £120 for the whole month.

ṢAWM

Note: In order to postpone or to pay ransom for missed fasts one must seek an accurate prognosis (i.e. the possibility of recovery from the illness) from a good Muslim physician (someone who does not commit major sins). A fast can also be broken if thirst and hunger become so severe that they cause anxiety and pain.

Diabetics and Fasting

Diabetes is due to the failure of the beta-cells of the pancreas to control the levels of blood sugar. Normally, these cells produce enough insulin to control the levels of glucose in the blood. However, diabetic patients either produce none (Type 1), produce very little (Type 2) or that which is produced is ineffective (as in the overweight diabetic). The lack of insulin or its effect causes a build up of glucose in the blood. Due to the nature of this illness, the question arises, what should the Muslim diabetic do in Ramaḍān?

Dr. Shahid Athar (MD, Prof. of Medicine, Indiana University, USA) has this advice:

CRITERIA ALLOWING DIABETICS TO FAST DURING RAMAḌĀN:

1. All male diabetics over the age of 20.
2. All female diabetics over the age of 20, if not pregnant or nursing.
3. Diabetics with a normal or above normal body-weight.
4. Absence of infection or co-existing unstable medical condition, i.e. coronary artery disease, severe hypertension, kidney stones, emphysema etc.
5. Diabetics that are diet controlled or using oral hypoglycaemics.
6. Diabetics with a fasting blood glucose of under 160mg/100ml (9.0mmol/l).
7. Diabetics with mild to moderate obesity, hypertension or hyperlipidaemia may still fast.

CRITERIA DISALLOWING DIABETICS TO FAST DURING RAMAḌĀN:

1. Juvenile Type 1 brittle and unstable diabetics.
2. Haemoglobin A.I.C. below 6 or over 12.
3. History of frequent ketosis of hypoglycaemia.
4. The presence of an infection, heart disease, gall bladder disease, pregnancy, lactation, renal disorders, colic or emphysema.

Such criteria have to be reviewed by the patient's physician (preferably a Muslim) and the patient be certified for fasting if he or she agrees in writing to comply with the physician's instructions during Ramaḍān.[4]

Note: The Ḥanafī jurists rule that having an injection, including insulin, does not nullify one's fast.

Travellers

It is permissible to postpone the fast if a person is on a journey equivalent to or greater than 48 miles from home. Allah Most High, says:

> *Whoever amongst you is ill or on a journey (let him fast) a number of other days.*[5]

We must remember that at the time of revelation of this verse the amount of travelling required to qualify for this exemption would be three days and nights spent mounted and on foot. Today on our fast motorways it would be less than an hour's journey, while even, for instance, the eight-hour flight between London and Islamabad (4800 miles) is relatively comfortable. Before taking this dispensation, we should reflect deeply as to whether it is really justified by our circumstances. In this, we can also observe the Qur'ānic wisdom contained at the end of the same verse:

And that you fast is better for you, if you were only to know.[6]

The Elderly

Old people who are weak and unable to fast at the time of Ramaḍān may perform their fasting at another time of the year. Those who are unable to fast at any time, and there are no prospects for them gaining enough strength, are exempt from fasting. However, they must pay the *fidyah* (ransom). If they cannot afford to pay it then they should seek forgiveness from Allah for their shortcomings.

Pregnant and Nursing Women

A pregnant or a nursing mother who is worried that her fasting may harm the child or herself can postpone fasting until she is capable of it. Again in this situation, it is proper to seek qualified medical advice.

Menstruating Women and Those in the Period of Post-Natal Bleeding

Women experiencing their *ḥayḍ* (monthly menstruation up to a maximum of 10 days) or *nifās* (post-natal bleeding up to a maximum of 40 days) cannot fast those days of *Ramaḍān* that happen to coincide with it. Unlike their prayers, however, they must later make up for all the fasts missed for this reason.

What is the Fast and when does it Begin and End?

The fast is to completely abstain from eating, drinking and sexual intercourse from the start of dawn (i.e. *fajr* time) until sunset (i.e. the entrance of *maghrib* time). It must be accompanied by an intention to fast, as it is an act of worship – someone who happens not to eat or drink, without intending to fast will neither receive a reward from Allah, nor have fulfilled their *farḍ* duty. The intention should be made the night before each fast as follows, 'I intend to fast for the sake of Allah tomorrow in the month of Ramaḍān.' If one forgets to do this, he may still make an intention to fast for that day before the entrance of *ẓuhr* time, as long as he has not eaten or drank anything. A person who forgets to do even this, must make up for the fast later, but will not be liable for atonement (see below).

What nullifies the Fast?

A fast can be nullified in two ways: firstly by a mistake/legitimate excuse and secondly by intentional eating, drinking or sexual intercourse. When a fast is invalidated by mistake it has to be made up (*qaḍā'*) later on. But if it was intentionally broken, then one has to make an atonement (*kaffārah*) for it, as well as performing a *qaḍā'*.

Situations in which only Qaḍā' *is required*

The Ḥanafī *fiqh* manual *Nūr al-Īḍāḥ* by Imām al-Shurunbulālī, lists 57 different situations in the fast will be nullified and therefore be in need of *qaḍā'* at a later date, without reaching the level of requiring *kaffārah*. Here are some examples which show the general pattern of this category: things eaten by mistake, or with some sort of excuse:

1. Mistakenly swallowing an unusual thing like seeds, cotton etc.
2. Taking necessary medicine for his illness or eating food because he was in agony or travelling.
3. Partially fulfilling one's sexual desire by ejaculating without insertion of the sexual organ.

Situations in which Kaffārah *and* Qaḍā' *are required*

More serious offenses during the fasting of Ramaḍān carry, in addition, a much more severe punishment – *kaffārah* (atonement). This is essentially an obligation to fast for two consecutive months outside of Ramaḍān, (see below for more details). Here are some important examples of this category:

1. To eat, drink or smoke without an acceptable reason.
2. To intentionally take part in sexual intercourse.

The Rulings of *Kaffārah* (Atonement)

Divine laws are for the benefit of mankind. Once they are accepted, these laws must be treated seriously and not casually. To flout and show contempt for them is a serious offence and any violation by word or action has a severe consequence on one's internal state and relationship with Allah. When a person realises his offence and turns to Allah for forgiveness he must atone (i.e. reconcile himself) with Allah by making amends. This will compensate for his offence and act as a purification. Allah Most High says:

> *Surely good deeds will erase evil deeds.*[7]

In the case of intentionally nullifying the fast of Ramaḍān a specific atonement has been legislated, which is to fast, in the *sunnah* manner, continuously for two months. This should be by the Islamic calendar, although one does not have to start from the beginning of any particular month. In other words, if a person is liable for *kaffārah*, they should note the day of the Islamic month that they wish to start and begin fasting. They must fast every day – without a break – until the same date two months hence. It is important that the two months that they choose for this purpose neither include a day of ʿĪd or the days of *tashrīq*, as fasting is prohibited on them. The first choice for atonement which was originally practised, was the freeing of a slave, however, this is impossible nowadays for obvious reasons. If two months of fasting is too difficult (due to a valid medical excuse), then an act of charity will suffice, sixty needy people should be given two meals each. Alternatively, one person could be given two meals a day for sixty days or amounts of money by which so many meals can be purchased. It should go without saying that in the condition that we currently find ourselves, the practice of two months of fasting as atonement teaches us a lot more about self-discipline and the sanctity of the fast of Ramaḍān than merely paying for food, despite the undisputed merits of this act.

What does not break the Fast?

1. To eat, drink, smoke or to have sexual intercourse forgetfully will not break the fast. Allah Most High says in regard to a different matter:

   > *There is no blame on you if you make a mistake therein, what counts is your intention.*[8]

2. Vomiting, whether a small amount or a full mouthful, will not break the fast.
3. To swallow something that was stuck between the teeth if it was smaller than the size of a chickpea will not break the fast.
4. A wet dream, or remaining in state of impurity (*junub*: when one must have a bath), does not break the fast.
5. If fine dust particles, a fly, or an insect get into the throat and are swallowed, then the fast will not be broken.
6. Permissible activities during the fast include:

   i. To smell scent and use perfume.
   ii. To brush the teeth using *miswak* or toothbrush (toothpaste should be avoided).
   iii. To rinse the mouth and nose regularly (no water should go all the way down the throat or up the nose).
   iv. To use *kohl* (*surma*/antimony) for the eyes, oil for the hair or facial make up.

What is Undesirable (*Makrūh*) whilst Fasting?

1. To kiss one's spouse if one is unable to control his lust and there is the possibility that they would get carried away and this would lead to sexual intercourse.
2. Accumulation of saliva in the mouth and then swallowing it.
3. To taste something except in the case of absolute necessity. For instance, a person who is cooking can taste the food to ensure it is not spoilt.
4. To chew something unnecessarily. Using chewing gum will break the fast.
5. Any activity that will exhaust and weaken a person so much that he will not be able to continue fasting must be avoided. Examples are: strenuous physical exercise, carrying heavy loads, blood donation etc. However, if a person is not weakened by any of these activities then they are not *makrūh*.

The Meaning and Practice of *Tarāwīḥ* Prayer

One night during the month of Ramaḍān, the Prophet, may peace and blessings be upon him, stayed in the *masjid* after *'ishā'* prayer and performed additional *ṣalāh*. Some of his *ṣaḥābah* (companions) joined him in this. The next night he did the same accompanied by even more *ṣaḥābah*. The third night saw an even greater number of believers assembled in the Prophet's *masjid*. However, on the fourth night he left the *masjid* immediately after praying the *farḍ* prayer. The next night he did the same and gradually the number of companions remaining in the *masjid* after *'ishā'* diminished. When he was asked about this new practice he said that he didn't want them to regard the extra prayer as obligatory. He said, *'I don't want to burden my followers.'* During his lifetime he would sometimes offer these extra prayers and avoid them on other days.

When 'Umar, may Allah be pleased with him, became *khalīfah*, he saw large numbers of people staying behind after *'ishā'*, praying individually. After consulting scholarly *ṣahābah*, he established the *tarāwīḥ* prayer as a regular congregational prayer during Ramaḍān. He instructed that it should be lead by a competent *ḥāfiẓ* (person who has memorised the Qur'ān), so in this way the whole Qur'ān would be heard by the entire community of believers at least once a year.

The congregational *tarāwīḥ* that has been established by 'Umar and perpetuated by the community of Muslims after him consists of 20 *rak'ah*s of *ṣalāh*, performed two at a time. The Ḥanafī jurists state that after this is completed, the *witr* prayer should be performed in congregation (something only done at this time of year) and not left to after *tahajjud* prayer, even if this is ordinarily a better practice. It is usual for there to be a rest period between every four *rak'ah*s, which was originally used for making *ṭawāf* (circumambulation) of the Ka'bah in Makkah and performing *dhikr* in Madīnah. Some *masjid*s organise speakers for these times, while others perform a group *dū'ā'*.

How did the Blessed Messenger fast?

Allah Most High tells us:

> *In the Messenger of Allah there is a beautiful example to follow.*[9]

The life pattern of the beloved Messenger, peace and blessings be upon him, is offered as a beautiful pattern to follow. Drawing closer to Allah depends on adopting his way:

> *Say! 'If you love Allah, follow me, Allah will love you and forgive you your sins.'*[10]

So it is important for the believer to ask, 'How did he fast?' *Aḥādīth* tell us that he would prepare himself for the next day's fast by making the intention to fast in these words: *'I intend to fast tomorrow in the month of Ramaḍān.'*

He would wake up early for the *tahajjud* (night vigil) pouring out his heart in devotion and longing to be near to his Majestic Lord.

He would eat the *suḥūr* (dawn meal) and would say *'Eat the dawn meal since it is full of barakah'* (spiritual influence). He urged people to have this meal so as to make fasting easier, *'None of you should miss it even if it is a sip of water since Allah and his angels bless those who have the dawn meal.'*[11]

Physiologically, the dawn meal is very important since it provides the energy required for the morning's work. The Prophet's day would be spent in devotion, prayer, *dhikr*, service, teaching and admonishing people. He would make his prayers in the *masjid*. 'Ā'ishah, may Allah be pleased with her, the wife of the Prophet, peace and blessings be upon him, reports that 'He would strive to do good deeds during the last ten days of Ramaḍān more than any other time of the year.' From many other *aḥādīth* we learn that he would retire to the *masjid* immersed in total remembrance of Allah. This temporary and complete dissociation from worldly affairs is known as *iʿtikāf*. Muslims around the world practice this *sunnah* by secluding themselves in the *masjid* for the last ten days of Ramaḍān.

When the time for ending the fast drew near he would pray: *'Oh Lord I fasted for you and believed in you and relied upon you and I end my fast with your food.'* He was hasty in opening the fast soon after sunset with dates and water. Once he said, *'My nation will continue to be good as long as they open their fast quickly and delay the morning meal* (within its permissable time!).'[12]

Notes

1 Narrated in *Saḥīḥ al-Bukhārī.*
2 See footnote 1, p. 101.
3 *Sūrah al-Baqarah* (Q2: 184).

4 Athar, S., *Health Concerns for Believers* (Kazi, 1995).
5 *Sūrah al-Baqarah* (Q2: 184).
6 *Sūrah al-Baqarah* (Q2: 184).
7 *Sūrah Hūd* (Q11: 114).
8 *Sūrah al-Aḥzāb* (Q33: 5).
9 *Sūrah al-Aḥzāb* (Q33: 21).
10 *Sūrah Āli ʿImrān* (Q3: 31).
11 Narrated in the *Musnad* of Aḥmad ibn Ḥanbal.
12 Narrated in the *Musnad* of Aḥmad ibn Ḥanbal.

CHAPTER 13

I'tikāf: Spiritual Retreat

Objectives of this section *to learn*:

- The meaning and virtues of *i'tikāf*.
- The three types of *i'tikāf*.
- The acts that nullify one's *i'tikāf*.
- The permissable reasons to temporarily leave *i'tikāf* (so that it is not nullified).
- The undesirable acts in *i'tikāf*.

The Meaning and Virtues of *I'tikāf*

The noun *i'tikāf* is derived from the Arabic verb *i'takafa* that means to isolate oneself, to devote oneself assiduously to a task, or, as we shall translate it, to go into retreat. In the *sharī'ah,* it means to stay in the *masjid* with the intention of worshipping Allah. The *masjid* used for this purpose should be one in which the daily prayers are established. Women can also go into retreat at home by staying in one room or in a corner of a room which is reserved for the prayer. 'Ā'ishah, may Allah be pleased with her, says:

> The Messenger, may peace and blessings be upon him, used to go into retreat during the last ten

> days of Ramaḍān, he continued this practice until he died and after him his wives used to do it.[1]

The retreat is an effective means for spiritual development since the devotee temporarily disassociates himself from worldly affairs, spending his day and night immersed in remembrance of the Allah, constantly praying, supplicating, reciting the Glorious Qur'ān and meditating. He longs and yearns to be near his Lord. This highly charged spiritual state of the devotee is graphically captured in *Zād al-Mād*:

> As the heart becomes attached to Allah Most High, one attains inner composure and equanimity. The preoccupation with the mundane things of life ceases and absorption in the eternal reality takes its place, and the state is reached in which all fears, hopes and apprehensions are superseded in the anxiety for Him and every thought and feeling is blended with the eagerness to gain His nearness. Devotion to the Almighty is inculcated instead of devotion to the world, thus it becomes the provision for the grave where there will be neither a friend nor a helper. This is the lofty purpose of *i'tikāf.*[2]

Shāh Walī Allāh comments on the value of *i'tikāf* in these words:

> *I'tikāf* in the *masjid* is a means to peace of mind and purification of the heart and it is an excellent opportunity for forging an identity with the angels and having a share in the *barakah* (spiritual benefit) of *Laylat al-Qadr* and for devoting oneself to prayer and meditation. This is a *sunnah* for the pious and virtuous slaves.

The devotee in retreat can be likened to the beggar who sits at the gates of a king's palace. He refuses to move until he is granted his wish, similarly this devotee is practically saying, 'Oh Lord! Forgive my sins for I shall not go away until I am cleansed.'

The Messenger, peace and blessings be upon him, described two benefits of *i'tikāf*:

> *The devotee is protected from committing sins and he gets the rewards of deeds like those who do them.*[3]

The first benefit of spiritual retreat is quite obvious: one is saved from sins, as being secluded for 24 hours a day in the clean environment of the *masjid*, he has no opportunity to be sinful. Secondly, his Generous Lord rewards him for deeds he is unable to perform like visiting the sick, attending a funeral, serving parents and family, as though he had done them.

The Three Types of *I'tikāf*

Obligatory (Wājib)

This is when a person takes an oath or makes a pledge that he will go into retreat for so many days if his wish is fulfilled, his illness is cured or he achieve this or that. If his pledge is fulfilled by Allah, then he must go into retreat. Unless a certain time was specified, this obligation can be fulfilled at any given period, although, as with all duties owed to Allah, the earliest possible performance is superior.

Recommended (Sunnah)

This is highly recommended for the entirety of the last 10 days in the month of Ramaḍan. It is an emphatic *sunnah* that at least one person in a locality goes into *i'tikāf*.

Desirable (Nafl)

This is whenever a person enters the *masjid* and makes the intention of a short retreat. This lasts as long as he remains inside and effectively has no minimum duration. This is an easy way of earning spiritual blessings, as the reward of all activities done in the *masjid* are multiplied. The intention of *nafl i'tikāf* is required if eating and sleeping within any *masjid* are not to be *makrūh*.

> *Note:* ▸ Fasting is a condition for the *i'tikāf* in Ramaḍān.
> ▸ For a woman to do *i'tikāf* she must be free from menstruation and post-natal bleeding.

What nullifies the *I'tikāf*?

The following things will nullify one's *i'tikāf*:

1. To leave the *masjid*: if one is doing the obligatory or *sunnah i'tikāf*, then one cannot leave the mosque except for a legitimate reason (see the section below). However, if one is doing a *nafl i'tikāf*, then it is permissible to leave the *masjid* when one likes, because there is no set limit on how long one is staying.
2. Sexual intercourse, intentionally or unintentionally, even without ejaculation. Allah says:

   > *Do not have intercourse with them [your wives] when you are in retreat at the* masjid. *These are the bounds of God, so do not go near them.*[4]

   However, while other sexual activities that cause sexual arousal do not nullify the *i'tikāf*, they are nevertheless absolutely forbidden at this time.
3. Becoming unconscious or insane nullifies the *i'tikāf*.

The Permissable Reasons to temporarily leave *I'tikāf*

Some permissible reasons to leave the *masjid* during *i'tikāf* (so it is not nullified):

1. The need to go to the toilet, do ablution, or to take a *ghusl*.

2. To go to a *jāmi' masjid* for Friday prayer if it is not held in the *masjid* in which one is staying.
3. If there is fear or danger of the *masjid* collapsing one can leave it to continue *i'tikāf* in another one.

The Undesirable Acts in *I'tikāf*

1. Silence becomes undesirable if one believes that it is an act of worship in itself. If one does not think that, but remains silent through absorption in *dhikr* and meditation, then it is not undesirable, as controlling the tongue can prevent one from great sins.
2. To bring merchandise into the *masjid* for selling. It is permissable in the *masjid* to make a contract of sale, but other kinds of business agreements are not permitted at this time.

Notes

1 Narrated in *Saḥīḥ al-Bukhārī.*
2 Ibn al-Qayyim, *Zād al-Mād.*
3 Narrated in *Sunan Ibn Mājah.*
4 *Sūrah al-Baqarah* (Q2: 187).

CHAPTER 14

Laylat al-Qadr: The Night of Power

Objectives of this section *to learn:*

- The significance of the Night of Power.
- The issues surrounding the question of when this night is.
- The wisdom in keeping the exact date of this night secret.
- What happens on this night.
- The devotions to be best performed on this night.

The Significance of the Night of Power

One of the special features of Ramaḍān is the Night of Power (or Decree). This night is one of the gifts of Allah granted to Muslims. Allah Most High says:

> *We indeed revealed it [the Qur'ān] on* Laylat al-Qadr. *And what will make you understand what* Laylat al-Qadr *is?* Laylat al-Qadr *is better than a thousand months. The angels and the* Rūḥ *[Jibrīl] descend in it*

> *by the permission of their Lord. [For every affair there is] Peace until the rising of the dawn.*[1]

Qadr means destiny, or power. Here it is possible to take both meanings. This is not an ordinary night, but that great night on which the revelation began of the unique Book that was to change the destiny, not of one tribe alone, but of all those who willingly accept its message. Here the majesty and the grandeur of that night is being described in which the Book of guidance was revealed. It is thus said that, 'to worship in this night is better than 83 years as angels and spirits continue to descend all night bringing blessings and peace.'[2]

The Messenger, peace and blessings be upon him, described its blessings in the following *ḥadīth* narrated by Anas, may Allah be pleased with him:

> When the month of Ramaḍan came, the Messenger, may Allah bless him and grant him peace, said *'A month has dawned upon you which has one night that is better than a thousand months. Whoever misses this night it is as though he has been deprived of all goodness and only the really unfortunate one is deprived.'*[3]

Indeed only the very unfortunate and unlucky person will ignore such a blessed night. A security guard will stay awake all night for a small payment, so if one can achieve the reward of 83 years of devotion in a single night, then who can afford to miss it except the unfortunate one. The fact is that in our communities there isn't always the zeal and the yearning for spiritual reward that there should be. We are used to material and immediate rewards; matters of the spirit are perhaps seem too esoteric for us to be concerned with them. The Messenger, peace and blessings be upon him, had already been promised Paradise and the highest rank of all creation called *al-maqām al-maḥmūd*, but despite all this he would stay awake long into the night standing in humility before his Lord, his feet would become swollen and his fine blood vessels would fill with blood. ʿĀ'ishah, may Allah be pleased with her, would pitifully demand:

> Why do you do this? Haven't you been promised forgiveness?

He would simply say,

> *Should I not be a grateful servant of my Lord?*

ʿUmar, may Allah be pleased with him, would return home from *ʿishā'* prayer in the *masjid* and start his night vigil till dawn. Abū Hanīfah's night prayer from *ʿishā'* until *fajr* for forty years is legendary. When someone wanted to know the secret of his power to stay awake all night he told him, 'I practise the *Sunnah* of the Prophet, peace and blessings be upon him, and I have a nap in the afternoon.'

He would sob so bitterly in his prayer that his neighbours would begin to cry too. Imām al-Shāfiʿī completed the recitation of the Qur'ān 60 times in Ramaḍān and it is reported that Ibrāhīm ibn Adham would not sleep at all during the month. So those who love their Lord can find plenty of time for Him, especially whilst immersed in the blessings of this peerless month.

When is this Night?

The Messenger, may peace and blessings be upon him, said:

> *Search for the night of power in the odd nights of the last ten days of Ramaḍān.*[4]

According to this *ḥadīth*, *Laylat al-Qadr* could be the 21st, 23rd, 25th, 27th or 29th of Ramaḍān. The Messenger, peace and blessings be upon him, went into spiritual retreat during the last 10 days of Ramaḍān, thus making sure he wouldn't miss this special night. There are many scholars who have held the opinion that it is the 27th night of Ramaḍān, while others have not been so sure. The following *ḥadīth* explains why there is a degree of uncertainty over its exact date:

> One day the Messenger came to the *masjid* to tell people the actual date of *Laylat al-Qadr.* As he entered, he saw two men quarrelling. He said, *'I came to tell you the date of* Laylat al-Qadr, *but so and so were quarrelling, and consequently the exact date will not now be disclosed. Perhaps there is some good in this for you, so search for it on the 29th, 27th and 25th.'*[5]

This *ḥadīth* makes three important points:

1. It practically illustrates the evil of in-fighting and quarrelling amongst ourselves. Because the Messenger, peace and blessings be upon him, saw these two men quarrelling he decided to withhold the date of this special night. What a great pity! The Qur'ān warns:

   > *Do not quarrel with one another, for you will lose heart and become weak.*[6]

   Bickering, debating, suspecting and plotting against one another is condemned in Islam, it has divided the *ummah* in the past and is continuing to divide the Muslims today. Ramaḍān is a month of mercy, forgiveness and generosity. We need to cultivate these positive traits and abandon those negative attitudes!
2. It demonstrates the Prophet's, peace and blessings be upon him, humility and submission to Allah's decree. *'Perhaps,'* he says, *'There is some good in this for you.'*

ṢAWM

Although he came out to tell the people the exact date, now he was ordered to keep it a secret and submitted to the Divine command.

3. Finally, the *ḥadīth* gives us hope that nonethless we can find *Laylat al-Qadr* and indicates some possible dates.

What is the Wisdom in keeping the Exact Date Secret?

As we have just mentioned, the Messenger, peace and blessings be upon him, suggested that there is some benefit in the date of *Laylat al-Qadr* not being known definitively. A part of this is the fact that people will search for this night and keep vigil for at least three nights thus earning enormous blessings, whereas if the exact date were known people would just worship on that night. Another wisdom could be that if the exact date was known then whilst the devotees would earn their reward the sinners who ignore the night would be liable for Allah's great wrath. Allah's benevolence doesn't permit such a thing, therefore the Gracious Lord decided to keep it secret.

What happens on this Night?

Anas, may Allah be pleased with him, narrates 'On *Laylat al-Qadr*, Jibrīl descends to earth with an army of angels and they bless every person who is busy in devotion.' Another *ḥadīth* says, '*The angels shake hands with the faithful*.'[7] It is also related that the angels bring down the command or *amr* on this night, which includes the decree (*qadr*) of all that will happen in the next year, hence its name.

Is there any Special Devotion on this Night?

Allah can be remembered in many ways: through *nafl* (voluntary) prayers, recitation of the Qur'ān, chanting His beautiful Names and through supplication. 'Ā'ishah, may Allah be pleased with her, asked the blessed Messenger, peace and blessings be upon him, 'What should I pray on *Laylat al-Qadr*?' He replied, '*Pray like this:*

اَللّٰهُمَّ إِنَّكَ عَفُوٌّ تُحِبُّ الْعَفْوَ فَاعْفُ عَنِّي

Oh Lord! You indeed are the Forgiver and You love forgiveness so forgive me.[8]

Notes

1 *Sūrah al-Qadr* (Q97: 1-5).
2 Quoted in Shah, Pir Mohammad Karam, *Ziā al-Qur'ān.*
3 Narrated in *Sunan Ibn Mājah*.
4 Narrated in *Saḥīḥ al-Bukhārī.*
5 Narrated in *Saḥīḥ al-Bukhārī*. Other *aḥādīth* also mention two other possible nights, the 21st and the 23rd.
6 *Sūrah al-Anfāl* (Q8: 46).
7 Narrated by Ibn al-Kathīr.
8 Narrated in the *Musnad* of Aḥmad ibn Ḥanbal.

CHAPTER 15

ʿĪd al-Fiṭr: A Time for Celebration and Charity

Objectives of this section to learn:

- Why ʿĪd is a time to celebrate and its place in the *Sunnah*.
- The almsgiving at the end of Ramaḍan: *ṣadaqah al-fiṭr*.
- To whom *ṣadaqah al-fiṭr* should be given.
- The reward of giving *ṣadaqah al-fiṭr*.
- When *ṣadaqah al-fiṭr* should be given.

A Time to celebrate

Anas, may Allah be pleased with him, reported that:

> At the time when the Messenger of Allah came to Madīnah, there were two days of festivity [each year]. He asked, *'What are these two days?'* We replied, We used to play and enjoy ourselves on these two days, during the days of ignorance. He then said, *'Allah has given you two better days, ʿĪd al-Fiṭr and ʿĪd al-Aḍḥā, in exchange for these two.'*[1]

Shāh Walī Allāh comments as follows:

> ʿĪd is the day of rejoicing, and the occasion to display the strength of the Muslims as everyone congregates for the ʿĪd assembly. The *ṣadaqah al-fiṭr* [obligatory charity due on this day] promotes this cause as well as perfecting the fast.[2]

ʿĪd al-Fiṭr, the first day of Shawwāl (the month following Ramaḍān), and ʿĪd al-Aḍḥā, the 10th of Dhū al-Ḥijjah, are the two days of celebration and festivity in Islam. The word 'ʿĪd' literally means 'the recurring happiness' since it is celebrated every year.

All religions have special days, which are designated for festival and celebration. The Christians celebrate the birth of Jesus at Christmas, the Hindus celebrate Diwali, and the Jews celebrate Yom Kippur etc. The Islamic celebration of ʿĪd has its own distinctive rituals and manners – in fact, the two ʿĪds, although sharing much in common, each have unique practices marking them out from every other day of the year. One of the most important of these is the congregation in the morning for the ʿĪd Prayer. This is a large gathering where all the local people congregate to listen to their leaders speak, pray and give thanks, all the while praising and glorifying their Lord. Also there is the payment of *ṣadaqah al-fiṭr* for the needy by all members of the household on ʿĪd al-Fiṭr and the sacrificing of an animal and its meat distributed to family, friends and the poor on ʿĪd al-Aḍḥā. Hence we notice that, even on festival days, when the mood is relaxed and one of enjoyment, the Muslim still keeps devotion to his Lord and care for others at the top of his agenda. Part of his own pleasure and happiness is to give to others.

Jabir, May Allah be pleased with him, reports:

> One day I was with the Prophet on the day of ʿĪd. We began [the day] with a congregational prayer followed by a sermon. There was neither the *adhān*,

> nor the *iqāmah*. Once the prayer was completed, he stood up and, leaning against Bilāl, he praised the Lord and glorified Him and counselled the people, reminding and urging them to obey Him. He then moved towards the women accompanied by Bilāl and told them to be God-fearing and reminded them of their duties."[3]

This *ḥadīth* clearly illustrates that the ʿĪd prayer would set the tone for the celebrations of the day.[4] The gathering and meeting of men and women in one place to listen to their leader's advice is in itself a festive event: it boosts the morale of the followers to see other brothers and sisters and an air of warmth, relationship and fellowship is created. It is interesting to learn that women also attended the ʿĪd prayers in large numbers, and the Prophet, may peace and blessings be upon him, would come and address them separately. May Allah give the communities and *imāms* of today the ability to practice this *sunnah*!

Muslims should enjoy God's favours, be happy, generous and cheerful all the time, but even more so on the days of ʿĪd. The beloved Messenger, peace and blessings be upon him, certainly has set us this example.

ʿĀ'ishah, may Allah be pleased with her, reports in the *Book of* ʿĪd that:

> The Messenger came into my apartment whilst two girls were singing the songs of war. He lay down on the mattress and covered his face. Then Abū Bakr came and he was angry with me and said, 'The flutes of the devil near the Prophet!' But the Prophet turned toward him and said 'Leave them both alone.' When he was paying no attention to them, I signalled to them and they left.[5]

Ibn al-Ḥajar comments in *Fatḥ al-Bārī* regarding this *ḥadīth* that the two girls' names were Hammāmah and Zaynab. In some other versions of the same *ḥadīth*, in addition to the two girls singing, it mentions they were playing tambourines. 'The flutes of the devil' refers to the singing and tambourines as these amusements can be a means of diversion and distraction from God's remembrance. Abū Bakr, may Allah be pleased with him, thought that the Prophet, peace and blessings be upon him, was asleep, so admonished his daughter for this intrusion. He also thought such amusements and singing were prohibited. The Prophet, peace and blessings be upon him, quickly corrected him and clarified the reason for allowing singing and tambourines – it was ʿĪd, a day for celebration.

Such activities should not be disapproved of on these days, as they are not disapproved of on wedding days. Ibn al-Ḥajar argues, however, that 'the permissibility of using tambourines on a weeding day and other festive occasions does not make other musical instruments permissible.' The *ḥadīth* also indicates towards being more generous and less strict in regard to one's family on ʿĪd days, in order to make them happy and cheerful, which is the correct *sunnah* at the times of festivals and celebrations.

These stories from the life of the Prophet, may peace and blessings be upon him, show that ʿĪd is a day of thanksgiving and praise for Allah, sharing and giving to the needy, visiting one another, being cheerful and enjoying permissable entertainment. Hammudah Abdulati makes just this point in writing about 'the proper meaning of an Islamic ʿĪd: a day of peace and thanksgiving, a day of moral victory, a day of good harvest and remarkable achievements and a day of festive remembrance. An Islamic ʿĪd is all this and much more, because it is a day of Islam and a day of God.'[6]

Almsgiving at the End of Ramaḍān: *Ṣadaqah al-Fiṭr*

Generosity is a fundamental characteristic of a Muslim and something that should increase even more in the month of Ramaḍān. Allah says:

You cannot achieve real good until you spend that which you love.[7]

Anas ibn Mālik tells the moving story of Abū Ṭalhah, may Allah be pleased with them both. Abū Ṭalhah had the largest orchard of palm trees in Madīnah which was called Bayrah. The beloved Messenger, peace and blessings be upon him, visited it quite frequently. When the above verse was revealed Abū Ṭalhah went to the Messenger of Allah, peace and blessings be upon him, and said:

> Oh Messenger, Allah has revealed that, *'You cannot achieve real good until you spend that which you love'* and I love my orchard Bayrah the most. I want to donate it in order to see Allah's reward and pleasure. The Messenger, peace and blessings be upon him, was very pleased and said, *'I've heard what you have said, go and distribute it amongst your close relatives.'* Abū Ṭalhah went away and distributed it amongst his cousins.[8]

On the day of ʿĪd al-Fiṭr , immediately following Ramaḍān, there is a special obligatory (*wājib*) almsgiving that should be made by all Muslims with enough wealth to be liable for *zakāh* (i.e. the *niṣāb* as defined in chapter 9). The wisdom of this *ṣadaqah al-fiṭr* includes the fact that it helps the needy and poor to join in the celebration of ʿĪd; that it acts as a kind of atonement for any shortcomings in a person's worship throughout the month that has just passed; and of course that it earns his Lord's Grace and Pleasure on this auspicious day.

To Whom should Ṣadaqah al-Fiṭr be given?

The most deserving recepients of this charity, like *zakāh*, include one's own family, the needy and the orphan, providing they are poor or destitute.

Abū ʿAbdullāh ibn Thawbān, may Allah be pleased with him the beloved Messenger, peace and blessings be upon him said:

> *The best dīnār is the one spent on one's family and the one spent on one's means of transport and the one spent on one's friends in Allah's path.*[9]

The Messenger of Allah, peace and blessings be upon him, once asked:

> *Shall I not tell you who deserves to enter Paradise? All those who are weak and needy – if they were to invoke Allah, Allah would grant them their needs.*[10]

The Reward of Almsgiving for the Sake of Allah

Sahl ibn Saʿd, may Allah be pleased with him, says the blessed Messenger, peace and blessings be upon him, said, '*The sponsor and guardian of an orphan and I will be like this in Paradise,*' and he indicated with his index and middle finger.[11]

Abū Hurairah, may Allah be pleased with him says, the beloved Prophet, peace and blessings be upon him, said,

> *The person who sponsors the needy and the widows will be like the one who does* jihād *in the path of Allah.*[12]

Abū Dardā, may Allah be pleased with him, reported him as saying,

> *Seek one [to help] amongst the weak people, [for] it is because of them that you earn victory and sustenance.*[13]

When should it be given?

In general, it is meritorious to give *ṣadaqah* at any time, although additional rewards are obtained due to the blessing of the month. *Ṣadaqah al-fiṭr* should be paid before praying the ʿĪḍ prayer, as has already been mentioned. Its amount is explained in the following *ḥadīth*:

> ʿUmar, may Allah be pleased with him, says the Messenger, peace and blessings be upon him, ordered us to pay *zakāh al-fiṭr*, or give either one *ṣāʿ* (1.1kg) of dates or one *ṣāʿ* of barley for every member of our family, old and young alike.[14]

The current value of one *ṣāʿ* (1.1kg) of dates or barley is approximately £1.50. The head of the household has to pay this amount for each dependant member of his household – even for the child born on the same day. If possible, it should be paid as early as possible in Ramaḍān so that the needy could also prepare for their ʿĪd. People in richer countries often take their blessings for granted and cannot imagine that many Muslim families in other parts of the world will not even get a two-course meal for ʿĪd, let alone a new set of clothes.

In the luxury of our homes we seldom remember the orphans, the sick, the widows and the ailing elderly. By imposing *ṣadaqah al-fiṭr* , Allah and His blessed Messenger, peace and blessings be upon him, want us to share our wealth with these deprived people so they too can celebrate and rejoice.

Notes

1 Narrated in *Sunan Abī Dawūd.*
2 Quoted from al-Dihlawī, Shāh Walī Allāh, *Ḥujjat Allāh al-Bālighah,*
3 Narrated in *Sunan al-Nisāʾī.*
4 The rules for ʿĪd prayers, including the *sunnahs* to be practised on the day are to be found in Chapter 7.
5 Narrated in *Saḥīḥ al-Bukhārī.*
6 Abdulati, H., *Islam in Focus,* (El-Falah Foundation, 1997), pp. 146-7.
7 *Sūrah Āl ʿImrān* (Q3: 92).
8 Narrated in *Saḥīḥ al-Bukhārī.*
9 Narrated in *Saḥīḥ Muslim.*
10 Narrated in *Saḥīḥ al-Bukhārī.*
11 Narrated in *Saḥīḥ al-Bukhārī.*
12 Narrated in *Saḥīḥ al-Bukhārī.*
13 Narrated in *Sunan Abī Dawūd.*
14 Narrated in *Saḥīḥ al-Bukhārī.*

5th
Pillar

ḤAJJ

(The Pilgrimage)

On the Path of Divine Love

CHAPTER 16

The Meaning and Significance of *Ḥajj*

Ḥajj – A Journey Back to Our Roots

A tree stands firm if its roots are sunk deep in the earth – then even the strongest storms and gale-force winds cannot break it.

A man too 'stands firm if his roots are well sunk in one place ... his own particular location, his property, his home. These things are like extensions of his own body; stripped of them he is a tortoise without its shell – a flayed, pulpy creature, and a ready prey for the predators.'[1]

Likewise, the soul too needs a home, a place of rest, and its own roots. Where is this located? Before we answer this let us go back in history and look at the man after whom we derive our title of 'Millah Ibrāhīm' (Nation of Ibrāhīm). The Prophet Ibrāhīm, may peace be upon him, the great patriarch looked up to by the Jews, Christians and Muslims, is referred to in the glorious Qur'ān as follows:

> *Indeed , Ibrāhīm was a man who combined within himself all virtues, devoutly obeying God's will, turning away from all that is false, and not being of those who ascribe divinity to aught beside God.*[2]

He wandered in the fertile valley of Bakkah hemmed in on all sides by the rugged black mountains of Faran. He was attracted by this site, and witnessed Divine manifestations here. In fact, if we are to go further back to pre-history – the Adamic descent from Paradise – tradition tells us that the first man and woman met near here at ʿArafah.

In his life, which was one of pivotal importance for the history of human beings on Earth, Ibrāhīm, may peace be upon him, prayed to Allah to bless this valley with safety and abundant sustenance. It is said that upon hearing the following Divine command, Ibrāhīm, may peace be upon him, stood on the mountain and proclaimed the *ḥajj*:

> *Make a proclamation of* ḥajj *(pilgrimage) to mankind: they will come to you on foot and on lean camels from every distant quarter, so that they may witness the benefits which are made available here for them; and (they will) pronounce the Name of Allah over the cattle which We have provided as food for them on the appointed days, then eat meat themselves and feed the indigent and needy.*
>
> *Then let them complete the rites prescribed for them, perform their vows, and (again) circumambulate the Ancient House. Such (is the pilgrimage): whoever honours the sacred rites of Allah, for him it is good in the sight of his Lord."*[3]

But who heard him? There where no shepherds, no caravans, and no nomads. Who heard the cry of the Prophet Ibrāhīm? *Every single human soul.* But not every human soul heeded his proclamation – only the blessed souls in their primordial state answered back *'Labbayk'*, yes we have heard and accepted the invitation.

Thus the souls of the pilgrims are urging them to fulfill the promise that they had made in their primordial state, as though the soul is saying, 'Go back to your roots, stay connected and linked with them.'

No wonder the Messenger, may Allah bless him and grant him pace, urged Muslims to hasten to perform the *ḥajj* as soon as they are capable of it, spurring the souls to return to that place of Divine manifestations and blessings where Ibrāhīm had lived. The visiting of this sacred place guarantees freedom from the burden of sins. *'He returns home'* the *ḥadīth* tells us, *'like a newborn child, sinless and pure.'*

The utterance of the chorus, 'I am here Lord! I am here Lord!' is the song of submission – a pledge of loyalty, obedience and proclamation of love. The pilgrim carefully treks the path trodden by Ibrāhīm, may Allah grant him peace, following his journey of sacrifice, reminiscing about that most heroic sacrifice that a young boy, Ismā'īl, may Allah be pleased with him, volunteered to make for the pleasure of his mighty Lord.

Ḥajj is about honouring, remembering and visiting these sites trodden by great men, the chosen ones, thus demonstrating with one's wealth, body and spirit that one is a true Muslim. Indeed, the Messenger is reported to have said, *'Whosoever dies without performing the* ḥajj *(and he was able to do it) let him die as a Jew or a Christian.'*

The *ḥajj* teaches us to live simply, frugally, spend in moderation and to avoid arrogance. Moreover it is a renewal of the covenant with our Lord. It is also an opportunity to see the diversity of the *ummah*, the unity of the Muslims from all over the world, and the equality of the rich and poor, big and small in these simple and timeless rituals.

Whenever he prays, the Muslim turns his face towards the sacred Ka'bah in Makkah. Five times a day he should imagine himself in front of this most ancient House of God, his heart full of yearning to see it with his own eyes. He waits and prepares himself for this majestic encounter. By praying, giving *zakāh* and fasting, he is making the preparation for a journey of a lifetime. Eventually he is called to his Lord.

We shall look at the detailed *fiqh* rulings about how to perform this journey, as well as where and when to go. But first let us look at why the faithful have to embark on this arduous and expensive journey. This is a spiritual journey with manifold religious, social and political values.

Firstly, the pilgrimage is an outward confirmation of the commitment of the believer to God and that he is always ready to forsake his worldly interests for His pleasure. The pilgrimage is performed in the Holy Land of the Ḥijāz, the birthplace of the beloved Messenger, may Allah bless him and grant him peace, and the cradle of Islam. Many of the *ḥajj* rituals are re-enactments of momentous events. So *ḥajj* thus provides an opportunity to learn about the harsh environment in which Islam took root. Visiting these historical places gives inspiration and deepens one's faith in the truth of Islam.

Some of the *ḥajj* rituals, like the sacrifice of an animal and the stoning the *shayṭāns*, are a means of reliving or commemorating the actions of Ibrāhīm and Ismā'īl, may peace be upon them. *Ḥajj* is a show of unity, brotherhood and equality of all mankind, where class, language and colour barriers disappear. All dressed in two white cloths, all chanting the same words and all together for one reason: to please their Lord.

Ḥajj is not a holiday in a far-off place. It is a demanding course of spiritual and moral enrichment, including opportunities to learn new experiences and see brothers and sisters in faith from all over the globe.

The Spiritual Benefits and Importance of *Ḥajj*

In view of these tremendous blessings of *ḥajj*, the Messenger, may Allah bless him and grant him peace, urged the Muslims to undertake this auspicious journey. Abū Hurayrah, may Allah be pleased with him, reports the Messenger God saying, '*Whoever performs the pilgrimage for the sake of Allah and does not sin whilst performing it, returns home cleansed of all sins like the day he was born from his mother's womb.*'[4] On another occasion he, may Allah bless him and grant him peace, enlightened the companions about the enormous reward of *ḥajj* with these words: '*The only fitting reward for a* ḥajj *properly done* ḥajj *is Paradise.*'[5] Once he honoured the pilgrim by likening him to a guest of Allah, saying, *'There are three guests of God, the* mujāhid *(warrior) and the person doing* ḥajj *and* 'umrah.'[6] Explaining the reason for doing *ḥajj*, he said, *"Do not delay performing* ḥajj *and* 'umrah *since* ḥajj *and* 'umrah *remove sins and poverty like the furnace which purifies the iron and cleanses gold and silver of contaminants.'*[7] 'Ā'ishah, may Allah be pleased with her, the beloved wife of the Messenger, may Allah bless him and grant him peace, once sought permission to take part in *jihād* (holy war) and he said to her, 'Ḥajj *is your* jihād.'[8]

'Abd Allāh ibn 'Abbās, may Allah be pleased with him, reports that a man came to the Messenger, may Allah bless him and grant him peace, and said, 'My mother had pledged to do *ḥajj* but she has died.' The Messenger asked him, *'If she had a loan would you repay that on her behalf?'* He said, 'Yes.' He told him, *'Now repay God's loan, this is more important.'*[9]

'Abd Allāh ibn 'Abbās, may Allah be pleased with him, reports the blessed Messenger, may Allah bless him and grant him peace, said: *'Do not sit with other women in seclusion and women should not travel alone without the company of a* maḥram (unmarriagable kin).' At that point one of the companions said 'I have been ordered to go on so and so expedition and my wife has just left for the *ḥajj*.' The Messenger, may Allah bless him and grant him peace said, *'Go and join your wife to do the* ḥajj.'[10]

During *ḥajj*, the many millions of Muslims from all over the world meet in one place. This is the largest gathering of its kind in the world, where people of different races, colours and languages worship Allah together and live as brothers and sisters. *Ḥajj* is full of *barakah*, blessings such as:

- *Ḥajj* gives Muslims the opportunity to concentrate on Allah for a number of days, putting aside material concerns which often make people forget their duties to Allah.
- It helps Muslims to remain conscious that they are always in the presence of Allah, who sees all creatures, at all times, though we do not see Him.

- The walk between Ṣafā and Marwah symbolises the desire and eagerness of the humble servant towards his Master.
- It reminds Muslims of the need to fight the temptations of *Shayṭān* in all their various forms, to the best of their ability, as did the Prophet Ibrāhīm, may peace be upon him. This is represented by the act of pelting the *Shayṭān*, which symbolises success in routing the devil's incitements.
- It teaches patience, perseverance and forgiveness since arguments, insults and petty worldly matters are forbidden during *ḥajj*.
- It promotes equality and unity as the pilgrims wear a dress of two sheets which all look alike, say the same prayers in the same language, and do many other things to complete their *ḥajj* in the same way, despite differences of race, colour, country, language and social status.
- The gathering on ʿArafah reminds Muslims of the resurrection when all human beings will be assembled before Allah for judgement.
- The concentration of spiritual and emotional energy leads to love and unity.
- The meat from the animals sacrificed is sent to help poor Muslims across the world.

Notes

1 Eaton, G., *King of the Castle* (The Islamic Texts Society, 1990), p. 43.
2 *Sūrah al-Nahl*, (Q16: 120).
3 *Sūrah al-Ḥajj*, (Q22: 27-30).
4 Narrated in *Saḥīḥ Muslim.*
5 Narrated in *Saḥīḥ al-Bukhārī.*
6 Narrated in *Sunan al-Nisāʾī.*
7 Narrated in *Sunan al-Tirmidhī.*
8 Narrated in *Saḥīḥ Muslim.*
9 Narrated in *Saḥīḥ al-Bukhārī.*
10 Narrated in *Saḥīḥ al-Bukhārī.*

CHAPTER 17

An Overview of the *Ḥajj*: Rules and Conditions

Objectives of this section to learn:

- The three types of *ḥajj*.
- On whom *ḥajj* is obligatory.
- The conditions for performing the *ḥajj*.
- The rules for performing *ḥajj* on the behalf of somebody else.
- The five days of *ḥajj* in brief.
- The conditions for the soundness of *ḥajj*.
- The obligatory (*farḍ*) rites of *ḥajj*.
- The necessary (*wājib*) rites of *ḥajj*.

The Types of *Ḥajj*

There are three ways of performing *ḥajj*:

1. *Ḥajj al-Ifrād* (Single) – this means entering into *iḥrām* only for the *ḥajj* and taking it off only on the day of sacrifice.
2. *Ḥajj al-Qirān* (Combined) – this means entering into *iḥrām* for both *'umrah* and *ḥajj* at the same time and not taking it off until the day of sacrifice at Minā. In

Ḥajj al-Qirān one has to stick to the restrictions of *iḥrām* for a longer period of time.

3. *Ḥajj al-Tamattuʿ* (Interrupted) – in this way, you first perform *ʿumrah*, and then take of the *iḥrām* and wear normal clothes. On the 8th of Dhū al-Ḥijjah, the *iḥrām* is then worn again for the days of *ḥajj*. The procedure for performing the *ʿumrah* is shown in Chapter 20.

On Whom is *Ḥajj* Obligatory?

Every Islamic act of worship has three requirements: Islam, maturity and sanity.

In addition to these three requirements, *ḥajj* becomes compulsory when the following condition is met:

- Affordability – an individual having the financial means to travel and stay in Makkah and leaving sufficient provisions for one's dependants.

> *Note:* *Ḥajj* is only obligatory once in a person's lifetime and after being successfully completed this obligation is discharged.

The Conditions for the Performance of *Ḥajj*

The following conditions must also be fulfilled before *ḥajj* can be performed:

1. Health – an individual undertaking *ḥajj* must be well enough to be able to withstand the strains that it puts on the physical body.
2. Security of route – such that one's life and wealth are safe.
3. A woman must be accompanied by her husband or a *maḥram* (if the period of travelling is more than three days) – a *maḥram* is a male member of the family whom she is not allowed to marry under the *sharīʿah*. However, a women can travel in the company of other trustworthy women if she has no *maḥram* (according to an opinion of the Mālikī and Shāfiʿī schools of jurisprudence).

When these conditions are fulfilled then *ḥajj* becomes compulsory that same year. To delay *ḥajj* unnecessarily is very sinful. If someone met the conditions above, having had the means to go, but died before fulfilling this duty, he would be responsible for not performing a *farḍ* action.

Performing *Ḥajj* on the Behalf of Somebody Else

If a person is financially capable of affording *ḥajj* but is permanently disabled or severely ill, he can send someone else to do it on his behalf. In this case he has to pay for all his expenses, including travelling, accommodation and food. Similarly all penalties incurred will be paid by the sender. If someone has written in his will that *ḥajj* should be performed on his behalf, then if one third of his inheritance suffices for *ḥajj* expenses then it will performed. However, if this amount is not sufficient then his will shall not be executed until the heirs agree to provide the balance. If a person dies without doing one *ḥajj* and without leaving a will for *ḥajj* he has sinned as mentioned above. His heirs may still perform *ḥajj* on his behalf.

The Five Days of *Ḥajj* in Brief

Before we explain the rules of *ḥajj*, here is a brief overview of the sequence of events, so we can orient ourselves to this unique set of rituals.

- Day One (8th Dhū al-Ḥijjah) – The *imām* of Masjid al-Ḥarām gives a sermon after *maghrib* on the 7th Dhū al-Ḥijjah in which he outlines the rites of *ḥajj*. After the sermon, people start leaving Makkah for Minā. They stay in Minā for the whole of the 8th Dhū al-Ḥijjah.
- Day Two (9th Dhū al-Ḥijjah) – After sunrise, pilgrims go to ʿArafah. They pray *ẓuhr* and *ʿaṣr* combined and remain at ʿArafah till sunset. Then after sunset they make their way back to Minā via Muzdalifah, where they pray *maghrib* and *ʿishā'* together.

- Day Three (10th Dhū al-Ḥijjah) – Yawm al-Naḥr. After praying *fajr* at Muzdalifah the pilgrims return to Minā. Four important rites of *ḥajj* are carried out: stoning the *shayṭāns*, sacrifice of an animal, trimming hair or shaving the head and revisiting the Kaʿbah.
- Day Four (11th of Dhū al-Ḥijjah) – The *shayṭāns* are pelted and the night is spent at Minā. The time for stoning is after midday until sunset.
- Day Five (12th of Dhū al-Ḥijjah) – The *shayṭāns* are pelted and the pilgrims can now return to Makkah for their farewell *ṭawāf*.

> *Note:* If a person travelling to *ḥajj* arrives and stays in Makkah for less than fifteen days before the days of *ḥajj*, then he will be considered a *musāfir* (traveller) during it and will have to do *qaṣr* of *ṣalāh*, which means that four *rakʿah farḍ* prayers will be shortened to two *rakʿahs*. If he prays behind an *imām* who is not a *musāfir*, however, he will follow him in all four *rakʿahs*.

The Five Days of Ḥajj

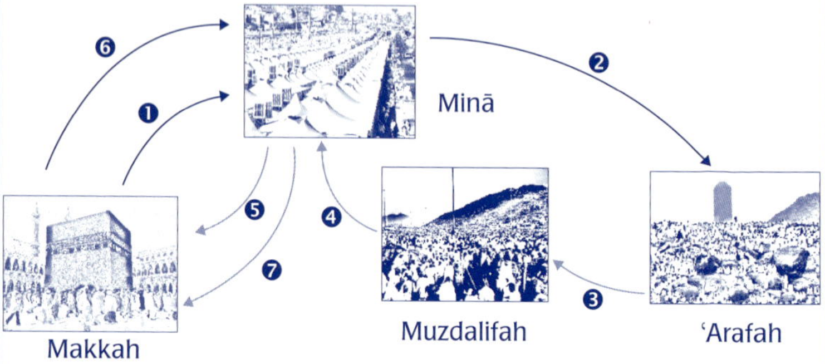

1. Leave Makkah for Minā on the 8th Dhū al-Ḥijjah.
2. Leave Minā for ʿArafah on the 9th Dhū al-Ḥijjah.
3. Leave ʿArafah for Muzdalifah on the 9th Dhū al-Ḥijjah after sunset.
4. Leave Muzdalifah for Minā on the 10th Dhū al-Ḥijjah before sunrise.
5. Leave Minā for Makkah on either the 10th, 11th or 12th Dhū al-Ḥijjah and perform *ṭawāf al-ziyārah or al-ifāḍah*.
6. Leave Makkah for Minā and complete *ramy*.
7. Leave Minā for Makkah. Perform *ṭawāf al-wadāʿ* and then depart for home.

The Conditions for the Soundness of *Ḥajj*

These three conditions must be fully met by anyone seeking Divine pleasure through the *ʿibādāt* of *ḥajj*.

1. To wear the *iḥrām*, which includes the *niyyah* (intention) and *talbiyah* (special *dhikr*).
2. To do this in the times that have been specified for *ḥajj*.
3. To not have sexual intercourse with one's spouse before the stay at ʿArafah.

The Obligatory (*Farḍ*) Rites of *Ḥajj*

These obligatory (*farḍ*) rites of *ḥajj* make the *ḥajj* invalid if omitted:

1. Staying at ʿArafah, even if only for a brief moment.
2. *Ṭawāf al-ziyārah or al-ifāḍah*. This is the revisiting of the Kaʿbah and circumambulating it after staying at ʿArafah. This can be performed anytime from *fajr* on the 10th of Dhū al-Ḥijjah.

The Necessary (*Wājib*) Rites of *Ḥajj*

These necessary (*wājib*) rites of *ḥajj* are integral to its soundness. If they are ommited a *damm* (sacrifice of atonement) is required by way of penalty.

1. Wearing *iḥrām* from the Mīqāt boundaries.
2. Staying (*wuqūf*) at ʿArafah until sunset (on 9th Dhū al-Ḥijjah).
3. To stay in Muzdalifah, even if for a moment, between the beginning of *fajr* time and the sunrise of 10th Dhū al-Ḥijjah.
4. *Ramy* – Stoning the *shayṭāns*.
5. *Qurbānī* – Sacrificing a sheep, goat or taking a seventh part in the sacrifice of a large animal (cow or camel)

in *Ḥajj al-Tamattuʿ* or *Ḥajj al-Qirān* after *ramy* but before *ḥalq/qaṣr*.

6. *Ḥalq* or *qaṣr* – Shaving the head or trimming locks of hair after *ramy* and *qurbānī*.
7. Performing *ṭawāf al-ziyārah or al-ifāḍah* during the 'days of sacrifice', i.e. 10th-12th Dhū al-Ḥijjah.
8. *Saʿy* – Running between Ṣafā and Marwah seven times in the months of *ḥajj*.
9. To do the farewell *ṭawāf*: *ṭawāf al-wadāʿ/al-ṣadar*.
10. To abandon everything prohibited by *iḥrām*.

CHAPTER 18

The Rites of *Ḥajj*: Meaning and Practice

Objectives of this section to learn:

- The meaning and practice of *iḥrām* – the state of sanctity.
- The meaning and practice of *wuqūf* – the staying at ʿArafah.
- The meaning and practice of *ṭawāf* – circumambulation around the Kaʿbah.
- The meaning and practice of *saʿy* – running between Ṣafā and Marwah.
- The meaning and practice of *ramy* – the stoning of the *shayṭāns*.
- The meaning and practice of *qurbānī* – the sacrifice.
- The meaning and practice of *ḥalq/qaṣr* – the shaving/cutting of the hair.
- The *jināyāt* – *ḥajj* offences and their penalties.

Iḥrām – The State of Sanctity

The literal meaning of *iḥrām* is 'to make *ḥarām*' (forbidden). When a pilgrim dresses in the *iḥrām*, makes a *niyyah* (intention) of *ḥajj* (and/or *'umrah*) and utters the *talbiyah*, certain usually *ḥalāl* (permissable) things become *ḥarām* for him.

The spiritual significance of *iḥrām* is that the pilgrim entering into a state of sanctity for the sake of Allah, in which there is a much stricter set of ritual observances in obedience to Him. This practice leads the individual to a more simple and less wordly state of being in which ideally every moment is transformed into worship. Also, the *iḥrām* emphasises the unitary nature of the Muslim *ummah* as people from every kind of background wear an identical garment.

The Talbiyah

لَبَّيْكَ اللَّهُمَّ لَبَّيْكَ لَبَّيْكَ لَا شَرِيْكَ لَكَ لَبَّيْكَ إِنَّ الْحَمْدَ وَالنِّعْمَةَ لَكَ وَالْمُلْكَ لَا شَرِيْكَ لَكَ

Here I am at Your service, Oh Allah! Here I am. Here I am at Your service and You have no partner! To You alone is all Praise, all Bounty and Sovereignty! You have no partner!

The *talbiyah* is the sweet chorus of the pilgrims, which they recite constantly. It is the response to the call of the Prophet Ibrāhīm to establish the *ḥajj* and its continual echoing around the valleys in which the pilgrimage takes place is a re-affirmation of the primordial covenant established between Allah and the souls of humanity.

All around Makkah there are boundaries, called the Mīqāt, and the pilgrim must wear the *iḥrām* before entering these boundaries. These boundaries are shown below:

The Mīqāt Boundaries

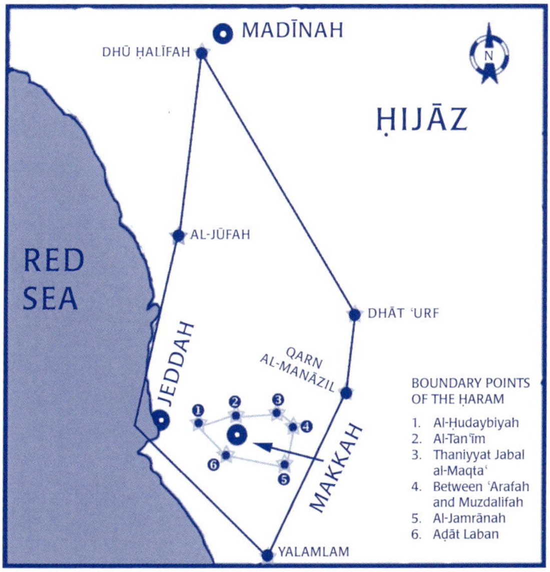

How to enter into Iḥrām

The pilgrim must be wearing *iḥrām*, before crossing the Mīqāt. The combined action (*niyyah* and *talbiyah*) is called *iḥrām*. The two sheets that a pilgrim wears are figuratively also known as *iḥrām* but the real *iḥrām* is to be found in the *niyyah* and *talbiyah*.

If someone wears these two sheets and does not declare his intention and utter *talbiyah*, he does not become a *muḥrim* (person in *iḥrām*) . That is why, before his *niyyah* and *talbiyah*, he can cover his head during two *rak'ahs* of *nafl* prayer, an act which is not allowed in the real state of *iḥrām*.

The *iḥrām* is simply two pieces of cloth: one for wrapping around the waist so that it covers the lower part of the body, the second piece is for the upper part of the body. Only sandals should be worn which leave the top of the feet bare, the head should also remain uncovered. Women wear their normal clothes, although the hands, feet and face should remain uncovered.

Before wearing the *iḥrām*, one should cut one's nails, trim one's hair and shave the hair from the private parts, and then have a bath before putting it on.

After wearing the *iḥrām*, it is *sunnah* to pray two units of *sunnah* al-*iḥrām*. Now make the intention for *ḥajj* or *'umrah* and then recite the *talbiyah*.

Forbidden Activities during Iḥrām

Whilst wearing the *iḥrām*, the pilgrim must avoid these activities:

1. Clipping nails, cutting, combing or pulling out hair
2. To use perfume or anything which contains fragrance
3. Hunting
4. Quarrelling or using obscene language
5. To have sexual relations
6. The male must not wear sewn garments, even underwear, gloves or socks

Note: 1. It is permissible to use an umbrella to get shade and to have a bath to cool oneself.
2. There are penalties to be paid for breaking the sanctity of *iḥrām* and for various other errors made during *ḥajj*. These usually take the form of a specific amount of *ṣadaqah* (almsgiving to the poor), or a *damm* (sacrificial atonement). See specific instances in Chapter 17, or the section on *jināyāt* (offences) for details.

'Arafah – Preparation for the Day of Judgement

This means going to 'Arafah and staying there whether asleep or awake, sitting or standing, walking or stationary. The time of stay must be between midday and sunset on 9th Dhū al-Ḥijjah.

This ritual, in which the pilgrims stand for hours under the beating sun, represents the long wait for judgement that will take place on Yawm al-Qiyāmah (literally the Day of Standing). The pilgrim should supplicate sincerely to his Gracious Lord in these hours, mindful that He may choose to lessen the wait on the future Plains of Judgement for whosoever He wishes and permit entry into Paradise. Allah Most High says:

> *Then when you pour down from (Mount) ʿArafah, celebrate the praises of Allah at the Sacred Monument, and celebrate His praises as He has directed you, even though before this, you went astray.*[1]

The Sunnahs of staying at ʿArafah

1. To have a bath
2. For the *imām* to deliver two sermons
3. To combine the *ẓuhr* and *ʿaṣr* prayers
4. To not fast
5. To be in a state of *wuḍūʾ*
6. To concentrate on supplicating to Allah Most High
7. To stay near the 'black rocks' where the Messenger, may Allah bless him and grant him peace, stood. If that is not possible then one should stay as close as one can.
8. To raise and spread open the hands whilst supplicating

Ṭawāf – Turning around the Spiritual Pivot of the World

Ṭawāf consists of seven circuits of the Kaʿbah, beginning each time at the Black Stone (al-Ḥajar al-Aswad). It is significant that Muslims always pray towards this House of Allah from every corner of the Earth. The pilgrim should be mindful of the reality that he is at the epicentre of all this worship and understand the symbolic and spiritual power of his act. Even as our planet circles the Sun and the electrons in the atoms that make up our bodies circle their nucleuses,[2] so we too as spiritual beings are called to perform a special type of orbit in glorification of our Creator. This is the *ṭawāf*. Allah, Almighty, says:

> *Behold! We gave the site, to Ibrāhīm, of the (Sacred) House (saying): "Associate not any thing (in worship)*

with Me; and sanctify My House for those who circle around it, or stand up, or bow, or prostrate themselves (therein in prayer).[3]

The Wājibāt (*Necessary Aspects*) *of* Ṭawāf:

1. To begin the *ṭawāf* from the Black Stone such that the Ka'bah is on the left-hand side and to proceed around seven times anti-clockwise.
2. For the *'awrah* (private parts) to be covered. This is from the navel to the knee for men and everything except the face, hands and feet for women.
3. Not to enter the Ḥatīm since it counts as part of the Ka'bah. The Ḥatīm is is the horse-shoe shaped wall by one side of the Ka'bah.
4. To walk during the *ṭawāf*, unless unable to. The disabled can use a wheelchair or a stretcher.
5. To pray two *rak'ah*s of prayer after the seven circuits have been completed. Preferably behind the station (*maqām*) of Ibrāhīm, may peace be upon him.
6. To be in a state of *wuḍū'* and not to be in need of a bath. Some jurists have said this is a *sunnah*. In any case, if *ṭawāf* is done without *wuḍū'*, then *ṣadaqah* must be given.

The Sunnahs of Ṭawāf:

1. To wear the upper part of the *iḥrām* such that it covers the left shoulder only and passes under the right armpit.
2. To march briskly in the first three circuits only. This involves taking small strides and moving the shoulders as well.
3. To kiss the Black Stone at the end of each circuit. If this is not possible due to overcrowding then raising both hands towards it is sufficient. It is disliked to push one's way through towards the Black Stone, as it is against the whole spirit of *ḥajj* to push or jostle fellow *ḥajjīs*.

How to perform the Ṭawāf

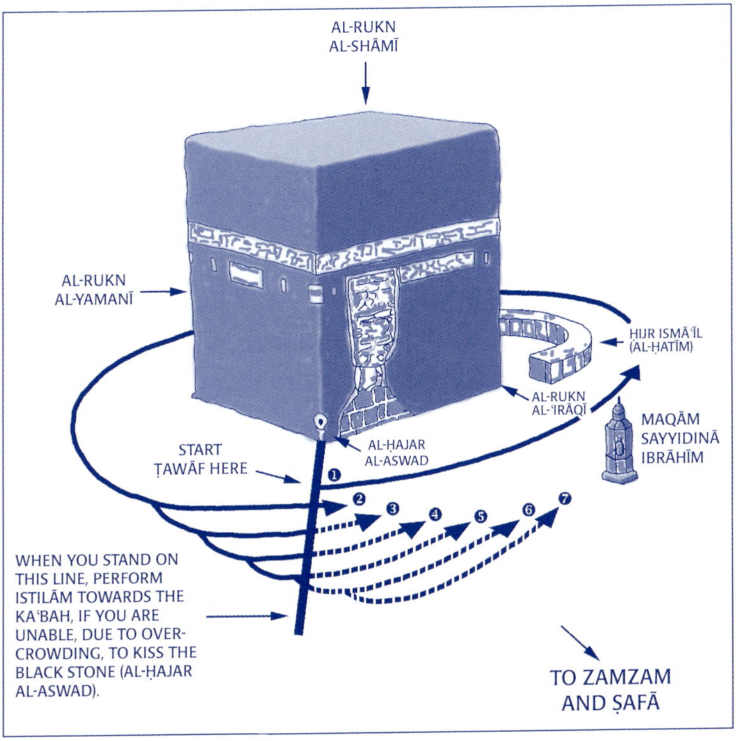

Saʿy – Running between Ṣafā and Marwah

The literal meaning of *saʿy* is 'to run' and 'to make effort', but in the context of *ḥajj* and *ʿumrah*, it refers to the ritual walking back and forth seven times between the hillocks of Ṣafā and Marwah which are situated to the south and north of the Kabʿah respectively. Now there are only signs of these hillocks and the whole route between them is enclosed in a long gallery.

Saʿy has a historical background. Prophet Ibrāhīm, peace be upon him, left his wife Hajrah and infant son Ismāʿīl in the wilderness of Makkah at the command of Allah. The mother and son lived for five days on the food and water they had. When the water was completely finished, the mother ran frantically seven times between the hillocks of Ṣafā and Marwah in search of water for her son. Suddenly the spring of Zamzam gushed miraculously forth near the feet of the young Prophet Ismāʿīl. *Saʿy* is included in the rites of *ḥajj* and *ʿumrah* to commemorate this event of the search and struggle of a loving mother.

It is necessary (*wājib*) for the completion of *ḥajj*.

The Wājibāt *of* Saʿy

1. To perform *saʿy* after the *ṭawāf*, not before it.
2. Starting *saʿy* from Ṣafā and finishing it at Marwah.
3. Completing all seven trips.
4. To perform it on foot, unless one has an excuse, in which case it can be made riding. Thus the disabled may use their wheelchairs and so on.
5. During the *saʿy* of *ʿumrah*, it is obligatory to be in the state of *iḥrām*. One must also be in *iḥrām* for the *saʿy* performed after the *ṭawāf* of arrival (*qudūm*) in *ḥajj*, but it is a *sunnah* to perform the *saʿy* after the *ṭawāf* of visiting (*ziyārah*) in ordinary clothes. *Saʿy* is performed only once during *ḥajj*, either after the *ṭawāf* of arrival (*qudūm*) or, better, the *ṭawāf* of visiting (*ziyārah*).

The Sunnahs of Saʿy

1. To be in a state of *wuḍūʾ* and free from all impurities. As this is not *wājib*, women during their menstruation can perform *saʿy*, although they are not allowed to enter al-Masjid al-Harām, pray *ṣalāh* or perform *ṭawāf*. They can enter the place of *saʿy* from the outside entrance.
2. To climb the hillocks of Ṣafā and Marwah and, facing the Kaʿbah, raise the hands for prayer.
3. To march more briskly between the two green lights.
4. To glorify, supplicate and praise Allah, as well as sending blessings on His Messenger, may Allah bless him and grant him peace.

5. To kiss the Black Stone before leaving for Ṣafā.
6. To start *sa'y* immediately after *ṭawāf*. As this is not *wājib*, if *sa'y* is delayed for some reason, there is no penalty.

> *Note:* It is *makrūh* to do business during the performance of *sa'y*, but one can talk if the need arises.

How to perform Sa'y

To perform *sa'y*, begin with the *istilām* of the Black Stone (al-Ḥajar al-Aswad). This is the raising of both hands towards al-Hajar al-Aswad so that the palms are facing it. Then say:

بِسْمِ اللهِ، وَالْحَمْدُ للهِ، وَلَا إِلٰهَ إِلَّا اللهُ، وَاللهُ أَكْبَرُ

In the name of Allah, all Praise is for Allah, there is no god but Allah, and Allah is the Greatest.

Now proceed towards Ṣafā, begin to climb it and make the intention (*niyyah*) for *sa'y*:

اَللّٰهُمَّ إِنِّيْ أُرِيْدُ السَّعْيَ بَيْنَ الصَّفَا وَالْمَرْوَةِ فَيَسِّرْهُ لِيْ وَتَقَبَّلْهُ مِنِّيْ سَبْعَةَ أَشْوَاطٍ للهِ تَعَالىٰ عَزَّ وَجَلَّ

Oh Allah! I intend to perform sa'y *between Ṣafā and Marwah seven times for Your sake. Make it easy for me and accept it from me.*

Now recite:

إِنَّ ٱلصَّفَا وَٱلْمَرْوَةَ مِن شَعَآئِرِ ٱللَّهِ فَمَنْ حَجَّ ٱلْبَيْتَ أَوِ ٱعْتَمَرَ فَلَا جُنَاحَ عَلَيْهِ أَن يَطَّوَّفَ بِهِمَا وَمَن تَطَوَّعَ خَيْرًا فَإِنَّ ٱللَّهَ شَاكِرٌ عَلِيمٌ

Behold! Ṣafā and Marwah are among the symbols of Allah. So anyone who performs ḥajj *or* ʿumrah *to the House, there is no blame if one goes around both of them; and anyone who does good voluntarily should know that surely Allah is Responsive, All-Knowing.*[4]

After this, climb Ṣafā to the point from where you can see the Kaʿbah, then facing it, raise your hands in supplication and say *'Allāhu Akbar'* three times and ask Allah for whatever you wish.

Now proceed towards Marwah. Come down from Ṣafā and move towards Marwah while reciting this supplication:

سُبْحَانَ اللهِ، وَالْحَمْدُ للهِ، وَلَا إِلَـهَ إِلَّا اللهُ، وَاللهُ أَكْبَرُ،
وَلَا حَوْلَ وَلَا قُوَّةَ إِلَّا بِاللهِ الْعَلِيِّ الْعَظِيمِ

Glorified is Allah, all Praise is for Allah, there is no god but Allah, and Allah is the Greatest. There is no power nor strength except from Allah the Most High, the Greatest.

You may also praise Allah and ask for His mercy in your own language or use supplications taken from the Qur'ān and *Sunnah*.

When you reach the first of the two green lights, men should begin to march briskly until they reach the other one, while women keep walking at their normal pace. When on top of Marwah, praise Allah facing the Kaʿbah and repeat the same supplications that were recited at Ṣafā. One trip is now over, the second trip will be back to Ṣafā, the third once again to Marwah and so on.

In this way, the seventh trip will end at Marwah, with each being performed as descibed. If it is not an undesirable (*makrūh*) time, one should offer two raka'ats of *nafl ṣalāh* in the Ḥaram upon completing *sa'y*.

How to perform Sa'y

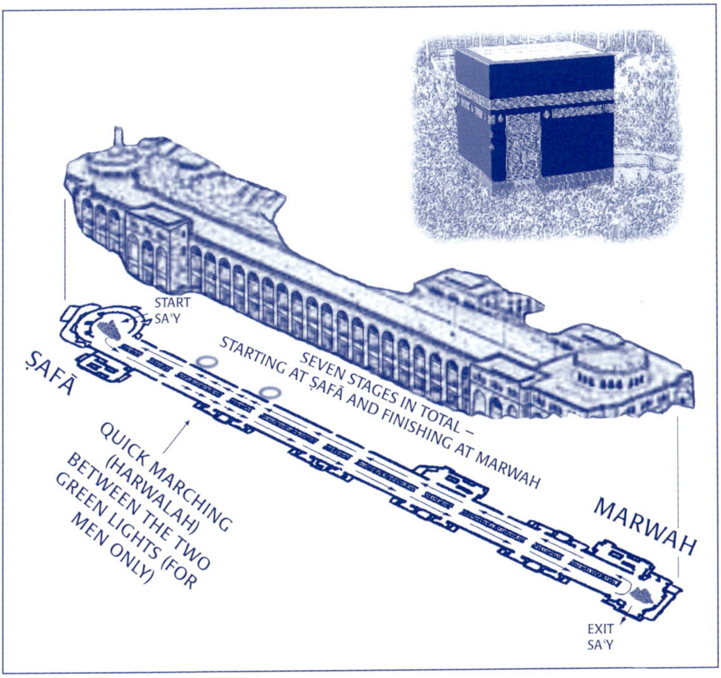

Ramy – The Stoning of the *Shayṭāns*

Ramy is the act of stoning the pillars in Minā, which symbolically represent the locations where the devil tried to tempt and steer Ibrāhīm, peace be upon him, away from the path of Allah. These are referred to as the Jamarāt.

The names of the three pillars are:

- The first (small) pillar: al-Jamarah al-Ṣughrā or al-Jamarah al-Ūlā.
- The second (middle) pillar: al-Jamarah al-Wusṭā.
- The third (large) pillar: al-Jamarah al-Kubrā or Jamarah al-'Aqabah.

In brief, seven pebbles are thrown at Jamarah al-ʿAqabah on the 3rd day of *ḥajj* (10th Dhū al-Ḥijjah) and seven at each of the pillars on the two subsequent days. This adds up to 7 + 21 + 21 = 49 pebbles altogether. Further description of the method for this practice can be found in the following chapter.

When throwing the pebbles, the pilgrim should not only remember the steadfast example of Prophet Ibrāhīm, peace be upon him, but also use the ritual as a way of affirming his own faith that Allah will protect him from satanic influence.

Qurbānī – The Sacrifice

On Yawm al-Naḥr (The Day of Sacrifice), which is 10th Dhū al-Ḥijjah, or on 11th/12th, it is *wājib* for the pilgrims performing Ḥajj al-Tamattuʿ or Ḥajj al-Qirān (*mustaḥabb* for Ḥajj al-Ifrād) to sacrifice a sheep or goat or take a seventh part in the sacrifice of a large animal (cow or camel). If one knows in advance that one cannot afford it, one must fast for any three days of the months of *ḥajj* (Shawwāl, Dhū al-Qaʿdah and the days before 10th Dhū al-Ḥijjah) and any seven days after completing the other rituals and the days of *tashrīq* (11th-13th Dhū al-Ḥijjah). For those members of the Islamic *ummah* not taking part in *ḥajj*, the 10th Dhū al-Ḥijjah is the day of ʿĪd al-Aḍḥā in which it is *wājib* for every legally responsible Muslim whose wealth reaches the *niṣāb* that makes them liable for *zakāh*, to offer a sacrifical *qurbānī* also.

This practice of sacrifice commemorates the utter submission of Prophet Ibrāhīm to Allah, through which he was ready to sacrifice his own son, Ismāʿīl, who also demonstrated complete obedience to Allah:

> *Then when (his son) was old enough to work with him, (Ibrāhīm) said, 'Oh my dear son, I have seen in a dream that I must sacrifice you, what is your view?' He said, 'Oh my father do as you are commanded! Allah willing, you shall find me of the steadfast.' So when they had both*

ḤAJJ

submitted (to Allah), and he had laid him on his forehead, We called out to him, 'Oh Ibrāhīm! You have already fulfilled the vision.' Thus do we reward those who do good. Indeed, this was a clear trial and we ransomed him with a tremendous sacrifice.[5]

The sacrifice mentioned here according to the exegetes was a large ram, sometimes said to have come from Paradise. It should be remembered that this was a test appropriate for a guided Prophet, which Allah used to perfect his faith and obedience to Him. In another part of the Qur'ān, Allah alludes again to His testing of Ibrāhīm by means of His commands and then goes on to link the significance of Ibrāhīm being chosen as a leader of humankind with the very rituals of *ḥajj* that characterise the Muslims that follow him in submission to their Lord:

And remember that Ibrāhīm was tried by his Lord with certain commands, which he fulfilled He said: 'I will make thee an imām *to the nations.' He pleaded: 'And also (*imāms*) from my offspring!' He answered: 'But my promise is not within the reach of evil-doers.'*

Remember We made the House a place of assembly for men and a place of safety; and take you the station of Ibrāhīm as a place of prayer; and We covenanted with Ibrāhīm and Ismā'īl that they should sanctify My House for those who circle it or use it as a retreat, or bow, or prostrate themselves (therein in prayer).

And remember Ibrāhīm said: 'My Lord make this a City of Peace, and feed its people with fruits – such of them as believe in Allah and the Last Day.' He said: '(Yea) and such as reject faith – for a while will I grant them their pleasure, but will soon drive them to the torment of fire – an evil destination (indeed)!'

And remember Ibrāhīm and Ismāʿīl raised the foundations of the House (with this prayer): 'Our Lord! accept (this service) from us; for Thou art the All-Hearing the All-Knowing. Our Lord! Make of us Muslims bowing to Your (Will) and of our progeny a Muslim people bowing to Your (Will) and show us our rites; and turn unto us (in Mercy); for Thou art the Oft-Returning, the Most-Merciful.'[6]

It is important to also note that there is also a charitable dimension to the sacrifices made both on *ḥajj* and at home, in that it is highly recommended that at least a third of the meat is given to the poor. In the case of *damm* sacrifices made as a penalty for breaking one of the rules of *ḥajj*, all of the meat must be distributed to the poor. Again we should recall that:

It is not their meat nor their blood that reaches Allah: it is your piety that reaches Him. He has thus made them subject to you, that ye may glorify Allah for His guidance to you; and proclaim the good news to all who do right.[7]

Ḥalq and *Qaṣr* – Shaving and Cutting the Hair

The ritual of having one's hair shaved off, or at least clipped short, is an important milestone in the completion of the *ḥajj*, as it marks the end of formal *iḥrām* (with the exception of the prohibition of relations between husband and wife, which is only lifted by *ṭawāf al-ziyārah or al-ifāḍah*). The significance of this ritual lies in the utter humble obedience to Allah and the submission of the egoistic self to His Will. The hair, which stands at the summit of a human being, represents one's feeling of pride and self-worth, and so, to cut it short indicates one's determination to rededicate oneself to the service of Allah. In the Glorious Qur'ān, Allah Most High says:

Truly did Allah fulfil the vision for His Messenger. You shall enter the Sacred Masjid, if Allah wills, securely, your heads shaven, hair cut short and not fearing.[8]

While men should preferably get their whole head shaved (*ḥalq*), it is permissible to cut the hair (*qaṣr*) of their whole head equal in length to a joint of a finger (about an inch). It is also permissible to cut the hair (about an inch) of one fourth of the head. Women are prohibited to shave their head and the ritual in their case is more symbolic. They should cut about an inch of hair from one fourth of her head, but, according to some scholars, it is sufficient to have just a lock of hair clipped. The exact time and place in which this practice should be done is described in the following chapter.

Jināyāt – *Ḥajj* Offences and their Penalties

We have already mentioned that the sanctified state of *iḥrām* and the other rites of *ḥajj* obligate a special degree of caution. When the the boundaries Allah has stipulated are crossed in these ritual matters it is necessary to pay a penalty. We can divide these penalties into the following categories:

Actions which make Jināyāt wājib:

1. A *Damm* – the sacrifice of a sheep, goat or seventh of a larger animal, with all the meat distributed for charity.
2. *Ṣadaqah* – almsgiving of half a *ṣāʿ* (0.55kg) of grain to the poor.
3. Minor *Ṣadaqah* – almsgiving of a smaller discretionary amount.
4. *Qīmah* – in the case of prohibited hunting, a pilgrim must find out the local value of the animal they have killed and make *ṣadaqah* or a sacrifice equal to this.

Actions which necessitate a Damm

A *damm* is required if a mature *muḥrim*:

1. Applies perfume to a (full) limb.
2. Dyes his head with henna, or other dyes containing perfume.

3. Rubs himself with oil etc.
4. Wears sewn clothes or covers his head for a complete day (or night).
5. Shaves a quarter of his head, nape, neck, one of his armpits, or pubic region (before the time of *ḥalq*).
6. Cuts the nails of his hands and feet, or even a hand or foot.
7. Performs *ṭawāf al-ziyārah or al-ifāḍah* without *wuḍū'*.
8. Kisses or touches his partner with desire. (If they have sexual intercourse before the *wuqūf* of 'Arafah, their *ḥajj* is not valid and they are both liable for sacrificing a goat. However, they must continue with the rites of *ḥajj* and make *qaḍā'* later. If the intercourse is after the *wuqūf* of 'Arafah, the *ḥajj* remains intact, but they must both sacrifice a large animal.
9. Leaves a *wājib* act as we have previously mentioned.

Note: If one uses perfume, wears sewn clothes or shaves with an excuse, they can choose between:

1. Performing a sacrifice.
2. Giving a *ṣadaqah* amount (half a *ṣā'*) to six poor people.
3. Fasting three days.

Actions that necessitate Ṣadaqah

Ṣadaqah is required if a mature *muḥrim:*

1. Applies perfume to less than a (full) limb.
2. Wears sewn clothes for covers his head for less than a complete day (or night).
3. Shaves less than a quarter of his head.
4. Cuts a nail, or even more, from any combination of hands and feet (so long as it does not reach five on any one). He is liable for the *sadaqah* amount for each such nail until it reaches the total value of a *damm,* in which case he can reduce it as he wishes (since he must make the sacrifice as a penalty).

5. Performs *ṭawāf al-qudūm* or *ṭawāf al-wadā'/al-ṣadar* without *wuḍū'*.
6. Leaves a circuit off from *ṭawāf al-wadā'/al-ṣadar.*
7. Leaves throwing a pebble at one of the Jamarāt. He is liable for the *ṣadaqah* amount for each such pebble, until it reaches the total value of a *damm* (as above).
8. Shaves another's head, or cuts his nails.

Actions that necessitate Minor Ṣadaqah

Small discretionary *ṣadaqah* is required if a mature *muḥrim*:

1. Kills a louse, locust, or similar small creature.

Qīmah - *Paying the Price of a Hunted Animal*

If a *muḥrim* hunts an animal or even indicates the position of an animal to another who kills it, he becomes liable for *qīmah.* This means two upright local people must value the animal hunted. If it comes up to the price of a slaughterable animal, he has the following choices:

1. Buy an animal of this value and slaughter it.
2. Buy food totalling this amount and give a number of poor people the *ṣadaqah* amount (half a *ṣā'*) each.
3. Perform a day's fast for every feeding that would have been made in two.

Note: 1. If less than a *ṣadaqah* amount is left over, one may also give it away, or fast a day.
2. Water-game is permitted for hunting.
3. A (vicious) dog, wolf, kite, crow (or feeder on carrion), snake and scorpion may be killed, as these animals attack on their own to cause injury.

Notes

[1] *Sūrah al-Baqarah* (Q2: 198).

[2] The position of the human being within Allah's created order is quite exquisitely balanced, both physically and spiritually. The astronomer Martin Rees notes that the 'human scale is, in a numerical sense,

poised midway between the masses of atoms and stars. It would take roughly as many human bodies to make up the mass of the Sun as there are atoms in each of us.' [Rees, M., *Just Six Numbers*, (Phoenix, 2000), p. 7.]

3 *Sūrah al-Ḥajj*, (Q22: 26).

4 *Sūrah al-Baqarah* (Q2: 158).

5 *Sūrah al-Ṣāffāt* (Q37: 102-7).

6 *Sūrah al-Baqarah* (Q2: 124-8).

7 *Sūrah al-Ḥajj*, (Q22: 37).

8 *Sūrah al-Fatḥ* (Q48: 27).

CHAPTER 19

Performing *Ḥajj*

The Five Days of *Ḥajj*

This chapter describes in details the itinerary and practices to be followed by the pilgrim during the five key days that constitute *ḥajj*, building on the descriptions and rules presented in the previous chapter. As these are at times fairly complex, the emphasis here will be on the outward forms of the rituals, i.e. doing the right thing at the right time. The sense of spirituality that should infuse the whole journey of *ḥajj* has been dealt with in Chapters 16 and 18.

Before 8th Dhū al-Ḥijjah: The Months of *Ḥajj*

Traditionally, the months of *ḥajj* started after Ramaḍān at the beginning of Shawwāl and included Dhū al-Qaʿdah and, of course, Dhū al-Ḥijjah. This was to allow the pilgrims time to make the long and often arduous journey to Makkah. In fact, sometimes individuals would have leave their homes in Dhū al-Qaʿdah of the year prior to the *ḥajj* that they wanted to attend!

Nowadays, as the methods of transport have become vastly quicker, it has become possible for a prospective pilgrim to arrange arrival in Makkah at the end of Dhū al-Qaʿdah, within the first few days of Dhū al-Ḥijjah, or even for the exact start of the *ḥajj* itself. However, such an individual still has to choose which of the three types of *sunnah ḥajj* they will perform: al-Ifrād, al-Qirān and al-Tamattuʿ (described in Chapter 17) Of the three, al-Tamattuʿ is usually chosen as it includes the reward of also performing *ʿumrah* (missed by al-Ifrād), yet gives the individual the ease of leaving *iḥrām* between completing their initial *ʿumrah* upon arrival in Makkah and starting their *ḥajj* on the 8th Dhū al-Ḥijjah (al-Qirān does not allow this). For this reason, Ḥajj al-Tamattuʿ will be described in the sections that follow as the default method, with differences arising from the other methods explained where necessary.

Arrival in Makkah

A pilgrim undertaking either Ḥajj al-Tamattuʿ or al-Qirān will arrive in Makkah before the days of *ḥajj* in *iḥrām* and will perform a complete *ʿumrah* (described in Chapter 20). The *ṭawāf* of *ʿumrah* performed here, will take the place of the *ṭawāf* of arrival (*qudūm*). Upon completing this *ʿumrah*, the pilgrim will remove his *iḥrām* if upon al-Tamattuʿ and remain bound by its rules if upon al-Qirān. In either case they should take the opportunity to do as much *ʿibādah* as possible within al-Masjid al-Ḥarām and wait for the beginning of *ḥajj*.

The pilgrim upon Ḥajj al-Ifrād, will enter the Mīqāt around Makkah in *iḥrām* for *ḥajj*. The *ṭawāf* that they will perform in Makkah will be the *ṭawāf* of arrival (*qudūm*). They may perform *saʿy* at this point, but it is better to wait until after *ṭawāf al-ziyārah or al-ifāḍah* to perform the single *saʿy* that they are allowed to make during *ḥajj*.

8th Dhū al-Ḥijjah: The First Day of *Ḥajj*

Ḥajj *Preparations*

The date of 8th Dhū al-Ḥijjah starts after the *maghrib* prayer of 7th Dhū al-Ḥijjah. Complete all final *ḥajj* preparations during these night hours.

Preparation for Iḥrām *by Pilgrims upon Ḥajj al-Tamattu*ʿ

Pilgrims upon Ḥajj al-Tamattuʿ, unlike those of the other two methods of *ḥajj*, will not be in *iḥrām*. For that reason they should get ready in the following ways:

- Comb the hair, shape the beard, trim the moustache, cut the nails, and remove unwanted body hair.
- Take a bath (*ghusl*) with the intention of *iḥrām*, or otherwise do *wuḍū'*.
- *Iḥrām*: men should wear a sheet of white cloth around the waist and cover the upper body with the other sheet. Women's ordinary clothes are their *iḥrām*. Both should wear flip-flops, or other sandals, that do not cover the middle bones of the upper part of the feet.
- *Nafl* ṣalah: if it is not a *makrūh* (undesirable) time, then men offer two *rakʿah*s of *nafl* for *iḥrām* in the Ḥaram, in which their heads are covered. Women can also offer these *nafl* at their accommodation.

Intention and Talbiyah

After praying the *nafl ṣalāh*, uncover your head and declare your intention saying:

اللّٰهُمَّ إِنِّيْ أُرِيْدُ الْحَجَّ فَيَسِّرْهُ لِيْ وَتَقَبَّلْهُ مِنِّيْ، نَوَيْتُ الْحَجَّ وَأَحْرَمْتُ بِهِ مُخْلِصًا لِلّٰهِ تَعَالَىٰ

Oh Allah! I wish to perform ḥajj. *Please make it easy for me and accept it from me. I have intended to perform* ḥajj *and have entered into* iḥrām *sincerely for Allah Most High.*

Immediately after that utter the words of *talbiyah* three times and as often afterwards as possible. Men should say it in a loud voice and women should say it more quietly.

Prohibitions of Iḥrām

Now the prohibitions of *iḥrām* start. Recall their details and follow the rules to avoid incurring penalties. From this point on, men cannot cover their heads for the duration of *iḥrām*.

Departure to Minā

After sunrise proceed towards Minā. On the way, pronounce *talbiyah* as often as you can and also utter other supplications. It is also acceptable to follow the procedure of your *mu'allim* (guide) who usually arranges for pilgrims to leave for Minā during the night after *'ishā'* prayers.

Spend the whole day and night in Minā offering *ẓuhr*, *'aṣr*, *maghrib*, *'ishā'* and *fajr* prayers.

9th Dhū al-Ḥijjah: The Second Day of *Ḥajj*

Departure for 'Arafah

Offer the *fajr* prayer in Minā and begin saying *takbīr al-tashrīq* after every *ṣalāh* (see Chapter 7), which will continue until the 13th Dhū al-Ḥijjah, and the *talbiyah*.

Get ready and reach 'Arafah by *zawāl* (declining of the sun and the beginning of *ẓuhr* time). Take a bath, if possible, otherwise perform *wuḍū'* and have a meal. Packages of food are usually provided by the *mu'allim*. Also take some rest.

Wuqūf al-'Arafah (*The Stay at 'Arafah*)

The *wuqūf* (stay) is started at the beginning of *zawāl* and ends at sunset. Spend this time uttering *talbiyah*, repenting from your sins, seeking the forgiveness and mercy of Allah, saying *darūd sharīf* and making as many supplications (*du'ā's*) in Arabic and your own language, as possible. It is better to do *wuqūf* while standing, but sitting down is also allowed.

Ẓuhr and *'aṣr* prayers in 'Arafah take place in Masjid al-Namrah, led by the *imām* in the combined (*jam'*) and shortened (*qaṣr*) form in the time of *ẓuhr* with one *adhān* but separate *iqāmahs*. At other places in 'Arafah, some people similarly combine these two *ṣalāhs*, but it is advisable that away from Masjid al-Namrah, they are offered at their proper times with *jamā'ah* as recommended by most scholars.

Departure for Muzdalifah

When the sun sets in 'Arafah, proceed to Muzdalifah without offering *maghrib* prayer, reciting *dhikr* and *talbiyah* on the way.

Maghrib *and* 'Ishā' *Prayers in* Muzdalifah

In Muzdalifah, offer *maghrib* and *'ishā'* prayers together at the time of *'ishā'*. For both prayers there is one *adhān* and one *iqāmah*.

First offer the *farḍ* prayer of *maghrib* with *jamā'ah*. Then say the *takbīr al-tashrīq* and *talbiyah*. Immediately after that offer the *farḍ* prayer of *'ishā'* with *jamā'ah*. After this offer the two *sunnah* of *maghrib*. Then offer the two *sunnah* of *'ishā'* followed by *witr* prayer. Offering *nafl* prayer is optional.

Dhikr and *du'ā'*: this is a very blessed night in which one should glorify Allah, recite *darūd sharīf*, read the Qur'ān, utter *talbiyah* and supplicate very humbly. Also take some rest.

Collecting of Pebbles

Pick up 49 pebbles the size of chickpeas if *ramy* (stoning the pillars in Minā) is to be performed for three days, and 70 if you intend to stay for four days.

Pray *fajr* in Muzdalifah and make a short *wuqūf* (stay) at the place known as the Sacred Monument (al-Mash'ar al-Ḥarām), but proceed back to Minā when the sun is about to rise.

10th Dhū al-Ḥijjah: The Third Day of *Ḥajj*

Ramy *of* Jamarah al-'Aqabah

In Minā, do *ramy*, which on the first day involves hitting the *Jamarah al-'Aqabah* with only seven pebbles one after the other. This may be done between sunrise and sunset on this day (unlike the 11th and 12th when it should be between noon and sunset), with it being *makrūh* between sunset and *fajr*. On account of risk of injury, the old, weak or sick persons may perform *ramy* a little before sunset or at night. However, pilgrims who do not perform *ramy* themselves but appoint others as representatives to perform it for them are breaking an obligatory act of *ḥajj*. This representation is not valid and whoever does this must give a sacrifice (*damm*). However, those persons who are unable to walk to the Jamarāt or are to ill or too weak, it is permissible for them to appoint someone as a representative.

Mere overcrowding is not a valid excuse for failing to perform the *ramy*. The best solution for a person who cannot endure the crowds is that he goes after the *sunnah* time and if there is great inconvenience he can do the *ramy* in the *makrūh* time. It will not be regarded *makrūh* for them.

Stop saying *talbiyah* when you throw the first pebble. Also don't stop for *duʿā'*, but just go to your residence and perform the *qurbānī* (animal sacrifice).

Qurbānī (Animal Sacrifice)

There are three days designated for the *qurbānī*, i.e., 10th, 11th or 12th Dhū al-Ḥijjah. It can be done any time during the day or night. It is usually easy to sacrifice an animal on 11th Dhū al-Ḥijjah. Do the *qurbānī* yourself or ask a reliable person to do it for you.

Ḥalq *and* Qaṣr *– Shaving and Cutting the Hair*

After the *qurbānī*, the *ḥalq* or *qaṣr* can be performed. If the sacrifice is postponed until the next two days, *ḥalq* or *qaṣr* is also postponed because it must come after the sacrifice. It also can be delayed up until the 12th Dhū al-Ḥijjah even if the sacrifice is not postponed. After *ḥalq* or *qaṣr* all prohibitions of *iḥrām* are lifted except for the private relations between husband and wife which become permissible after *ṭawāf al-ziyārah or al-ifāḍah*.

Ḥalq or *qaṣr* in Minā is a *Sunnah*. But you are allowed to do it anywhere in the Ḥaram. If done outside the precincts of the Ḥaram, it requires a *damm*.

You have to make sure that *ramy*, *qurbānī*, then *ḥalq* or *qaṣr* are performed in the order in which they are listed otherwise a *damm* is required as a penalty.

Ṭawāf al-Ziyārah (Ṭawāf al-Ifāḍah)

Now perform *ṭawāf al-ziyārah*. It can be performed any time, day or night, from 10th Dhū al-Ḥijjah to the sunset of 12th Dhū al-Ḥijjah. Usually it is convenient to do it on 11th Dhū al-Ḥijjah. Its procedure is the same as the *ṭawāf* of *ʿumrah* which is described in detail in Chapter 20 and it is essential that you have performed *wuḍūʾ*. According to the *Sunnah*, this *ṭawāf* is to be performed after *ramy*, sacrifice and shaving or clipping of the hair, and every effort should be made to do that, but the *farḍ* stands discharged even if *ṭawāf al-ziyārah* is performed prior to all these practices. As mentioned earlier, *ḥalq* or *qaṣr* after *qurbānī* lifts all the prohibitions of *iḥrām*, except the private relations between husband and wife that are permitted only after this *ṭawāf*.

Note for ladies: If before the *ṭawāf al-ziyārah* or *ṭawāf al-ifāḍah*, a woman's menstruation begins and according to her travel arrangements it is not possible for her to be clean to perform this *ṭawāf* (i.e. to first finish her menses and perform *ghusl*), then it is important that she try everything possible to delay her journey in order to perform this *ṭawāf* in the state of purification (even if this goes beyond the 12th Dhū al-Ḥijjah).

However, if all efforts fail and her journey home is imminent before being clean, then she can perform *ṭawāf al-ziyārah* in the state of menstruation. This *ṭawāf* will be considered valid under the *sharīʿah*. However, she must give a *badanah* (sacrifice of a large animal) because of perpetrating an offence and this sacrifice must be offered within the boundaries of the Ḥaram.

Sa'y *of* Ḥajj

After this perform *sa'y*. Its procedure has been described in Chapter 18 and it is a *sunnah* to make sure that your *wuḍū'* is intact. As mentioned earlier, if it was already performed during the *ḥajj* after the *ṭawāf* of arriving (*qudūm*), it is not to be done again. *Sa'y* performed as part of an earlier *'umrah* (in Ḥajj al-Qirān and al-Tammatu') does not count in this.

Return to Minā

Return to Minā when *sa'y* is done and spend the night there.

11th Dhū al-Ḥijjah: The Fourth Day of *Ḥajj*

Ramy *of* Jamarāt

Throw seven pebbles on each of three Jamarāt after *zawāl* (decline of the midday sun). If there is intense crowding it may be easier to do *ramy* a little before sunset. It is permissible to do *ramy* at night if the crowds mean there would be a a risk to life during the day.

Supplicate and then throw seven pebbles at al-Jamarah al-Ūlā. Then move a little forward, and then with your hands raised and facing the *qiblah*, praise Allah and recite Arabic *du'ā's* or supplicate in your own words. There are no prescribed *du'ā's*.

Supplicate and then throw seven pebbles at al-Jamarah al-Wusṭā. Here too, facing *qiblah*, praise Allah and earnestly seek His mercy and blessings. No particular *du'ā's* are prescribed here either.

Then throw seven pebbles on Jamarah al-'Aqabah. But this time do not supplicate at all, and after the *ramy* is complete return to your place of stay.

Other Practices for this Day

There is a second chance for *ṭawāf al-ziyārah*. If you could not do *ṭawāf al-ziyārah* yesterday, do it today and return to Minā for the overnight stay.

Also make sure that you are continuously in *dhikr* and *ʿibādah*, savouring the preciousness of these moments as a pilgrim and guest of Allah. At your residence, recite the Qurʾān, glorify Allah and repent, seeking forgiveness. Ask Allah for whatever you want and refrain from committing any sins.

12th Dhū al-Ḥijjah: The Fifth Day of *Ḥajj*

Ramy *of* Jamarāt

Throw seven pebbles on each of the three Jamarāt following exactly the same procedure as described for the previous day.

Last Chance for Ṭawāf al-Ziyārah

If you could not do *ṭawāf al-ziyārah* earlier, it is essential to do it on this day before *maghrib*.

An Option to return to Makkah

After today's *ramy*, there is an option to return to Makkah before sunset. But if the sun sets before you are able to depart, remain in Minā for the third night and throw pebbles the next day in the same order.

Ṭawāf al-Wadāʿ

After *ḥajj*, when you intend to return home from Makkah, it is *wājib* (necessary) to perform *ṭawāf al-wadāʿ* (farewell *ṭawāf*). Its procedure is the same as that of a *nafl ṭawāf*.

The Steps of *ʿUmrah* and *Ḥajj*

1

- Perform *ghusl*
- Put on *iḥrām*
- Make intention for *ʿumrah*
- Recite the *talbiyah*
- Avoid prohibited acts during *iḥrām*

2

- Perform *ṭawāf* of the Kaʿbah
- Pray two *rakʿahs nafl* behind Maqām Sayyidinā Ibrāhīm
- Perform *saʿy* between Ṣafā and Marwah
- Trim hair
- Take off *iḥrām*

Congratulations, you have completed your *ʿumrah*!

Steps for Ḥajj

1

- Perform *ghusl*
- Put on *iḥrām*
- Make intention for *Ḥajj*
- Perform *fajr* prayer in Makkah
- Leave for Minā on 8th Dhū al-Ḥijjah
- Perform *ẓuhr*, *'asr*, *maghrib* and *'isha'* prayers in Minā
- Spend the night in Minā

2

- Leave for 'Arafah on 9th Dhū al-Ḥijjah after performing *fajr ṣalāh* in Minā
- Stay within the bounds of 'Arafah until sunset
- Pray, offer *du'ā'*s and ask for forgiveness
- Offer shortened *ẓuhr* and *'asr* prayers

3

- Leave for Muzdalifah after sunset on 9th Dhū al-Ḥijjah
- Offer shortened *maghrib* and *'ishā'* prayers at Muzdalifah
- Collect pea-sized pebbles at Muzdalifah
- Stay overnight and perform *fajr* prayer

4

- Shortly before sunrise, leave for Minā on 10th Dhū al-Ḥijjah
- Stone al-Jamrah al-'Aqabah with seven pebbles
- Offer *qurbānī*
- Men should shave their heads
- Ladies should cut off about an inch/1.5cm of hair
- Take off *iḥrām*
- All *iḥrām* prohibitions lifted except for marital sexual relations

5

- Go to Makkah and perform *ṭawāf al-ziyārah*
- Peform *sa'y* between Ṣafā and Marwah
- All *iḥrām* restrictions are now lifted
- Return to Minā

6

- 11th Dhū al-Ḥijjah: Perform *ramy* of the Jamarāt, starting with the small pillar and ending with the large one
- 12th Dhū al-Ḥijjah. Perform *ramī* of the Jamarāt, starting with the small pillar and ending with the large one

7

- After performing *ramy* on 12th Dhū al-Ḥijjah, leave for Makkah before sunset
- If you can't leave before sunset, spend on more night in Minā and offer *ramy* again, and then leave for Makkah

Congratulations, you have completed your *ḥajj*!

ḤAJJ

CHAPTER 20

Performing *ʿUmrah*

The Rites of *ʿUmrah*

Performing the *ʿumrah* simply consists of the following four rites:

1. Entering the state of *iḥrām*.
2. *Ṭawāf* of the Kaʿbah.
3. *Saʿy* between the hills of Ṣafā and Marwah.
4. *Ḥalq* or *qaṣr* – shaving or clipping the hair.

As these have been described in significant detail already, this information will not be repeated here, with the exception of the *ṭawāf* of *ʿumrah*, in which a look at in greater depth is beneficial. It will perhaps also be recalled that this *ṭawāf* is identical to *ṭawāf al-ziyārah* and so the following information can be applied within the *ḥajj* as well.

How to perform *ʿUmrah*

Iḥrām *for* ʿUmrah *and entering* al-Masjid al-Ḥaram

One should wear the *iḥrām* for *ʿumrah* before entering Makkah. Prepare as for *ḥajj*, but make the following *niyyah* (intention):

اللَّهُمَّ إِنِّيْ أُرِيْدُ الْعُمْرَةَ فَيَسِّرْهَا لِيْ وَتَقَبَّلْهَا مِنِّيْ، وَأَحْرَمْتُ بِهِ مُخْلِصًا لله تَعَالَىٰ

Oh Allah! I wish to perform ʿumrah, *so make it easy for me and accept it from me. I have entered into a sanctified state in sincerity for Allah Most High.*

Note: An *āfāqī* pilgram (one who resides outside the boundaries of the Mīqāt) doing *Ḥajj al-Tamattuʿ* can perform as many *ʿumrahs* as he wishes before putting on the *iḥrām* of *ḥajj*.

Entering al-Masjid al-Ḥaram

While reciting the *talbiyah*, enter al-Masjid al-Ḥaram preferably through Bab al-Salām with the right foot first. Supplicate to Allah and proceed towards the Kaʿbah. You may recite the following supplication which is usually used before entering a mosque:

بِسْمِ الله وَالسَّلَامُ عَلَى رَسُوْلِ الله، اللَّهُمَّ افْتَحْ لِيْ أَبْوَابَ رَحْمَتِكَ

In the Name of Allah and peace upon the Messenger of Allah, Oh Allah! Open the gates of Your Mercy for me.

First Sight of the Kaʿbah

At the first sight of Kaʿbah, keep your eyes fixed at the Noble Baytullāh and standing at one side, it is suggested that you do the following:

- Say (x3) اَللّٰهُ أَكْبَرُ – *'Allah is the Greatest'* three times.
- Say (x3) لَا إِلٰهَ إِلَّا اللّٰهُ – *'There is no god except Allah'* three times.

Proclaim *ṣalawāt* (*darūd sharīf*) upon our beloved Prophet, may Allah bless him and grant him peace, and very humbly and with tears in your eyes supplicate to Allah for whatever you wish. This is a special time for the acceptance of prayers.

The idea is to praise and glorify your Creator before proclaiming *ṣalawāt* and supplications. Therefore, in lieu of *'Allāhu Akbar'* and *'Lā ilāha illa'llāh'*, you may recite some other similar holy verses if you so desire. After this, whilst uttering the *talbiyah*, move forward to perform *ṭawāf* of the Kaʿbah.

Ṭawāf *of* ʿUmrah

Ṭawāf means circling around something. Here it means moving around the Kaʿbah seven times with extreme love and devotion. The following are the steps by which it performed:

Preparation

1. Pass the upper sheet of *iḥrām* from underneath the right arm and put it on the left shoulder. This act bares the right shoulder and is known as *iḍṭibāʿ*.
2. *Wuḍū'* is necessary (*wājib*) for *ṭawāf*.
3. Recitation of *talbiyah* is stopped when you reach al-Ḥajar al-Aswad, the starting point of *ṭawāf*.
4. *Niyyah* (intention) – Stand in front of the Kaʿbah facing al-Hajar al-Aswad (the Black Stone) in such a way that the whole of it is on your right side. To achieve this end, you may get help from the black line on the floor. This line should be on your right side. Then without raising your hands make the *niyyah* for *ṭawāf*.

Istilām

1. Now moving towards the right, come in front of al-Ḥajar al-Aswad and kiss it if possible, or touch it with a stick and kiss the stick. If that also is not possible, raise your hands to your ears keeping your open palms towards al-Ḥajar al-Aswad and say:

> بِسْمِ اللهِ، وَالْحَمْدُ لله، وَلَا إِلٰهَ إِلَّا اللهُ، وَاللهُ أَكْبَرُ
>
> *In the name of Allah , all Praise is for Allah, there is no god but Allah, and Allah is the Greatest.*

2. Now drop your hands down. Point the palms of your hands again towards al-Ḥajar al-Aswad and kiss them. This act of kissing al-Ḥajar al-Aswad or pointing towards it is called *istilām*.

> *Warning:* The authorities often apply perfume to al-Ḥajar al-Aswad, Rukn Yamanī (Yemeni Corner) and Multazam. If so, do not touch them whilst in the state of *iḥrām*, otherwise a *damm* will be required as a penalty.

Start *Ṭawāf*

After *istilām*, turn right and start *ṭawāf* counterclockwise. During *ṭawāf*, it is not permissible to face or turn your back towards the Ka'bah except when you are kissing or pointing towards al-Ḥajar al-Aswad.

Ramal

For the first three circuits of the *ṭawāf* of *'umrah* and the *ṭawāf* of arrival, men are required to move their shoulders and walk with quick short steps. This act is called *ramal* and is a *sunnah*. They are to walk normally during the remaining four circuits.

Supplications of Ṭawāf

There are no fixed supplications for *ṭawāf*, but there are several recommended supplications listed in the books of *ḥajj* and *ʿumrah* out of which the following supplication is easy to memorise if it is not already known:

> سُـــبْحَانَ اللهِ، وَالْـحَمْـدُ للهِ، وَلَا إِلَـٰهَ إِلَّا اللهُ، وَاللهُ أَكْبَرُ،
> وَلَاحَـــوْلَ وَلَا قُوَّةَ إِلَّا بِاللهِ الْعَلِيِّ الْعَظِيْمِ
>
> *All Glory is to Allah, all praise is for Allah, there is no god except Allah and Allah is the Greatest. There is no power nor strength except that from Allah, the Most High, the Almighty.*

The Prophet Muḥammad, may Allah bless him and grant him peace, has said that there are two *kalimah*s (statements) that are light on the tongue, yet weigh heavily on the scale on the Day of Judgement and are beloved to Allah. These are:

> سُبْحَانَ اللهِ وَبِحَمْدِهِ، سُبْحَانَ اللهِ الْعَظِيْمِ
>
> *Glory be to Allah and Praise is to Him! Glory be to Allah, the Almighty.*

You may also use supplications used in the daily *ṣalāh* or you may seek forgiveness of Allah and ask Him whatever you wish in your own language.

The Ḥatīm

The Ḥatīm is a semi-circular half-built wall which was originally a part of the Kaʿbah but which could not be included in the main structure when the Kaʿbah was rebuilt. It is necessary to go around the Ḥatīm also whilst performing *ṭawāf*.

Rukn Yamānī and its Supplications

After passing the three corners of the Kaʿbah you reach the fourth corner known as Rukn Yamānī. Touch it with both hands or with the right hand, if it is not too crowded. There is a beautiful supplication, repeatedly recited by our beloved Prophet, peace and blessings be upon him, which is to be used while walking between Rukn Yamānī and al-Ḥajar al-Aswad:

رَبَّنَا آتِنَا فِي الدُّنْيَا حَسَنَةً وَفِي الْآخِرَةِ حَسَنَةً وَقِنَا عَذَابَ النَّارِ وَأَدْخِلْنَا الْجَنَّةَ مَعَ الْأَبْرَارِ يَاعَزِيْزُ يَاغَفَّارُ يَارَبَّ الْعَالَمِيْنَ

Oh our Lord! Grant us good in this world and good in the Hereafter, and save us from the chastisement of the Fire, and let us enter Paradise with the righteous ones. Oh Glorious One! Oh All Forgiving! Oh Lord of the Universe!

The first circuit is complete when you arrive back at al-Ḥajar al-Aswad.

Seven Circuits

At al-Ḥajar al-Aswad, start the second circuit by kissing it or pointing towards it as you started the first circuit, i.e. come in front of al-Hajar al-Aswad, raise both hands to your ears with open palms towards it and say:

بِسْمِ اللهِ، وَالْحَمْدُ لله، وَلَا إِلَهَ إِلَّا اللهُ، وَاللهُ أَكْبَرُ

In the name of Allah , all praise is for Allah, there is no god but Allah, and Allah is the Greatest.

Now kiss both palms and drop your hands. After this go around the Kaʿbah as you did before and similarly complete the seven circuits.

The End of Ṭawāf

At the end of seven circuits, do *istilām* of al-Ḥajar al- Aswad or point towards it an eighth time, which is *sunnah mu'akkidah* (an emphatic *sunnah*). Also say:

بِسْمِ اللهِ، وَالْحَمْدُ للهِ، وَلَا إِلَهَ إِلَّا اللهُ، وَاللهُ أَكْبَرُ

In the name of Allah , all praise is for Allah, there is no god but Allah, and Allah is the Greatest.

Īḍṭibāʿ *finished*

Now *iḍṭibāʿ* is finished, therefore, you cover both your shoulders with upper portion of the *iḥrām* sheet. This does not apply to women who did not perform *iḍṭibāʿ* in the first place.

Multazam

Now, come to Multazam which is a place five or six feet in length between al-Ḥajar al-Aswad and the door of the Kaʿbah. This is a highly sacred place where prayers are accepted. Among a large crowd of people, if it is possible to reach Multazam, cling to it pressing your chest and cheeks, and whilst trembling and crying with devotion and with all humility seek the Mercy of Allah, His blessings and ask Him whatever you wish. If you are unable to come close to Multazam, just face towards it and supplicate from a distance.

Important Note: Due to the fervent devotion of pilgrims, the sacred area around the Kaʿbah, particularly al-Ḥajar al-Aswad, Multazam and the Kaʿbah's door, are almost always incredibly crowded. This can make it very difficult to perform the most virtuous *sunnahs* in regard to them, which involves directly touching or kissing their blessed presence. Despite our desire to perform these rituals, it is vital that we recall that Allah alone is the Bestower of blessings and that in this situation, He will reward us for the intentions in our hearts and our spiritual, not material, proximity to His sacred symbols. Thus, to push other people out of the way, or to dangerously crush against them, in order to try to fulfil these *sunnahs*, is not only against the very spirit of *ḥajj* and *ʿumrah*, but the dangerously insulting manners of a bad guest at the House of Allah. We should fear that the entire reward of our pilgrimage could be lost by even one instance of this rude and dangerous behaviour.

Maqām Ibrāhīm

Next, offer two *rakʿahs* of *nafl* behind and close to Maqām Ibrāhīm without covering your head. If it happens to be one of the three times of day when prayer is not allowed (sunrise, noon and sunset), then you have to wait till this time has passed and then offer the prayer.

While making the *niyyah* (intention) for this *ṣalāh*, intend to offer two *rakʿahs* of *nafl wājib* al-*ṭawāf*. Recite *Sūrah al-Kāfirūn* (Q109) in the first *rakʿah* and *Sūrah al-Ikhlāṣ* (Q112) in the second *rakʿah*. These *sūrahs* are shown below:

قُلْ يَٰٓأَيُّهَا ٱلْكَٰفِرُونَ . لَآ أَعْبُدُ مَا تَعْبُدُونَ . وَلَآ أَنتُمْ عَٰبِدُونَ مَآ أَعْبُدُ .

وَلَآ أَنَا۠ عَابِدٌ مَّا عَبَدتُّمْ . وَلَآ أَنتُمْ عَٰبِدُونَ مَآ أَعْبُدُ . لَكُمْ دِينُكُمْ وَلِىَ دِينِ .

Say: Oh disbelievers! I worship not that which you worship. Nor do you worship that which I worship. And I shall not worship that which you worship. Nor will you worship that which I worship. Unto you your religion, and unto me my religion.

قُلْ هُوَ ٱللَّهُ أَحَدٌ . ٱللَّهُ ٱلصَّمَدُ . لَمْ يَلِدْ وَلَمْ يُولَدْ . وَلَمْ يَكُن لَّهُۥ كُفُوًا أَحَدٌ .

Say: He is Allah, the One! Allah, the Eternally Besought by all. He neither gives birth nor was born. And there is none comparable unto Him.

After this, supplicate to Allah in Arabic or in your own language. Ask Him whatever you wish and invoke His blessings.

If it is not possible to offer this *wājib* prayer near Maqām Ibrāhīm, it can be offered anywhere in the Maṭāf (place of *ṭawāf*), or in the Ḥatīm or anywhere in al-Masjid al-Ḥaram or even at any place in the Ḥaram of Makkah.

Zamzam

Now go to the Zamzam well situated in the basement of the Ḥaram about 200 feet from the Kaʿbah's door. There are separate sections for men and women. Zamzam is the best available water in the world. Drink this water to your fill while in a standing position after saying *bismillah*. Then supplicate to Allah:

اللَّهُمَّ إِنِّي أَسْأَلُكَ عِلْمًا نَافِعًا، وَرِزْقًا وَاسِعًا، وَشِفَاءً مِنْ كُلِّ دَاءٍ وَسُقْمٍ يَآ أَرْحَمَ الرَّاحِمِيْنَ

Oh Allah! I seek from You profitable knowledge and overflowing provisions and a cure from all ailments through Your Mercy, Oh Most Merciful of the Merciful.

HAJJ

Rules for the Ṭawāf *of* ʿUmrah

There are three conditions essential for the *ṭawāf* of *ʿumrah* and for all other kinds of *ṭawāf* as well, namely:

1. To be a Muslim.
2. *Niyyah* (intention).
3. To perform *ṭawāf* inside al-Masjid al-Ḥaram.

Note: Without a *niyyah*, *ṭawāf* is not valid. *Ṭawāf* can be performed in Maṭāf or on different floors of al-Masjid al-Haram or even on its roof.

- One must be in the state of *iḥrām* before starting the *ṭawāf* of *ʿumrah.*
- While performing *ṭawāf*, one should not look towards the Kaʿbah. One has to face Kaʿbah only when doing *istilām* of al-Ḥajar al-Aswad.
- If, after completing the seven circuits of *ṭawāf*, someone deliberately starts the eighth circuit, it becomes obligatory (*wājib*) for him to complete the second *ṭawāf* by doing six more circuits.
- Undesirable times for prayer are not considered undesirable for performing *ṭawāf.*
- If a person has to discontinue his *ṭawāf* because of it being time for prescribed (*farḍ*) prayer, or because a dead body is brought for a funeral prayer, or a need for fresh ablution (*wuḍūʾ*) arises, he can later resume his *ṭawāf* at the point where he discontinued.
- One must make sure to complete all seven circuits of *ṭawāf.*
- It is vital to make sure that all the *wājib* elements of *ṭawāf* are fulfilled.

Nafl Ṭawāf

Just as *ʿumrah* may be performed as often as one wants according to the procedure that is being described here, so too can a *nafl ṭawāf* be performed on its own. The difference is that a solitary *nafl ṭawāf* has no *iḥram*, no *iḍṭibāʿ*, no *ramal* and no *saʿy*.

Saʿy *and* Ḥalq *or* Qaṣr

In *ʿumrah, ṭawāf* should be soon followed by *saʿy* between Ṣafā and Marwah and then shaving or clipping of the hair. These rituals have been adequately described in Chapter 18 and so will not be repeated here.

After the cutting of hair, *ʿumrah* is complete and the restrictions of *iḥrām* no longer apply. The visitor to the House of Allah and to Makkah, upon finishing his *ʿumrah* (or *ḥajj*) should thank Allah for being given the opportunity to make such a great journey. He should also continue take advantage of the immense rewards available for worshipping in this blessed location and firmly steer clear of all sinful actions, remaining in obedience to his Lord both now and in the future. Shaykh ʿAbd al-Qādir al-Jilānī describes a type of spiritual pilgrimage that is not limited to a single time and place:

> As for the Pilgrimage of the Spiritual Path, its first requirement is provision for the journey and suitable means of transport. This is obtained by finding a qualified teacher and receiving spiritual instruction from him.[1]

After giving details of special devotions that mirror the rites of *ḥajj*, the Shaykh compares the removal of *iḥrām* that makes certain actions permissible with Allah's supreme promise of forgiveness:

> *Those who repent, and truly believe, and do righteous work – in their case, Allah will change their evil deeds into good deeds.*[2]

Notes

1 Al-Jilānī, ʿAbd al-Qādir, *The Book of the Secret of Secrets and the Manifestation of Lights*, (Al-Baz, 2000), p. 83.

2 *Sūrah al-Furqān* (Q25:70).

APPENDIX

Moon Sighting

The Lunar Calendar in the Sharī'ah

> *They ask you concerning the crescent moons. Say: they are time periods for humanity, and for the pilgrimage.*[1]

There is underlying wisdom in the *sharī'ah*'s use of the lunar calendar. By observing the moon even the simple nomads living in the desert can easily know the date. Also the use of the lunar calendar leads to the month of Ramaḍān rotating around the seasons of the year. Thus people can experience various lengths of fasting, as well as having the chance to perform the *ḥajj* and *'umrah* at an appropriate season.

Yet the peculiarities of the lunar calendar can lead to controversy, particularly in a country such as Britain that lacks both a widely-recognised Islamic religious authority and a universal consensus as to how exactly it is to be practically implemented. This is most pronounced in the case of the beginning and end of the month of Ramaḍān, as the obligatory fasting and celebration of 'Īd al-Fiṭr are shared by the whole of the Islamic community. What is particularly interesting is that the divergent perspectives that have divided the *'ulamā'* and common believers alike are all based on the above *āyah* of the

Qur'ān and the following *ḥadīth* narrated by Abū Hurayrah, may Allah be pleased with him. He reports that the Prophet, peace and blessings be upon him, said:

> *Fast after sighting the moon and end the month after sighting it, if it is cloudy then complete thirty days of Sha'bān.*[2]

Before looking at the different interpretations that have been made of this evidence from the Qur'ān and *Sunnah* it is important to take the time to look a little more deeply at the important place that the moon plays in Islamic timekeeping, the astronomical facts surrounding the sighting of the crescent and the distinctive features of the Islamic lunar calendar as compared to the lunar calendars adopted by other communities.

The Role of the Moon as Allah's Timepiece for Humanity

As the Qur'ānic verse and *ḥadīth* cited at the beginning of this chapter clearly indicate, the crescent moon has been legislated by Almightly Allah as the sign for Muslims to begin their months. In fact, Allah Most High calls the crescents 'periods of time for humanity'. Yet the meaning here is that they are Allah's sign that the month has started, the earliest formation of the crescent corresponding to the beginning point of the month. We are also told that the moon, as one of Allah's timepieces for humanity, fulfils its function precisely. He Most High says:

> *The sun and the moon follow precise courses.*[3]

> *It is He Who made the sun to be a shining glory and the moon to be a light, and measured out stages for it: that you might know the number of years and the count (of time).*[4]

> *And the moon, We have measured for it stages (to traverse) till it returns like the old dried curved date stalk.*[5]

It is clear from all the Qur'ānic evidence quoted that Ramaḍān, like any month, arrives upon the moon entering the stage of its monthly orbit that we can call the first visible crescent after its conjunction. The following diagrams illustrate how this happens:

Diagram of Conjunction

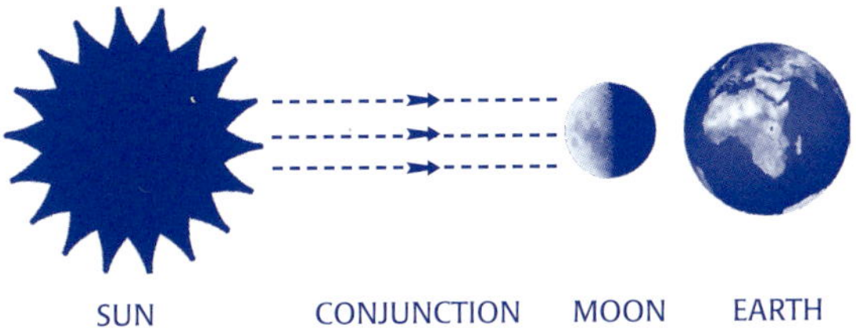

The moon is invisible until it moves out of this line, as shown in the next diagram.

Diagram of First Visible Crescent

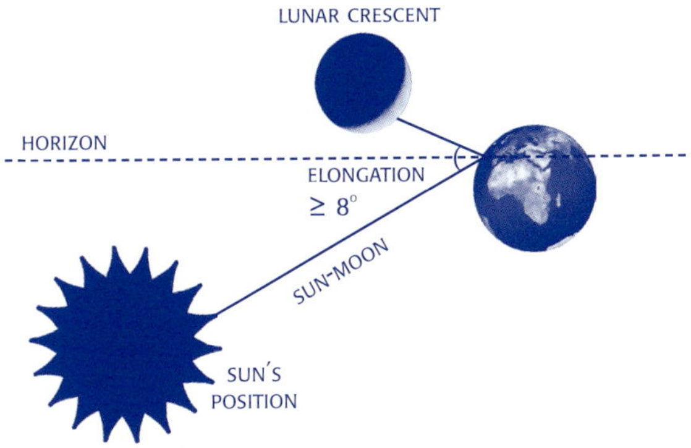

A sliver of the moon becomes visible as a crescent as it moves into the waxing phase.

The conjunction can be predicted very accurately. But when the moon becomes visible after conjunction is a crucial question. The moon can only be visible if the light reflected by it can be seen by an observer on the earth. This will happen if the moon is in a certain geometrical position relative to the sun and the earth.

We can list the following factors as determining the possibility of the sighting of the crescent:

1. The Sun-Moon elongation angle is greater than eight degrees.
2. The minimum age of moon after conjunction must be 17 hours high on horizon.
3. Weather conditions, clear or cloudy sky.
4. Use of telescopes (this advances sighting by about one day compared to the naked eye).
5. The moon set must be 40-50 minutes after sunset.

Defining the Lunar Month

There are at least three different ways of defining the lunar month:

The Conventional Month

The Arabs before Islam used this. According to this method, one month was thirty days and the next twenty-nine days. This was decided arbitrarily and it meant that the lunar year was exactly 354 days.

The Synodic Month

According to this system of classification, the lunar month is from the birth of the new moon to the birth of the next new moon or from one conjunction to the next conjunction. This is precisely 29.53 days (29 days, 12 hours and 44 minutes). This is commonly used by the Jewish community.

The Islamic Lunar Month

This begins from the sighting of the crescent to the next sighting, i.e. from crescent to crescent. The argument for this is that when the moon is in conjunction it is not a crescent and therefore not visible. The moon must move out of the Earth-Sun line and be visible. Many notable Muslim jurists like ʿAllāmah Subkī, Ibn Daqīq al-ʿĪd, Qāḍī Abū Bakr al-Jaṣṣāṣ and Ibn al-Rushd all hold this view. Amongst contemporary scholars are people like Dr ʿAbdul Wahhāb (Morocco), Dr Ḥussain Kamāl Uddīn (Riyadh) and Qāḍī Abū Khaikh Mismī. According to these people, the mere presence of the new moon is not sufficient evidence to begin the new month, it must be capable of being sighted in the manner we have indicated.

Interpretation of the Evidence

Practically speaking, and without yet delving into the *fiqh* arguments of each position, the evidence from the Qur'ān and *Sunnah* in regard to starting the month of Ramaḍān have been interpreted in Britain in at least six distinct ways, which are summarised below:

1. Global sighting – The proponents of this method hold that the crescent moon must actually be seen by witnesses, in the traditional manner, somewhere in the world. Once news of this is reliably transmitted, individuals in other countries may act upon it. Thirty days of the month are only to be completed if no reliable report of a sighting is to be found. A practical (and to some scholars essential) variant of this opinion holds that the sighting that is to be taken must be to the East, as a decision about the month must be made around *maghrib* time – otherwise the people are left in confusion and important practices such as *tarāwīḥ* are more difficult to organise. Obviously, locations significantly to the West would not have entered into their own *maghrib* yet and thus not be able to provide a sighting in time.
2. Regional sighting – This method proposes a certain region within which sightings should be carried out. In the case of Britain this could be the country itself, or perhaps could include Continental Europe as well. Again, an actual sighting must be reliably witnessed,

but if it comes from an area outside of the region it will not be counted.

3. Local sighting – This is the same as the previous two but the acceptable range of sightings is limited to one's locality, such as the city or town of one's residence.
4. Sighting with calculation to exclude impossible claims – This method is still fundamentally based on sightings and so be based on the principles of any of methods 1-3. The difference is that astronomical calculations are applied to make sure that no sighting is claimed that, according to the location in which it is made, the crescent moon is not sufficiently old to be seen by the naked eye/binoculars/telescope. However, according to this method, if the sky is completely cloudy, and no sightings have been reported, it is necessary to count 30 days in the month even if from calculations it is thought that the crescent would have been seen.
5. Calculation when sighting is not possible – This method accepts the validity of traditional sightings in locations that tend to have good visibility, but argues that in more cloudy climates, such as that of Britain, a different approach can be beneficial. This is that astronomical calculations can give an extremely accurate indication of what would be seen if cloud cover was not present and therefore, can be used to decide if 30 days should be counted. Like method 4, this perspective is able to include a number of variants, based on what type of sighting – global, regional or local – it utilises and whether it envisages calculation for a region as a whole, or just a locality.
6. Pure calculation – This method determines the lunar calendar solely based on astronomical calculation, with sighting reports, if used at all, playing purely a corroborative role. Again this can take a variety of forms, depending on whether it seeks to develop a global, regional, or local calendar and what parameters are set in place, for instance, in the minimum acceptable time

from the birth of the new moon until a new month can be established.

From the above descriptions it should be clear that very different interpretations can be made from the same basic evidence of the Qur'ān and *ḥadīth*. We shall now begin to address the particular case at hand, the condition of moon sighting in the UK, before explaining in more depth the reason for the different scholarly perspectives on this issue.

Moon Sighting in the UK

Where the new crescent can be easily and regularly seen, for instance in the Arabian Peninsula and the Subcontinent, there is no reason to depart from the traditional and beautiful practice of moon sighting by the naked eye, although it is useful to deploy calculations to exclude 'impossible' claims and as a guide for when to look. In the often cloudy northern hemisphere, for instance in the UK, it is fine to also attempt this *sunnah* practice, which can certainly be a spiritual experience, as a means to marvel at the exquisite creative power of Allah. However, it is an unfortunate fact that the atmospheric conditions often leave the observer disappointed, as it can be impossible to confirm a sighting, even if it is known that in a clear sky a crescent moon of the same age would have been possible to spot.

The Meaning of Ru'yah *(Sighting)*

Faced with cloudy UK skies, scholars have broadly divided into two camps on the interpretation of the *ḥadīth* quoted earlier. One group adhere to the literal meaning of *'ru'yah'* (seeing) as meaning *'mushāhadah'* (observing with the eye). They say that the moon must be sighted with the eye and there is no room for astronomical calculations in confirming any sighting (even if some permit them for the purpose of rejecting 'impossibly early' sightings.) Under this approach, it is possible that 30 days are recorded month after month and because of this the lunar calendar starts to behave strangely resulting in the need for a 28 day lunar month – something which should never happen. The other method for rectifying this problem is to take sightings from outside of the UK, whether they are regional or global and thus keep the situation pegged, as it were, to what is happening in a more easily observable sky. However, as the UK tends to lag in first seeing the crescent compared to less northernly countries, once this method is adopted, the crescent will virtually never be seen on the sunset of the 29th day. In a broad sense, we can term these scholars as either falling within methods 1-3 outlined earlier, in which case they could be called traditionalist, and method 4, which could be called semi-traditionalist.

Another group of *ʿulamā'*, argue that the *'ru'yah'* or the sighting of the moon mentioned in the above *ḥadīth* can be understood figuratively as not having to simply mean seeing with the eye. They argue that *ru'yah* has various meanings, e.g. the Prophet Ibrāhīm, peace be upon him, says to his son:

> *I saw in the dream that I will sacrifice you.*[6]

So here it means seeing in a state of dreaming. *'Ru'yah'* could also refer to something that is known but not necessarily seen with the eyes. In the Qur'ān, Allah asks the Messenger, peace and blessings be upon him:

> *Have you not seen what your Lord did to the people of the elephant?*[7]

Obviously the Prophet, may peace and blessings be upon him, had not seen the army of Abraha attacking the Kaʿbah since it took place two months before his birth. So here 'seen' means to know, as the Messenger, peace and blessings be upon him, had clearly heard about Abraha's attack. There are numerous other examples that could be given in this regard and based on this understanding these scholars argue that 'sighting' in the *ḥadīth* can also mean knowledge through astronomical computation.

However, some would argue against this interpretation citing the *uṣūlī* principle that it is impermissable to apply both the *majāzī* (figurative) meaning of a word at the same time as the *ḥaqīqī* (literal) meaning. The response that can be made to this is twofold. Firstly, although this is a valid position, mainly adopted by the Ḥanafīs, it is also the case that:

> The Shāfiʿīs and the *ʿulamāʾ* of *ḥadīth* have held, on the other hand, that the literal and the metaphorical meaning of a word can be simultaneously applied.[8]

Secondly, it can be argued that we should be wary of taking the literal meaning of the instructions from the beloved Messenger, peace and blessings be upon him, as an end in themselves, rather than comprehending their ultimate purpose, which is to guide us to awareness and obedience of Allah. In fact, this *ḥadīth* is not the primary evidence requiring Muslims to fast in the month of Ramaḍān, which instead comes from the Qurʾān:

> *So whoever from you witnesses the month, fast within it.*[9]

These scholars would go on to mention the other verses of the Qurʾān quoted above which establish the moon's regularity in motion and the definitive link between its crescent phase and the beginning of the Islamic month. From this perspective it can be argued that the function of the Prophet's command was to give an accurate and enlightened method for his companions to keep track of an astronomical month that is always between 29 and 30 days in length. A method so good in fact, that it is still being successfully used around the world. However, the critical difference that sets aside what can be called 'progressive' scholars (methods 5 and 6 above), is that they argue it is not necessary to stick unswervingly to this procedure in the cloudy conditions of the UK, when precise knowledge of the moon's phase can be obtained by other means – astronomical calculation. They also mention that searching to understand the workings of Allah's creation and the rhythms of the natural order that He maintains is entirely in the spirit of the Qur'ānic message as a whole.

However, the opponents of the validity of astronomical data quote many traditional supreme jurists, for example, Mullah ʿAlī Qārī, a Ḥanafī jurist, who says:

> There is a consensus in the *ummah* that calculations of astronomers are unacceptable.[10]

As a rejoinder to this, it can be said that the reason why jurists were sceptical about astronomical data was because in the past their methods were not refined and accurate. But no one can say that about astronomy these days, for it is an exact science. Dr. Yūsuf al-Qaraḍāwī argues in this regard:

> Since the reason (for not accepting astronomical calculation) is no longer valid, it is a requisite to use the calculations and prove the appearance of the crescent by astronomical computation.[11]

A Way Forward, or Continued Chaos?

There is no doubt that the varying *ijtihād*s made by our Islamic scholars in regard to this issue are sincere attempts to follow the commands of Allah and the *Sunnah* of His Messenger, may peace and blessings be upon him. However, without consensus or a recognised authority to enforce a particular approach, it is not surprising that chaos has reigned with regard to the issue of moon sighting in the UK, with each *masjid* or community group choosing its own preferred method and ending up with an entirely different calendar. Thus there are two overarching issues that we will discuss in this concluding section: the question of which method of moonsighting is in our opinion best for the UK Muslim community, and the issue of developing greater unity regardless of our juristic preferences.

It is our contention that the most appropriate moon sighting method for British Muslims to follow is a regionally-based variant of the formula 'calculation when sighting is not possible' (method 5 mentioned earlier). The way in which this would work is that the days on which the crescent moon is visible over any point in the UK would be calculated on a month-by-month basis.[12] If sightings can be carried out in the available weather conditions, then by all means the Islamic lunar month can be established by this in the traditional manner. If it is impossible to carry out a sighting, then reference can be made to astronomical calculations showing that the crescent would have been visible, which includes a minimum age of at least 17 hours. If even this would not be the case, then 30 days are counted. Note that if calculations state it should be sightable with the naked eye and despite good conditions it is still not seen anywhere in the UK, then 30 days are also counted. We know that the moon's visibility curves do not exactly correspond to national boundaries, but the UK is a small country and there would be no significant problems with using a single physical/calculated crescent sighting for all of it. The new month should be confirmed by a national council of *'ulamā'* representative of the entire British Muslim community and duly followed throughout the country.

This method has the following advantages:

1. No need to look for sightings outside of the UK.
2. A single physical/calculated crescent sighting for the entire UK.
3. If the conditions are not cloudy the crescent will actually be sightable on the 29th in Britain far more often than methods that take sightings from other countries and thereby make the genuinely first UK crescent of the next month always fall on the 30th or later.

Note: It should be made clear that because of the UK's position in the northern hemisphere, it will not have the same lunar dates as other places in the world (particularly those that are far away). This is a natural consequence of following a lunar calendar that is based on the movement of the moon, which can take several days to become visible all over the world after its conjunction.

We recognise that our proposal to include astronomical calculations within the moon sighting formula may be controversial to some of our more traditionally-inclined brothers and sisters. It is part of human nature and also the breadth of our religious law that we are able to legitimately differ in these matters. All of us wish to see unity in the Islamic calendar followed in the UK, however all sides want that unity to be on their own terms. With consensus on this issue still not reached, there may have to be compromises made and this will require continued discussion and dialogue between the scholarly representatives of the different positions. We certainly believe that it is vital that the British Muslim community work constructively towards observing our great days, such as the fasts of Ramaḍān and the ʿĪds, in unison. The founding of an inclusive and respected national council of *ʿulamāʾ* to definitively settle these matters would be a positive way forward regardless of which precise formula is ultimately adopted. Also, it should be reiterated that in the interest of avoiding *fitnah* (civil strife), it is generally best for believers to unite with their local *imāms* and communities and observe the same Islamic calendar as them, even if they are inclined to a different approach. In any case, if they do choose to differ in method, they should certainly not awaken dispute and argumentation on this subject. We all should heed the words of Allah, Most Majestic:

> *Hold fast to the rope of Allah all together and do not become divided amongst yourselves.*[13]

Notes

1 *Sūrah al-Baqarah* (Q2: 189).
2 Narrated in *Saḥīḥ al-Bukhārī.*
3 *Sūrah al-Raḥmān (*Q55: 5).
4 *Sūrah Yūnus (*Q10: 5).
5 *Sūrah Yā' Sīn (*Q36: 39).
6 *Sūrah al-Ṣāffāt* (Q37: 102).
7 *Sūrah al-Fīl* (Q105: 1).
8 Kamali, M., *Principles of Islamic Jurisprudence*, p. 162.
9 *Sūrah al-Baqarah* (Q2: 183).
10 Qārī, A., *Mirqāt Sharḥ Mishkāt.*
11 Qaraḍāwī, Y., *Kayfa Natmalu Mā Sunnah.*
12 Several websites provide such information and also sighting reports. The most prominent of these is *www.moonsighting.com*. There is also *www.crescentmoonwatch.org* and many others.
13 *Ṣūrah Āl ʿImrān* (Q3: 103).

APPENDIX

Selected Scholarly Biographies

Imām Abū Ḥanīfah

Abū Ḥanīfah Nuʿmān ibn Thābit was born in Kūfah, Iraq in 80 AH and was a *tābiʿ* (follower), i.e. he saw at least one companion of the Prophet, may Allah bless him and grant him peace; a giant in the subject of *fiqh*; and an important Sunnī theologian. He has been called al-Imām al-Aʿẓam (the Greatest Imām) in recognition of his extensive contributions to the development of the Islamic sciences of jurisprudence and *kalām*, his claim to have been the earliest founder of one of the four Sunnī *madhhab*s extant today and certainly the one with the most extensive following.

Inheriting the scholarly tradition established in Kūfah during the century preceding him, Abū Ḥanīfah can be credited with not only systemising its general approach to the derivation of legal rulings from the primary sources, but due to his prodigious intellect, developing it into a highly original methodology. This work, continued by his principle disciples, Muḥammad ibn al-Ḥasan al-Shaybānī and Qāḍī Abū Yūsuf and following generations of the school, is demonstrated by the Ḥanafī *madhhab*'s distinctive positions and arguments with regard to many issues. Particularly striking for the student of knowledge, is how often a ruling that is attributed directly to the Imām, is amongst the varying opinions of the scholars, the greatest in foresight and practical application to our time. These qualities are in no small part responsible for the eventual adoption of the school as the major source of law for the ʿAbbāsid, Mughal and Ottoman empires.

In the realm of theology, Abū Ḥanīfah is ascribed the authorship of *al-Fiqh al-Akbar*, a foundational Sunnī creedal text. This is considered by some to have influenced Imām al-Maturīdī, himself a Ḥanafī, in his formulation of the orthodox theological school of the same name, which, since its inception, has always had a particularly close link to the *madhhab*. During his life, Imām Abū Ḥanīfah became almost legendary for his piety, as well as his quick-wittedness and died in 150 A.H. in Baghdad to the *ummah*'s great loss.

Imām ʿUmar al-Nasafī

Al-ʿAllāmah Abū Ḥafs ʿUmar ibn Muḥammad al-Nasafī (d. 537 A.H.) was born in a town called Nasaf near Samarqand in Turkestan. He was a great Ḥanafī scholar and author of some one hundred books on such diverse topics as *fiqh*, literature, *tafsīr* and theology. Amongst his numerous titles are: *The Magnanimous Imām, Leader of the Muslims* and *Star of the Religion.*

He was one of the teachers of the famous al-Marghinānī, author of *al-Hidāyah* and would have thousands of students come to seek knowledge from him. As well as his mastery of many different Islamic sciences, he was known for his skill in composing poetry. In fact, his *al-Manẓūmah fī al-Fiqh* was a rewriting of the celebrated book *al-Jāmiʿ al-Ṣaghīr* by Imām Muḥammad ibn al-Ḥasan al-Shaybānī into verse form. His most influential work, however, remains his short creed *ʿAqāʾid al-Nasafī* which has been translated into English within the present volume.

Imām Saʿd al-Dīn al-Taftāzānī

E. E. Elder, the translator of *Sharḥ ʿAqā'id al-Nasafī* comments on al-Taftāzānī as follows:

> We know very little indeed regarding his life and environment. The following facts concerning him are mentioned in the *Encyclopaedia of Islam*. He was born in the month of Ṣafar, 722 A.H. ... at Taftāzān, a large village near Nasa in Khurasān. He is said to have been a pupil of ʿAḍud al-Dīn al-Ījī and of Quṭb al-Dīn. His earliest work was completed at the age of sixteen. The *Muṭawwal*, the *Mukhtaṣar al-Maʿānī* [a well-respected work on Arabic rhetoric] and the *Talwīḥ* were completed in 748, 756 and 758 respectively, at Harat, Ghujduwān and Gulistān. The commentary on *al-ʿAqā'id al-Nasafiya* was completed at Khwarizm in 768.[1]

He also quotes Ibn Khaldūn, who was a near contemporary, with words that show the prominence that al-Taftāzānī swiftly achieved:

> I found in Egypt numerous works on the intellectual sciences composed by the well-known person Saʿd al-Dīn al-Taftāzānī, a native of Harat, one of the villages of Khurāsān. Some of them are on *kalām* and the foundations of *fiqh* and rhetoric, which show that he had profound knowledge of these sciences. Their contents demonstrate that he was well versed in the philosophical sciences and fard advanced in the rest of the sciences which deal with Reason.[2]

Imām al-Shurunbulālī

Abu al-Ikhlāṣ, Ḥasan ibn ʿAmmār al-Shurunbulālī was born in Shurunbula, Egypt, in 993 A.H./1585 C.E. At the age of six he was sent to Cairo, where he memorised the Qur'ān and went on to study at al-Azhar under some of its most prestigious teachers. He specialised in the subject of *fiqh* and became a prominent Ḥanafī jurist, eventually becoming one of the reliable authorities of the later period of the school. It is said that he wrote about 60 books, the most famous being *Nūr al-Īḍāḥ*, an easy-to-understand work setting out the rulings pertaining to Islamic worship, which the present volume has used extensively. He also wrote an important commentary to it, *Marāqī al-Falāḥ*, which is now a standard text studied by those aspiring to gain detailed knowledge of ritual worship. He passed away in Cairo in 1069 A.H./1659 C.E.

Imām Abū Ḥāmid al-Ghazālī

Brilliance within the rational, intellectual disciplines of Islam and its mystical practice are embodied in the famous life of Abū Ḥāmid al-Ghazālī (d. 505 A.H.). Gifted with an immense intellect and relentless in his search for truth, he developed a singularly impressive pedigree in theology and law, something which his youthful attainment of a prestigious teaching position at the Niẓāmiyyah College in Baghdād was to confirm. Yet his eventual decision to leave this scholarly environment at the height of his influence in order to practice Sufism, graphically demonstrated where his ultimate loyalties lay. After ascending the ranks of spiritual knowledge, he returned to public life in order to present what was to become the definitive intellectual and practical fusion of the outer rituals of Islam and their inner meanings.

Al-Ghazālī's legacy looms large in the history of Islamic thought and he is a perpetual point of reference in diverse fields such as *uṣūl al-fiqh* (the principles of jurisprudence), Ashʿarī *kalām* (theology within the school of Abū al-Ḥasan al-Ashʿārī) and, of course, spirituality and mysticism, largely due to his magnum opus *Iḥyā ʿUlūm al-Dīn* (*The Revival of the Religious Sciences*). Amongst his achievements is the introduction of philosophical methods, including Aristotelian logic, into Islamic theology, whilst retaining a fundamental consistency with the school's orthodox tradition. This, however, is overshadowed by the impact of al-Ghazālī's articulation of Sufism, in which he showed how a deep spiritual practice could be cultivated in every part of a Muslim's life – from formal ritual worship to the sphere of one's social and family life.

Shāh Walī Allāh al-Dihlawī

Shāh Walī Allāh, the popular name of Quṭb al-Dīn Aḥmad Abu'l-Fayyāḍ, a revolutionary Indian thinker, theologian, pioneering Persian translator of the Qur'ān, and *Ḥadīth* scholar, and the first child of the 60-year-old Shāh ʿAbd al-Raḥīm al-ʿUmarī of Delhi, by his second wife, was born in 1114 A.H./1703 C.E. at Delhi, just before the death of the Moghul Emporer Awrangzeb. He was a talented child, who memorized the Qur'ān at age of seven and completed his studies with his father in the Islamic and other rational sciences by the age of 15. On the death of his father in 1131 A.H./1719 C.E., he succeeded him as the Principal of the religious college, Madrasah Raḥīmiyyah, which his father had founded, at Delhi. In later years, this institution produced many great scholars and was the forerunner of many other institutions such as the Dār al-ʿUlūm at Deoband. In 1143 A.H./1730 C.E., Walī Allāh performed the *ḥajj* and stayed in the Ḥijāz for 14 months before returning to India in 1145 A.H./1732 C.E. He took advantage of his stay in Madīnah to learn *ḥadīth* from scholars like Abū Ṭāhir al-Madanī, ʿAbd Allāh ibn Sālim al-Baṣarī, and Tāj al-Dīn al-Qalʿī. After his return to India, he devoted himself to writing and teaching. He died in 1176 A.H./1762 C.E., and was the author of more than 40 works.[3]

Among the important works of Shāh Walī Allāh is his *Ḥujjat Allāh al-Bālighah*, which attempts to reveal the deeper secrets of the religion of Islam and to develop a synthesis of a wide range of different disciplines and sciences. Also significant is his work on *uṣūl al-tafsīr* (the principles of exegesis) named *al-Fawz al-Kabīr*, and his Persian translation of the Qur'ān.

BIOGRAPHIES

Although one of the most exceptional Islamic thinkers of the last three centuries, Shāh Walī Allāh's ideas, perhaps because of their complex and radical nature, did not have the extent of influence in his homeland that he would have wanted. Nonetheless, he left a considerable scholarly legacy, which continues to be a source of inspiration for Islamic intellectual activity up until today.

Notes

1 Al-Taftazānī, *Sharḥ ʿAqā'id al-Nasafī*, translated as *A Commentary on the Creed of Islam*, by E. E. Elder, p. xxiii.

2 Ibid, p. xxiii.

3 Details taken from Bazmee Ansari, A.S. 'Al-Dihlawī, Shāh Walī Allāh.' *Encyclopaedia of Islam*, Second Edition. Edited by P. Bearman, Th. Bianquis, C.E. Bosworth, E. van Donzel and W.P. Heinrichs. (Leiden: Brill, 1960-2005)

Glossary

Al-ʿĀdah: A practice that is considered desirable, see *musta-ḥabb.*

ʿAdl: Justice and equity. It is one of the Divine Names, signifying that God is the Most Just.

ʿAqd: A contract. The Qur'ān teaches *'Oh believers! Fulfil your contracts.'*[1]

ʿĀm al-Ḥuzn: The Year of Sorrow.

ʿAlayhi al-salām: A phrase used to express appreciation and respect of the Prophets. It means *'may peace be upon him'*.

ʿĀlim: (pl. *'ulamā'*) A learned person who has studied the Islamic sciences of Qur'ān, *ḥadīth*, *fiqh*, *tajwīd* and *sīrah* etc. in a formal setting and has been granted a certificate to teach.

ʿAqīdah (pl. *'aqā'id*): Islamic beliefs; works on the subject of creed. It means 'to believe in something because of the certainty of its truth'.

ʿĀqil: Sane (therefore legally responsible).

ʿArafah: The plain eight kilometres east of Makkah where all pilgrims gather on the 9th day of Dhū al-Ḥijjah.

ʿĀrif: A spiritual term referring to someone with special powers of perception; a gnostic.

Adab: The acceptable manner of acting and behaving in social settings, based on the *Sunnah* and the customs of society. It expresses courtesy, respect and self discipline; Arabic literature.

Adhān: The call to prayer. It is one of the symbols of Islam.

Afḍal: A superlative term used for the best deeds.

Aḥad: One, solitary. A divine name that means the One, the Unique, Who is free of partners.

Aḥkām (sing. *ḥukm*): Laws, rulings.

Ahl al-Bayt: Family of the Prophet's household, which includes his wives, daughters, two grandsons and his cousin ʿAlī.

Ahl al-Sunnah wa al-Jamāʿah: People of the Prophetic Precedent and the Community, commonly known as Sunnīs. This comprises the majority of Muslims and is characterised by its acceptance of the *ḥadīth* narrated by the full body of Companions.

A'immah (sing. *imām*): Leaders.

Ākhirah: An important Qur'ānic term that refers to the spiritual realm of existence, the afterlife. The soul will experience this after death. Some other experiences of the *ākhirah* are, the *barzakh* (the intermediate place that a soul resides from death until the Resurrection), the Day of Judgement, the Scales, the Bridge, Hell and finally Paradise.

Akhras: A mute person.

Allah: God. The Creator and Sustainer of all. The Supreme Being. The Eternal Uncaused Cause of all that exists.

Amānah: Something given to someone for safekeeping; a trust.

Al-Amīn: A wonderful title of the Prophet, which means the trustworthy. Even his enemies in Makkah kept their valuables with him.

Amīn: May Allah accept it (said after a supplication).

Al-Anṣār: 'The Helpers' – title of the people of Madīnah who helped the Prophet and his companions when they migrated from Makkah to Madīnah.

Athār: Reports narrated by the Holy Prophet's companions. It sometimes also refers to *ḥadīth* in general.

ʿAwrāh: Parts of the body that must be covered: for men it is from the belly button to the knees; for women it is the whole body except the hands, feet and the face.

Āyah (pl. *Ayāt*): A verse of the Holy Qur'ān – 6236 in total.

Ayyām al-Tashrīq: Five days (9th–13th) of the twelfth month of the Islamic calendar (Dhū al-Ḥijjah). During these days a special *takbīr* is recited after the *farḍ* prayers.

Bāligh: A child who has reached puberty, a major.

Bāṭil: A Qur'ānic term meaning the false, mainly used to describe the state of *kufr*. In *fiqh* it means that an action is null and void and has to be repeated.

Dābbah al-Arḍ: The Beast of the Earth, a strange entity whose appearance is a sign of the approaching Day of Judgement.

Dajjāl: The False Messiah and Deceiver, a heinous figure who will appear near the end of time. Also a term used for any false prophet, or great liar. The Messenger, may Allah bless him and grant him peace, forecasted that there will be 30 such deceivers before the end of the world.

Dhikr: Remembrance. Having in mind thoughts of Allah, or praising Him, verbally and mentally. This is a state of being connected with the Lord, that leads to peace and tranquility.

Duʿā': Supplication to Allah, praying to Allah for forgiveness, for help, healing and good in the world and the best in the Hereafter. This is a personal and intimate conversation with the Lord.

Dunyā: The present, worldly life which is a temporary abode of testing, as opposed to the Hereafter which is permanent.

Darūd Sharīf: Salutations upon the Prophet, a way of expressing love of the Messenger and showing appreciation for all he has done for us, peace and blessings be upon him.

Faqīr: Poor person. However spiritually it means recognising the truth that as human beings we are all in a state of utter poverty. The Messenger said *'Poverty is something I am proud of.'* It produces a state of contentedness and freedom from worldly worries.

Farḍ: Obligation. This is a ruling that must be carried out and omitting it is a major sin.

Fatwā: A formal legal opinion delivered by a competent *'ālim* on religious matters based on his understanding of the *sharī'ah* as it pertains to that particular case.

Fī Sabīl Allāh: In the way of Allah. An action done purely for the pleasure of Allah.

Fiqh: Means 'to understand' and interpret the *sharī'ah* and the rulings of *sharī'ah*. Also used for Islamic jurisprudence and the principles of deriving laws from the *sharī'ah*.

Fitnah (pl. *fitan*): Temptation; trial; social disruption or tribulation.

Ghusl: To wash all the body thoroughly according to the *Sunnah*. It lifts one to the state of major ritual impurity.

Ḥadd (pl. *ḥudūd*): Divine boundaries. These are restrictions that a Muslim must not cross. Also used for punishments in criminal law.

Ḥadīth: Narrations and reports of the deeds, sayings, gestures, approvals, and disapprovals of the Prophet, peace and blessings be upon him.

Ḥadīth qudsī: A statement of the Prophet, peace and blessings be upon him, that is directly attributed to Allah.

Ḥajj: Pilgrimage to Makkah during the month of Dhū al-Ḥijjah.

Ḥajj al-Wadā': The Farewell Pilgrimage. This was when the Prophet bade farewell to his *ummah* in the eleventh year of *hijrah*.

Ḥalāl: Anything permitted by the *sharī'ah*; lawful.

Ḥanifiyyah: To devote oneself fully to Allah and completely surrender to His will. This is the name of the religion of Prophet Ibrāhīm, peace be upon him.

Ḥarām: Anything prohibited by the *sharī'ah*. Committing it is a major sin. This is the opposite of *ḥalāl*.

Hijrah: Literally means to leave one's place of residence for the sake of Allah. Usually refers to the specific migration of the Prophet, peace and blessings upon him, and his companions from Makkah to Madīnah in the thirteenth year of his prophethood.

Ḥikmah: Wisdom. The ability to make the right kind judgement in matters of life and conduct. The Qur'ān uses it to describe the *Sunnah* of the Messenger, as this is the wisest way of worshipping, behaving and conducting one's life.

ʿIbādah (pl. *ʿibādāt*): Worship that consists of loving adoration and obedience of Allah. Islamic worship is entirely based on the Prophetic *Sunnah*.

ʿĪd: Islamic day of celebration that occurs twice a year in two distinctive festivals.

Iḥrām: The sanctified state that is a requirement in the performance of *ḥajj* and *ʿumrah* and makes many normally acceptable actions subject to restrictions.

Ijmāʿ: Consensus and agreement on a particular issue among the *ʿulamā'*.

Ijtihād: The derivation of Islamic legal rulings by an expert jurist known as a *mujtahid*.

Ilhām: Inspiration in the heart given by Allah Most High to whom He wills of his servants.

Īmān: Faith and accepting the teachings of the Messenger, may Allah bless him and grant him peace, as the truth. Declaring this with the tongue and accepting it with the heart.

Imām: The person who leads the prayer. Also refers to the leader of Muslims.

Iqāmah: Call to prayer made inside the *masjid* that signals the start of *farḍ ṣalāh*.

Isʿāh: Offense. This ruling is between *makrūh taḥrīmī* and *tanzīhī* in terms of importance. It concerns acts that are offensive to do and doing it on a regular basis is sinful.

Ishrāq: Voluntary prayer, offered 15-20 minutes after sunrise.

Islam: The religion of submission to the will of Allah. It lays down a creed, forms of worship, as well as moral and social norms of behavior. In short not only the religion, but the complete way of life of Muslims.

Isrāf: Waste, overconsumption and excessive use of anything wealth, natural resources etc.

Istihāḍah: Non-menstrual vaginal bleeding which results in special rules for purification. The basic principle is that such a person makes only one *wuḍū'* for each prayer time. This term is sometimes also used for any other condition (such as a perpetual nosebleed) which takes its ruling.

Istinjā': Cleansing of the private parts after passing stool or urine. A very hygienic practice which prevents disease.

Janāzah: A funeral.

Jahannam: Hell.

Jāhiliyyah: The Age of Ignorance. This name was given to the period between Prophet ʿĪsā and Prophet Muḥammad when people forgot the teachings of the prophets, and violated the religious sanctities.

Jamāʿah: Congregation. A group of Muslims praying together, or a group gathered for any other reason.

Jannah: Paradise. The most beautiful and delightful place in the Hereafter – its pleasures can not be imagined. Here the good people will live in the Divine proximity. This will be given on the basis of their faith and increased due to good works done in the earthly life.

Jibrīl: Angel who brought Allah's revelation to the prophets.

Jihād: To struggle or fight in the way of Allah. This is to dedicate oneself to the Divine cause, expending every ounce of energy for self improvement, social transformation and general uplifting of humanity. *Jihād* also refers to a war that is declared by a Muslim state in self defence or liberation of the oppressed. It is not a concept of offensive war for the sole sake of plunder or occupation.

Jinn: Beings created by Allah from fire, which are invisible to human beings. They can change their shape. They are subject to the Islamic call. Among them there are believers and unbelievers.

Jumu'ah: The Friday afternoon prayer which is performed instead of the usual *ẓuhr* prayer. Its key purpose is the assembly before the prayer in which the *imām* delivers the sermon. This is a means of teaching, preaching and social engagement amongst Muslims.

Ka'bah: A cube-shaped building rebuilt by Prophets Ibrāhīm and Ismā'īl (peace be upon them). The first house built for the worship of Allah. Situated in Makkah, the direction all Muslims face when praying.

Kāfir: Someone who denies God, the Messenger and the life Hereafter. A person who denies the reality of the spiritual realm of existence and does not believe in a Divinely-ordained higher purpose in life.

Kafan: A shroud consisting of three pieces of unsewn cloth used for wrapping the dead after washing the body.

Kalimah: Literally a word, most often used to refer to the *shahādah* (testification of faith). It is also a title of the Prophet 'Isā, as well as being used for a collection of prophetic invocations known as the six *kalimah*s.

Khalīfah: Someone who comes after, or represents someone, a vicegerent. Most commonly refers to the leader of all the Muslims as a shortened version of *Khalīfah Rasūlillāh* (The Representative of the Messenger of Allah).

Khilāf al-Awlā: The undesirable.

Khilāl: Passing wet fingers through a beard, for example, whilst making *wuḍū'*.

Khiṭbah: Marriage proposal.

Khuffayn: A pair of leather socks that if worn in a state of purification and not removed, may be wiped over when performing it afresh. They must cover the ankles, be made of a sturdy waterproof material and stand up without being tied. The time limit for wiping is one day while resident and three days while travelling.

Khushū': Concentration and humble attention in prayer.

Khuṭbah: The Friday sermon.

Kufr: Disbelief in Allah and/or His Messenger, peace and blessings be upon him.

Madhhab: An established school of thought, usually referring to one of the four Sunnī schools of *fiqh*.

Madīnah: A city in Arabia 286 miles north of Makkah. The prophet Muḥammad, may Allah bless him and grant him peace, migrated to this city to escape persecution and lived here for 10 years until his death, and is buried here. Formally known as Yathrib.

Madrasah: School. The name of a traditional Islamic University. Now generally refers to the part-time Islamic school where Qur'ān reading is taught.

Maḥram: A close relative that one cannot marry. For a man this includes: daughter, sister, mother, aunt, niece; and for a woman: son, brother, father, uncle, nephew. Stepbrothers and stepsisters are also included as well as wet nurses and in-laws.

Makkah: A city in Arabia where the Holy Ka'bah is situated. The first holy sanctuary ever built.

Makrūh (pl. *makrūhāt*): An act which is disliked by Allah but not absolutely forbidden.

Makrūh taḥrīmī: An abominable action closer to *ḥarām* than to *ḥalāl.*

Makrūh tanzīhī: It is offensive and disliked, but at a more minor level.

Manārah: The lofty turret of a *masjid* from which the caller, i.e. the *mu'adhdhin* calls the people to prayer.

Mandūb: Another word for *sunnah*.

Mardūd: Rejected. Used to describe the *Shayṭān*, as God rejected him and threw him out of Heaven. Sometimes used for an apostate Muslim who has renounced Islam.

Masjid: Mosque. A place of Muslim worship, it is a dedicated space for public worship, where the five daily prayers are performed in congregation.

Mimbar: The pulpit. A three step chair from where the *imām* gives a sermon on Friday.

Miʿrāj: The Prophet's ascension. The celestial journey to the Seven Heavens and beyond to the Divine presence. The Prophet, peace and blesings be upon him, was shown all the different realms of existence. One of the great miracles of the Prophet and alluded to in the Qur'an at the beginning of *Sūrah al-Najm* (Q53). It is celebrated every year by Muslims on the 26th Rajab.

Miswak: Tooth-stick used for cleaning teeth.

Al-Muʿawwidhatayn: the name of *Sūrah al-Falaq* and *Sūrah al-Nās* together. Often read as a means of protection from evil.

Muzakkī: The person paying *zakāh*.

Mu'adhdhin: The caller of the *adhān*, inviting Muslims to prayer.

Mubāḥ: Permissable. This is something neither prescribed nor prohibited by the *sharīʿah*. It carries neither reward nor any punishment in itself.

Muḍārabaḥ: An agreement between two or more persons whereby one or more of them provide finance, while the other(s) provide entrepreneurship and management to carry on any business venture whether trade, industry or service with the objective of earning profits. The profit is shared by them in an agreed proportion. The loss is borne by the financiers only in proportion to their share in the total capital.

Muḍārib: The partner who provides entrepreneurship and management.

Muftī: One who delivers *sharīʿah*-compliant verdicts on various issues.

Muhājir: (pl. *Muhājirūn*) Title of the Prophet's companions who migrated from Makkah to Madīnah to escape the persecution. They are the most highest in status amongst all the companions. Most of their properties were confiscated and in some cases their wives and children were snatched from them.

Muḥaddith: An expert in the science of *ḥadīth*.

Mujtahid: One who researches Islamic issues and using the text and independent reasoning gives scholarly verdicts that affect the lives of Muslims.

Munkar and Nakīr: Two fearsome angels that visit each soul in its grave and ask three important questions: 'Who is your Lord, what is your religion and who is your prophet?' A correct response will lead to a pleasant experience in the grave, while an incorrect response will lead to punishment therein.

Murābaḥah: Sale at a special profit margin. The seller purchases the goods desired by the buyer and sells them at an agreed mark-up price. The payment being settled within an agreed time frame, either in instalments or lump sum. The seller undertakes all management needed for the purchase and also bears the risk for the goods until they have been delivered to the buyer.

Murtādd: A Muslim who changed his religion, see *mardūd* above.

Mushrik: A polytheist. One who associates others with Allah, which means assigning divinity and power to others besides Allah. This could be to one's ego, or to idols like the statues the Makkans worshipped.

Mustaḥabb: Desired activity under the sacred law. Reward is gained if it is performed and there is no sin for its ommitance.

Mutawātir: A continuously narrated report, which is affirmed by a number of people large enough for it to be inconceivable that they could have colluded upon a lie.

Nabī: A prophet who is commissioned i.e. chosen by Allah to guide his people according to a previous prophet's law.

Nabuwwah: The state of prophethood.

Nafl: Optional deeds a person undertakes voluntarily.

Najāsah: Impurity.

Najas (pl. *anjās*)*:* Impurity.

Nifās: The post-natal bleeding during which period women are exempt from prayer.

GLOSSARY

Niṣāb: A specific amount of wealth upon which *zakāh* is taxable.

Niyyah: Intention to do an action. It is an aim or a wish expressed in words or formulated in thought. It is the formula necessary to render an act of devotion acceptable. So the intention can be seen as the mobilisation of inner strength and energy to achieve one's wish and aim. The Prophet, said, *'The value of any deed depends on the nature of its intention.'*[2]

Al-Qaḍā': Allah's Decree. This refers to His Creation of all entities and actions by His Will, Desire, Command and Measure.

Qaḍā': Performance of an act of worship after its proper time, or its repetition if invalidated for some reason.

Qiblah: the direction a worshipper faces in prayer.

Qīmah: The equivalent value of something, such as the price of an animal needed to be given in *zakāh* or to be spent in buying a sacrifice if illegally hunting whilst on *ḥajj*.

Qur'ān: The Final Revelation from Allah to mankind. The Divine speech revealed to Prophet Muḥammad, may Allah bless him and grant him peace, and brought to him by the angel Jibrīl. It is preserved in its original form.

Qurbānī: The sacrifice offered on ʿĪd al-Aḍḥā, the day after the pilgrims stand on Mount ʿArafah in Mecca. (This is the 10th day of Dhū al-Ḥijjah in the twelfth month).

Rājih: Preferable, a term used in *fiqh* to signify a point of view that is preferred because it has stronger proofs

Rakʿah: One unit of a prayer, characterised by a single bow and two prostrations.

Ramy: Throwing pebbles at the Shayṭāns (Jamarāt); one of the distinctive rituals of *ḥajj*.

Rasūl: A messenger commissioned by the Almighty to guide humanity. In order to fulfil this purpose, Allah grants him revelation and a new *sharīʿah*.

Rasūlullah: The Messenger of Allah, may peace and blessings be upon him.

Ribā: Literally means increase or addition and refers to the 'premium' that must be paid by the borrower to the lender along with the principal amount as a condition for the loaner or an extension in its maturity. It is equivalent to usury/interest.

Al-Risālah: The divine message sent to mankind through the messengers. This is the channel of communication between God and mankind.

Rūḥ: The soul. Also called the spirit. The very essence of human being, which makes man special and distinct from other living things, his immortal and non-material essence. After God created Adam, may peace be upon him, He blew his *rūḥ* into him. The full reality of this vital force remains a mystery to us, but we know that it lives even after the death of the body.

Rukūʿ: Bowing position made in ritual prayer.

Saʿy: The running between the hillocks of Ṣafā and Marwah seven times that is one of the distinctive rituals of *ḥajj* and *ʿumrah*.

Ṣabr: Patience, particularly in the midst of turmoil or stress.

Ṣadaqah: Voluntary alms for the poor.

Ṣaḥābī (pl. *Ṣaḥābah*): A companion of the Prophet, may Allah bless him and grant him peace. This is defined as a person who saw the Prophet in state of faith and later died in that state.

Ṣahīh ḥadīth: A statement attributed to the Prophet, peace and blessings be upon him, that has been rigorously authenticated by the scholars, leading to a high degree of confidence about its accuracy.

Sajdah: See *sujūd*.

Sajdah al-Sahw: Prostration made for forgetfulness in prayer, so that a *wājib* action is accidentally omitted.

Sajdah al-Tilāwah: Prostration made whilst reading the Holy Qur'ān. There are 14 such prostrations to be made throughout the whole Qur'ān.

Ṣalāh: The ritual prayer. The second pillar of Islam that has to be performed five times daily.

Ṣawm: Fasting.

Sayyidunā: 'Our Master' – Honorific words preceding the name of a prophet or a companion.

Shafāʿah: Intercession. The prophets and the righteous in general, and the Prophet Muḥammad, peace and blessings be upon him, in particular, will be allowed by Allah to intercede for the sinful on the Day of Judgement.

Shahādah: The testification of faith in Allah and His Messenger, peace and blessings be upon him, which is the entrance into Islam and its first pillar.

Sharīʿah: Refers to the Divine guidance as given by the Qur'ān and the *Sunnah* and embodies all aspects of the Islamic faith, including beliefs and practices.

Shayṭān: The Devil; a devil.

Shirk: The act of associating partners with Allah. See *'mushrik'*.

Shirkah: Partnerships between two or more persons whereby, unlike *Muḍārabah*, all of them have a share in finance as well as entrepreneurship and management, though not necessarily equally.

Al-Ṣiḥāḥ al-Sittah: the six most authentic books of *ḥadīth*. They are famous because they used rigorous criteria to measure the credibility of narrators, therefore the authenticity of their reports is high. However, not all the *aḥādīth* in them are *ṣaḥīḥ*, they vary from *ṣaḥīḥ* (highly authenticated) to *ḍaʿīf* (weak). The six books were written by al-Bukhārī, Muslim, al-Tirmidhī, Abū Dawūd, al-Nisā'ī and Ibn Mājah.

Sīrah: The biography of the Prophet, may Allah bless him and grant him peace.

Suḥūr/seḥrī: Sunnah pre-dawn meal taken just before starting to fast.

Sujūd: The position of prostration made in ritual prayer.

Sūrah: A chapter of the Holy Qur'ān. There are 114 *sūrahs* in the entire Sacred Book.

Sunnah: Refers essentially to the Prophet's example, peace and blessings be upon him, as indicated by his practice of the faith. The major source for the *Sunnah* is the collection of *aḥādīth*.

Al-Sunnah al-Mu'akkadah: A code of life established by the Holy Prophet, which it is highly recommended to follow.

Tabiʿīn: Followers of the companions.

Tabzīr: To waste oneself in sinful activities.

Tafsīr: The exegesis or commentary of the Qur'ān. It is a human attempt to understand the Divine teachings. It uses a variety of methods, principally: language, grammar, reason and *aḥādīth*. The most useful resource for understanding the Qur'ān is the Qur'ān itself, including its internal organisation, elaboration and self-explanation.

Tahajjud: Night prayer offered in the early hours of the morning before the dawn. It is a powerful means of developing Divine love and connection.

Tajwīd: The art of correct recitation of the Glorious Qur'ān. It depends on the proper pronunciation of the letters and understanding the punctuation marks.

Takbīr: Saying *'Allahu Akbar'* (Allah is the Greatest).

Taqwā: Piety, or fear of Allah. It requires being God-conscious, aware of his commandments and prohibitions and ever attentive to Him. It means being spiritually awake.

Tasbīḥ: Saying *'Subḥānallāh'* (Glory be to Allah) or another similar phrase of glorification; a set of prayer beads, often consisting of 99 or 100 beads.

Tashahhud: Special salutations that are given whilst sitting in the second of each pair of *rakʿah*s in prayer, as well as in the final *rakʿah*. It is sometimes also used as the name of the distinctive position sat in when perfoming it.

Taṣdīq: Affirmation of the truth.

Ṭawāf: Circumambulation of the Kaʿbah made by the piilgrim on *ḥajj/ʿumrah*.

Tawakkul: Reliance on God. A person's faith is perfected to the extent that he relies totally on his Lord.

Tawbah: Repentance, seeking forgiveness, turning back to Allah after disobeying him.

Tawḥīd: The belief in the the absolute Oneness of Allah.

Tayammum: Dry ablution made as a substitute for *wuḍū'* and *ghusl* in certain circumstances.

Tilāwah: the melodious recitation of the Qur'ān. It is a *sunnah*.

'Umrah: A visit made to Makkah as a form of worship. It is a kind of smaller *ḥajj*, sharing some of its rituals, but takes a much shorter time to complete and may be done throughout the year.

Umm al-Mu'minīn: Mother of the Believer, a title given to the wives of the Prophet Muhammad because they are regarded as the mothers of all believers.

Ummah: A nation; the whole Muslim community, irrespective of colour, race, language or nationality.

Urf: Customary practice.

Wājib (pl. *Wājibāt*): Necessary; compulsory.

Wird: An individual's regular portion of Qur'ān recitation and prophetic invocations. Sometimes recommended by a spiritual director.

Ya'jūj and Ma'jūj (Gog and Magog): Fearsome people who are prophesised to emerge near the end of time. They are characterised by their unstoppable warlike behaviour and drinking of the world's water resources.

Yaqīn: Certainty of faith, charachterised by the absence of any doubt. The Qur'ān mentions three degrees of certainty: certainty through cognitive knowledge, certainty through sense experience; and absolute certainty gained through wisdom and Divine inspiration.

Zakāh: The fixed amount of money payable on net disposable wealth to poor and the needy.

Zamzam: Holy water that comes from the spring of the same name inside the sacred *masjid* in Makkah.

Zawāl: The point just before and after noon when the sun moves away from its zenith (highest point) and *ẓuhr* prayer becomes permissable. It is often erroneously used to mean the prohibited time just before when the sun was at its zenith, or for all three prohibited prayer times. The correct name for this noon-time is *istiwā´* (equally balanced) as it signals the exact midpoint between sunrise and sunset.

Notes

1 *Sūrah al-Mā'idah* (Q5: 1).

2 Narrated in *Ṣaḥīḥ al-Bukhārī.*

Bibliography

Islamic Source Texts

- *The Noble Qur'ān.*
- *Ṣaḥīḥ al-Bukhārī.*
- *Ṣaḥīḥ Muslim.*
- *Sunan Abī Dawūd.*
- *Sunan al-Nisā'ī.*
- *Sunan al-Tirmidhī.*
- *Sunan Ibn Mājah.*
- *The Musnad* of Aḥmad ibn Ḥanbal.
- *Mishkāt al-Maṣābīḥ.*
- Ibn Ḥibbān.
- Ibn al-Khuzaymah.
- Al-Ṭabarānī.
- Al-Dāraquṭnī.

Classical and Modern Scholarly Works

ʿAbd al-Ghanī al-Maydānī, *Al-Lubāb*, (Maktabah al-ʿIlm al-Ḥadīth, 2002).

Abdulati, H., *Islam in Focus* (El-Falah Foundation, 1997).

Ibn ʿĀbidīn, *Radd al-Muḥtār ʿalā Durr al-Mukhtār* (Dār al-Kutub al-ʿIlmiyyah, 1994).

Athar, S., *Health Concerns for Believers* (Kazi inc., 1995).

Al-ʿAynī, *ʿUmdat al-Qārī* (Dār al-Kutub al-ʿIlmiyah, 2001).

Birgivi, Imām, *The Path of Muḥammad: A Book on Islamic Morals and Ethics.*

Al-Dihlawī, Shāh Walī Allāh, *Ḥujjat Allāh al-Bālighah* (Dār al-Kutub al-ʿIlmiyyah, 1995).

Eaton, G., *King of the Castle* (The Islamic Texts Society, 1990).

Al-Ghazālī, *Iḥyā' ʿUlūm al-Dīn.*

Al-Ghazālī, *Inner Dimensions of Islamic Worship*, translated by Muhtar Holland, (The Islamic Foundation, 2000).

Al-Ghazālī, *Kimiyā-yi al-Saʿādat.*

Al-Jilānī, ʿAbd al-Qādir, *The Book of the Secret of Secrets and the Manifestation of Lights* (Al-Baz, 2000).

Kamali, M., *Principles of Islamic Jurisprudence*, (The Islamic Texts Society, 2003).

Ibn al-Kathīr, *Tafsīr al-Qur'ān al-Karīm.*

Kurāni, ʿAlī Muḥammad, *Falsafah al-Ṣalāh*, (Dār al-Zahdā', 1972).

Al-Marghinānī, *Al-Hidāyah* (Dār al-Kutub al-ʿIlmiyyah, 2000).

Al-Marghinānī, *Al-Hidāyāh* with commentary by al-Lakhnawī, (*Al-Miṣbāḥ*).

Al-Māwardī, *al-Aḥkām al-Sulṭāniyyah*, translated as *The Laws of Islamic Governance* by Asadullah Yate (Ta-Ha Publishers, 2005).

Mawlūd, M., *Ishrāq al-Qarar.*

Al-Miṣrī , Aḥmad ibn Naqīb, *Reliance of the Traveller*, translated with commentary by Nuh Ha Mim Keller (Amana Publications, 1994).

Nadwi, Abul Hasan Ali, *The Four Pillars of Islam* (Haji Arfeen Academy).

Al-Nasafī, *Aqā'id al-Nasafī.*

Nuʿmānī, Shibli, *Sirat-i-Nuʿmānī*, translated as *Imam Abu Hanifah: Life and Works*, by M. H. Hussain, (Darul Ishaat, 2000).

Pickthall, M., *Fasting in Islam*, (Islamic Review and Muslim India, v. 8, December 1920).

Qaraḍāwī, Y., *Fiqh al-Zakāh*, translated by Monzer Kahf (King Abdulaziz University).

Qaraḍāwī, Y., *Kayfa Natmalu Mā Sunnah.*
Qārī, A., *Mirqāt Sharḥ Mishkāt.*
Ibn al-Qayyim, *Zād al-Mād.*
Al-Rāzī, Fakhr al-Dīn, *Mafātīḥ al-Ghayb.*
Rees, M., *Just Six Numbers* (Phoenix, 2000).
Rumi, *Fīhi Mā Fīhi.*
Al-Samarqandī, *Baḥr al-ʿUlūm.*
Al-Sarakhsī, *Al-Mabsūṭ* (Dār al-Maʿrifah, 1978).
Al-Sarrāj, *Kitāb al-Lumaʿ fī al-Taṣawwuf,* (Leiden, 1914).
Shah, Pir Mohammad Karam, *Ziā al-Qur'ān.*
Shakir, Z., 'Flight From the Masjid' (*Seasons,* Spring/Summer 2003).
Al-Shaʿrānī, ʿAbd al-Wahhāb, *Asrār Arkān al-Islām.* (Dār al-Turāth al-ʿArabī, 1980).
Al-Shaybānī, *Kitāb al-Aṣl (al-Mabsūṭ)* (ʿĀlam al-Kutub, 1990).
Al-Shurunbulālī, *Nūr al-Īḍāḥ.*
Al-Taftazānī, *Sharḥ ʿAqā'id al-Nasafī,* (Maktabah Kulliyāt Azhariyyah, 1988).
Al-Taftazānī, *Sharḥ ʿAqā'id al-Nasafī,* translated as *A Commentary on the Creed of Islam* by E. E. Elder (Columbia University Press, 1950).
Weiss, B., *The Spirit of Islamic Law* (University of Georgia Press, 1998).

Reference Works and Internet Links

The Encyclopaedia of Islam, Second Edition.
The Encyclopaedia Brittanica.
Lane, E. W., *Arabic-English Lexicon* (Islamic Texts Society, 2003).
Prayer times: *www.Islamicfinder.org.*
Price of gold/silver: *www.24hgold.com/english.*
Moon sighting: *www.moonsighting.com,*
www.crescentmoonwatch.org.

BIBLIOGRAPHY